Reflections in the Mill Pond

Visit www.booksurge.com to order additional copies.

Reflections in the Mill Pond

Larry Wood

My precious friend Ashlee,

You are wonderful.

May you have the best of everything.

2007

Larry Wood

Reflections in the Mill Pond

ACKNOWLEDGEMENTS

A large number of individuals, living and deceased are in varying degrees responsible for the story you are about to read.

"Reflections in the Mill Pond" materialized in an attempt to document the lives of some very remarkable people. Few of the individuals who play major rolls in this story survive to see the story in print. Without their contributions however, there would be no "Reflections in the Mill Pond." I am grateful that I knew and loved each and every one of them.

As countless pages of clinical journals scribbled on legal pads, stenographer notebooks, and eventually cassette tapes began to take the form of a story, supportive people began to appear along the twenty three year journey it has taken from the first hand written line to a published book.

Initially, I would like to thank my dear friend, Laurie Medina, who literally gave me the strength and will to write this book. Another dear friend, the late Laura Meador convinced me that I had a story to tell and kept me on task during the early stages of writing.

In the early 90's, I moved from New Mexico across the

border into Colorado, and made a host of new friends whose support and encouragement kept me writing and recording the rather fascinating events of my life. I would like to specially thank my dear friends Jackie Lewis and Gaytha Frye who always had a smile and encouragement in times when it was needed.

Lois Booth, Director of Hospice del Valle, Alamosa, Colorado has done more than she will ever know to assist me in completing this task.

I am likewise grateful to Lynn Howard, Superintendent of Sangre de Cristo Schools who has been a tremendous support. I would also like to thank the hundreds of students of Sangre de Cristo schools who have fulfilled my lifelong dream of working with young people.

I want to thank my special friend Carmella Chavez-Villafranca, of Taos, New Mexico who always appeared miraculously with a word of encouragement when I thought I would never finish writing this story.

Douglas and Carol Carruth of Alamosa, Colorado have been the driving force behind getting this book in print. Without their friendship, support, and encouragement, you wouldn't be reading this.

There are very few remaining members of our family. I cannot express my appreciation enough to those few remaining who have always believed in me and been there for support. Mike, Pam, Mindy, Tyler, Blake, Skye, Aunt Bea, Uncle Dave, Aunt June, Sue, Don, Claudia...thank you for believing in me.

Last but certainly not least is my buddy, Linda Eavenson of Alamosa, Colorado who knows what catastrophic loss is all about. Her own personal tragedy gave me the courage to continue writing about mine.

PROLOGUE

A while back, I sat with a dear friend who inquired about the book project I had been working on for roughly two decades. The question arose, "How does one go about writing a book such as the one you have buried yourself in for so many years?" After pondering a bit, I responded,

"Simple! All you have to do is live a pretty difficult life for about 50 years, and live to tell about it!"

I suspect that no one's life is totally awful. Mine certainly wasn't. There were definitely high spots, and they were of such a magnitude that they made up for a great number of the difficult times. Unfortunately, the difficult times, like the high spots, were also of such a magnitude that they cast a somber shroud that made any light appearing at the end of a tunnel appear more like the proverbial oncoming train.

Somewhere along the journey, I reluctantly learned that life, in my humble opinion, is simply a matter of choices. We have a lot of help, good and bad, in making those choices, but ultimately the choices are ours and ours alone. Not all good choices are rewarded. Not all bad choices are punished. Sometimes, I have learned, really bad things happen to pretty good people. Alternately, some pretty decent things have come to some undeserving types. The choices are ours to make. The rewards seem to come randomly.

I have come to believe that sadness is simply a choice. If we choose to accept it, in fact, embrace it, it just might hang around for a while, like your whole life, for example. It's a choice! In this advanced stage of my life, I have come to believe that unhappiness, much like obesity, is sitting prostrate somewhere eating Twinkies. Unhappiness must love inactivity! It will sit idly with you as long as you care to embrace it. Misery loves company and all that!

Many years ago as I sat in a sanitarium pondering my miserable state, it came to me to share my difficult times in hopes that others might read my words and choose to elevate themselves. Surely some good must come from my misfortune, I thought. Interestingly enough, as I began to document chapter and verse, all the while feeling terribly sorry for myself, I began to recall the many good times which had preceded the disasters, and even followed them on occasion. Over the weeks, months and eventually years, those first few memoirs took on a life of their own, and became the book you hold in your hand.

"Reflections" is based on actual events of my life. Some accounts are exact; some are fiction. In the creation of the thing, I found that a number of events that "should" have happened along the journey didn't happen. I have taken the liberty to bend them, shape them, and create them into a roller coaster ride of actual and embellished events. Regrettably, the tragic accounts are actual excerpts from my journey. Though many names are changed, the characters are all very real. Along the journey, a number of persons must have been angels sent to accompany me. One of the forces compelling me to write this story is to document their existence. I believe there are angels among us. Certainly they were present in my life!

It is my hope that you enjoy reading my story. It is also my prayer that in doing so, you may be encouraged to make your day and everyone's around you a little brighter. Life is a gift. Cherish it!

Reflections in the Mill Pond
A Novel by Larry Wood

How strange it is that things today appear so small when compared to those images locked away in our childhood memories. Such was the Mill Pond and all its many reflections, indelibly inscribed into the lives of those who stood wonderingly at the marvels of its vastness, beauty, intrigue, and mystery.

It's not possible that we only visited the Mill Pond in the fall of the year as it was so much of our daily lives; the visitation, the fantasies shared there, the dreams of youth. But the eau now emitted from the pond wafted so pungently of its slightly musty autumn flavours that it surely takes me back to a fall day when the world basked in the fleeting rays of a long summer in preparation for the first frost which would inevitably, like myself, re-visit the Mill Pond.

Part I
Reflections in the Mill Pond

Chapter 1
My Birth

I'm not certain of my first real memories. I suspect none of us are. We do have those bits and pieces of things we might have thought we experienced, which could have been things from later in life, or even a movie for that matter. I do recall talk of the war and that almost everyone in my small circle of humans seemed to be much bigger, obviously older than I. Children, as I remember vaguely, were occasional and the source of pure fascination to discover beings roughly my own size. I remember those initial encounters, and have faith that they were actual events and not just my imagination. As a child, I was normally surrounded by adults, specifically my grandfather and his entourage of what I remember to be very dark and lovely ladies whom I knew simply as "abuelita" or Grandma.

The plurality of the previous statement might confuse some, but to understand I think it would have been necessary to live in a very special time and in a very special place, Taos, New Mexico in the middle of the twentieth century. Taos had been our ancestral home for many, many years, possibly centuries. I'll explain that later.

It's hard to recall when I first had friends. It must have been around the age of three or so as I do recall standing somewhat dumfounded on my feet, quite possibly adorned in cloth diapers still, but admiring another child figure standing directly in front of me. She was similarly clad but with longer, darker hair. She was "Rosa," Rosa Montoya, and she would figure rather significantly in my life. I do recall reaching out with a somewhat chubby hand and touching Rosa on the cheek. Life was good then.

As time passed, more children began to move into our little life circle which was centered at what is now the old abandoned trout hatchery located just a short distance from the Historic Plaza in Taos. These kids brought all the excitement that children seek, and with each one brought a new personality, charm, and oftentimes, language. We spent countless days exploring each others' secret hideouts and playing games that lay the groundwork for who we all were to become. By my fourth birthday celebration, my party was comprised of possibly six or seven of us. Thinking back to our little group, it must have looked to an outsider like a commercial for the Rainbow Coalition. We were Spanish, Tiwa, Tewa, French, Navajo, Anglo and me. I, and my first close associate, Roma were the lightest of the bunch. I imagine that we looked different; I being of French, Spanish, Native American and English decent, and Roma being whatever it was that she was. It's amazing how wonderfully people get along when it's never called to their attention that, "you look different." Maybe I should tell you about Roma but I think I will put that off until another time. Roma is more or less a book of her own.

Chapter 2
My Grandfather

My grandfather was a remarkable man to say the very least.

The first memorable account that I have kept with me through my life are the events of his second marriage. I must back up a moment and say a brief word about my maternal grandmother. It will, of necessity be brief, as I knew very little of her. I do possess a marriage certificate with the date March 14, 1900 which was given to my grandparents at the Wood's Ranch in northwestern Oklahoma. That was nine years prior to statehood, and my grandfather had been ranching a large area of this land since meeting my grandmother here during a cattle drive he made while working for a historic figure named Charles Goodnight. The trail was called the Goodnight-Loving Trail. After completing his third drive, he returned to the Oklahoma Territory, married my grandmother, and began ranching.

I knew my grandmother only as ABC. This was the point at which she began learning English after marrying my grandfather. Her name was pronounced "Ah-Bee-Sah." Her mother reportedly was a French woman, most likely descendent of the early French traders who lived in the area, and her father was thought to be a Kiowa chief of some notoriety named Lone Wolf. She lived with the Kiowa people who inhabited this region, and spoke the Kiowa language and French. I never knew her real name, and that has haunted me. In fact I know very little of her at all except that I am enormously proud of my native heritage and an old postcard showing her in native dress. She was an awesome beauty.

ABC choked on a peanut hull and died not long after the birth of my father, the youngest of four siblings. Heartbroken and quite possibly reeling from the loss of the children's mother, the family packed up, left the Oklahoma ranch, and returned to their ancestral home, Taos, New Mexico. It must have been around 1909 as I recall early discussions that the family would quite possibly lose the ranch anyway as Oklahoma Territory would soon become the State of Oklahoma and that the Wood's Ranch would soon become Wood's County, the second largest county in the new state. Regardless, my grandfather and his four children moved home to Taos, and my grandmother returned to the earth that the Kiowa people had roamed for centuries.

I remember being told that in some societies, when a husband loses his wife, it's customary to take a "mourning trip." During his absence the husband can deal with his pain and maybe not present such a forlorn picture to the surviving children and family members. This was done. I don't recall just how long it was following the loss of ABC and the move back home to Taos that my grandfather departed on his "mourning trip" with a destination of New Orleans, Louisiana. I do recall hearing that he rode horseback south through the Rio Grande Canyon and on to Santa Fe, and was there to catch a train to his faraway destination. I think it was the look of total disgust on the face of my Uncle Floyd Santisteven, an old time Taos lawyer and social straight arrow, when he would reluctantly re-tell the story that I remember best. According to Uncle Floyd, he was loading his fly rod into the car to do some trout fishing on the Little Rio Grande, one of his favorite spots, when he looked down the road and saw a man and woman approaching in a buggy.

This was the Sunday following the departure for New Orleans on Wednesday. I'm certain you have guessed by now that the man driving the buggy up the road was none other than my grandfather. The lady was Alicia, wife number 2. I still recall the look of bewilderment on Uncle Floyd's face as he tells the story.

As the account goes, my grandfather was awaiting the train when his thoughts were sidetracked by flamenco music coming from a nearby cantina. This was common in those days as the flavour of early New Mexico was pure Hispanica!

Grandma number 2 was named Alicia!! If ABC was not the most beautiful woman my grandfather had ever met, Alicia was! She didn't speak English either as she had recently migrated from Spain to pursue her career as a cantina dancer in the new world. Taos, New Mexico in 1910 must have been a great place to pursue it. I never knew her cither as she died long before my birth, but I do recall my aunt and uncles comments describing her arrival as "someone turning the lights back on!" She was a dazzler and is credited with initiating the party that lasted forty years.

Alicia, I'm told, succumbed to scarlet fever and died young, happy and still very beautiful. That must have been sometime in the 1920's.

My grandfather was always known as a very positive thinker. I'm sure it was this positive attitude that led him to believe, "If it worked once, it can again."

Mariposa was dancing at La Gallina, the very same cantina where he met Alicia. Peas in a pod! Her portrait is still found in paintings from some of the early Taos artists and photographers. I own a postcard of her which is lovely. Unfortunately, I didn't know her either. She did, reportedly live a wonderful and lively life with my grandfather and rests peacefully in the cemetery on the Pueblo end of town.

It was during Mariposa's life that things began to happen that defined my family as perhaps, "a little different." As the story goes, Mariposa and several of the Spanish ladies would dance every Saturday evening at our home, or at the La Fonda, a big hotel and cantina on the plaza. They were riotous events with music and dancing which lasted well into the mornings when the last piñon embers cooled in the kiva fireplaces. It was on one of these occasions that a cousin of a friend or some acquaintance of someone was being visited by a lady from Mexico. As fate would have it, she danced as beautifully as Mariposa and in no time they danced together, and related like long, lost sisters. Do you see where this is going?

Her name was Esmeralda. They called her Essie and when she joined the family things must have really kicked into high gear.

By the time Essie moved in, my dad and his siblings were old enough to venture out into the world, which they did. The Second World War was in full swing, and my dad went off to make his fortune in the trucking business carrying war materials. My Aunt Ruth remained in Taos and lived her life there in a lovely adobe home which is now a popular restaurant. My uncles went off to the war. My grandfather stayed home with Mariposa and Esmeralda.

I never understood exactly how Guillerma and Paca joined the group. It was sometime around 1940 and before my birth. Now they were 4; Mariposa, Esmeralda, Guillerma and Paca, all lovely, all flamenco dancers, and all present when I joined them shortly after my birth, in 1943.

Chapter 3
A Different Kind of Childhood

Acquaintances with whom I've shared parts of my story never quite understood how I ended up with my grandparents and not my parents, so soon after my birth. To fully understand, or at least accept how this happened, it would have been necessary to know my father, and to a lesser extent my mother.

My father was a brilliant man, graduating high school at age 12. From childhood, he spoke several languages as did everyone in my family and he also possessed a skill we now refer to as "total recall." The medical/psychological term for his actual condition was "savant," which you might recall from a popular movie back in the 80's concerning one of two brothers who had gifts. While the "gifts" are fairly remarkable, oftentimes the possessor has considerable deficiencies which can appear as gaping holes in the personality or intellect. In fact, years ago, the individuals identified with this condition were termed, "Idiot Savant" to more emphasize the gaping holes compared to the gifts. Diagnosis and medical descriptors are kinder these days. Anyway, my dad's biggest "gaping hole" was an inability to deal with children. Damn the luck!

Regardless of my mother's pleadings, so I'm told, I was packed off to my grandfathers as soon as I was old enough to make the trip. You ask, "Why did she allow that to happen?" My mother, bless her heart, was a lovely but very timid country girl from southern Oklahoma. My dad made all the decisions for both of them. They already had one child, an infant girl, my sister Judith, who provided all the children tolerated in the home. Enough said.

That I ever learned to walk was a miracle! I had 4 grandmothers! I must have been years into my childhood before I stopped raising my arms to be lifted when I was approached by an adult! I could best describe our home life with canvas and a palate of vibrant New Mexico colours. I've appreciated art my entire life and spent many hours winding through galleries throughout the world. In all candor I can say I've never viewed a canvas that even comes close to the colour, excitement, and "joie de vivre" that was the continuing scene in our little adobe hacienda in Taos during my youth. Our picture, however, was alive! Our picture resounded with music, laughter and all the pleasures life had to offer.

You're probably wondering about what it was like living in a home with a grandfather and 4 grandmothers. Yes, it does raise a couple of questions. It's a little hard to describe. At the time Esmeralda danced into Taos, it was basically just my grandfather and Mariposa. The kids were all gone and Esmeralda and Mariposa reportedly hit it off like sisters. I imagine that this union was such a success that there was little hesitation over the addition of Guillerma and Paca. By the time Guillerma and Paca joined the family, I imagine it was sort of a moot point about proprieties, customs, norms, legalities, what-have-you.

One of my favorite stories told by my Aunt Ruth was about a drinking session between the old priest at Ranchos Mission and my grandfather. As the story was related to me, Father Martinez, after a few too many tequilas slammed his fist on the kitchen table and roared,

"God damn it Sam, you're single handedly ruining the divorce statistics of the Catholic Church!"

It really didn't change anything, nor was the incident ever taken as factual as if all the grandmothers were somehow legally married which was impossible in our church. They certainly never divorced as they all remained until "in death they did part," which they did following the death of my grandfather some years later. As for legalities, formalities, etc., etc., no one seemed to care much at the time. That was early Taos. The only topic that brought everyone to attention was when talk began about paving the road into town. Then everyone got very excited and out came the guns.

So that's how I came to be in Taos in 1943. It was like a scene from an old western movie and that's where my earliest memories began.

Chapter 4
The Early Years

I vaguely recall the ending of the war and the sadness surrounding many of the families we knew. I vividly remember one of the grandmothers commenting sadly that "The poor Martinez family will be all on their own now that Mr. Martinez will not be returning from the war." This was all very confusing to a very young boy whose interest were basically focused within a 100 foot radius of our house, the pond, and the great swing that soared like an eagle from a limb of the giant willow beside the pond. There was no fear of tomorrow, any anticipation of loss, nor anxiety for things unknown. There was only the magic of Northern New Mexico, my beloved family, and playing around the mill pond.

I do have a faint memory of a small pair of cardboard Army boots that a friend had managed to procure from a cousin in Albuquerque. Leather had been rationed for the war effort and for a while there was an attempt to make kid's shoes from cardboard. The cardboard boots were a pretty hot item until the first time the boy attempted to cross Taos Creek with them. Bobby Yazzie was with him, and reported there was not much left but the strings. Our shoes mostly came from the Pueblo. They were made from deer or elk, and lasted forever.

I mentioned earlier that I would share with you at a later time my unique relationship with Roma. Her name was Roma Siler and her family lived in a big adobe directly across from ours at the old hatchery. Roma's dad obviously had money because the Silers had a car. Roma had webbed toes. Honest! I'm not sure whether it was the car or Roma's webbed toes that made her such an attraction. From my earliest memories, I knew Roma was "different." I'm comfortable that anybody who knew her at the time and over the next 50 years would agree that "Roma was different." Maybe webbed toes just make you follow roads less traveled, but regardless of the reason, she definitely did. At best, having webbed toes would make you very trackable. I must have been pretty young, possibly 3 or so when I first noticed those toes. Someone, possibly Tony Two Hats, a Taos Indian who was my grandfather's constant companion and our "Would you please help us?" man, had made for us a small raft on which two of us at a time could sail upon the pond. It was marvelous. It gave us the freedom to break away from being mere landlocked beings and sail upon the water alone or in pairs. I usually preferred pairs as it gave me an opportunity to be alone and in close proximity with Roma, the object of my fascination. It was on one of the early voyages that I broke away from those wonderfully captivating blue eyes and looking downward noticed that she had webbed toes. I commented something charming and engaging like,

"Hey, your toes are stuck together!"

I'm certain Roma responded in true Roma fashion with, "So?"

That was the end of it. The subject never came up again.

Though the warm months of the year were our special times, as I'm sure is true with most youths, the winters had their own magic. Fifty years ago streams and small ponds abounded all over the little community of Taos. The streams wove pristinely throughout the village and brimmed with trout eager to give up to any kid with a pole, hook and worm. Where the beavers built dams, the streams became small ponds which invited skaters in the winter months. At least most of us called it skating. Roma was quick to point out to us lesser beings that we "were only sliding," as you don't call it "skating" if you're wearing moccasins! This was very confusing to me and my young colleagues, and as many times previously, we didn't have a clue what she was talking about. You must remember, Roma's family had money. That was unique in Taos in 1940's. The whole skating thing came to a head on Roma's fifth birthday. It was between Christmas and New Years as I recall and out of this big gift wrapped box appeared a pair of white shoes with knives attached to the bottoms! I do recall my first thought was they were going to take those "knife shoes" and do something dreadful to her webbed toes. I and my young companions wanted no part of this if that's where these money people were headed. At times, Roma delighted in making us look like un-enlightened, provincial, backwoods, small town, minority kids. That seemed to work well for her because we were just that; un-enlightened, backwoods, small town, minority kids. Limited as we were however, we were savvy enough to know that when you've got webbed toes and your parents give you shoes with knives on them, something is in the wind. We were un-informed, not stupid!! I do remember the cake was wonderful and after opening about a zillion dollars worth of presents, it was time to put them to use. You cannot imagine our shock when Roma's first order of the day was that we would all go ice skating!

Now how crazy is that, when you've just been given a Red Ryder BB gun, a double holster with cap pistols, and a pirate gun that shoots projectiles with rubber stoppers that can stick to a victim's forehead??? Roma was DIFFERENT!

Walking in the snow a short 60 feet to the pond, our questions were soon answered. In the blink of an eye, Roma had on those knife shoes and was nudging out onto the ice. We marveled! In minutes she was streaking, gliding and circling us like a person possessed. It was one of the most spectacular things I had witnessed in my four or five years of life. She had really outdone us this time, and all we could do was just stand there in our freezing moccasins and look stupid. I vividly recall her breezing past us and shouting, "Look at me, I'm Sonja Henie!" Of course Sonny Spotted Horse had to open his mouth and yell out, "Who's Sona Hanky?" To compound our ignorance, Bobby Montoya had to plead with her, "Can I put them on and skate?" to which Roma curtly chastised him and responded, "Of course not silly, these skates are WHITE!"

A lot of things happen when you're a kid that you just can't seem to grasp the understanding. This was one. I'm not sure just how many years passed before I finally understood what she was trying to teach us that day. I've also likewise wondered if the other boys ever learned. Ice skating never caught on big in Taos. Several years later while attending the Ice Capades in Dallas, Texas I finally solved the Sonja Henie riddle. Too bad the Ice Capades never made it to Taos. My little buddies probably died in ignorance. It's likewise highly probably that they never understood about the white skates either.

Chapter 5
Horses!

It was about this same time I remember that suddenly our little band of renegades mobilized. Michael Castillo was the first of us to make the move to "greater mobility." Several of us were fishing in the pond when Michael and his dad arrived horseback. Seeing people horseback was very normal in town but seeing a friend on a small black pony no one recognized was news. Michael's dad who raised sheep out by Questa was grinning ear to ear. Michael was beaming so he was speechless. The pony was jet black with a long mane and tail. He was about as tall as the bed of a wagon as well as I remember. Michael was riding him bareback, but on the pony's head was a fancy beaded headstall with a silver bit. It had come, no doubt, from the Pueblo and made the steed look like something out of the movies we watched every Saturday at the matinee. Conversation was limited. We were spellbound.

Thus began the period when our group became unbearable. There was no conversation that didn't include a horse, pony, mule, donkey. The point being, "How do we get one?" It seemed like an eternity before the second group member broke down the resistance at home, and came trotting up on a bony little red creature he constantly prodded with, "Go Silver, go Silver!" Of course Roma was the first to remind us that the Lone Ranger's horse "Silver" was named "Silver" because he was pale in colour. Anyway the horse remained Silver for the next six months of his life until he succumbed to total exhaustion and very old age. That's when Bobby Lujan got "Red" as a replacement. Red was a dark bay.

By the time we rode Silver into his grave, Bobby Yazzie had acquired a big brown gelding he called Thunder. The storm had definitely passed as Thunder had only one speed and that was very, very slow. Tony Cantu was given Rocket by his grandfather. Wanka Moscua acquired Bandit from his older brother who it was rumored got sent off to jail in Santa Fe for drunkenness. Bandit was a good horse with his only fault being that he had a tendency to stop instead of just walking past a bar. Joseph Left Hand earned a horse named Pansa for weeding an entire field of squashes and corn. We helped a little, but it was very warm that summer and we preferred to play instead of weeding corn. Pansa's one attribute was that he could trot faster than Thunder. "I" could trot faster than Thunder!

Roma didn't have a horse. She apparently didn't want one which was fine for the rest of us in that it gave us an opportunity to just be boys and venture out with our newly acquired mobility. We often rode 3 to a horse. Oh yes, then there was me.

It was my fifth birthday party. I had not given up the begging, pleading, promising, deal making, anything to acquire myself a ride. It didn't seem to be getting me anywhere except with my Grandmother Paca. She had pled my case for weeks, seemingly getting nowhere as the common responses were: no money, he'll be gone all the time, he'll break his neck. It was endless. By this time, Michael Castillo had fallen off his pony and broken his arm which did little to advance my cause. I recall our sitting at the kitchen table and my excitement over the presents I had received, mostly homemade by my grandfather, or parents of my friends. Noticing his absence, I had inquired,

"Where's Tony Two Hats?"

Tony would never miss a party involving cake. Someone responded,

"He'll be along."

Shortly, we heard my Aunt Ruth's dog Rusty barking in front of the house. Rusty, a little red Cocker, always barked when horses arrived. I think he developed that habit from years of greeting my Uncle Curt returning from the bar. Looking through the frosted window pane on this January day, I did see horses. It was Tony. There in the snow in front of the house was Tony mounted on his old horse Skinny which Tony rode everywhere. Tony and Skinny were not alone. Next to Skinny and standing about half as tall was what appeared to be a long haired musk ox in a red and white coat. Frost spouted from his nostrils, and he stomped the ground repeatedly in an attempt to free the ice balls which clung to the long hair on his stubby legs. The emotion I felt at that moment has not left my memory these fifty plus years. Strangely, I did not bolt to the door but stood there motionless. It was if I dared to move this scene would expose itself as simply a fantasy. The only movement I recall were big tears rolling down my cheeks and spilling onto my two hands which held fast to the window sill as if to keep me from falling. Suddenly I felt a big, warm hand gently settling on my shoulder. I've never felt more loved than at that moment and in his low, gentle voice my grandfather said,

"He's Scout."

"Yes," I agreed. "He's Scout!"

Chapter 6
Beginning School and Other Trauma

I vividly recall the conversation between Father Martinez and my grandfather. Again they were sharing drinks at the kitchen table when the elderly priest questioned,

"Don't you think it's about time he started school?"

Of course the "he" they were discussing was "me," and the effect the topic had on "me" was about like Father Martinez had asked,

"Don't you think it's about time we chopped his head off with a dull ax?"

I knew a little about school. Roma told me. It wasn't good. The nuns make you stand up and repeat things you're supposed to know, and if you can't do it they beat you or worse, make you put on a pointy hat and sit in the corner of the room on a high chair. It was called a Dunce Hat. Up until now I had not really experienced anything dreadful in my life. I had been sick once and a nurse took my temperature in my bottom of all places. That was horrid but nothing to compare with the stories I had heard about school. My grandfather must have known it was horrid or he would have made me go sooner.

I was still five years old in the fall when I was forced to

begin school. Several of us started together at the old San Francisco Mission School in Ranchos. I dreaded it. We weren't even allowed to ride our ponies to school. We went in the back of Jimmy Martinez' dad's truck.

Jimmy was a midget. He and I were good friends and had very similar notions about attending school. Of all the kids we ran around with, Jimmy rode the biggest horse of any of us. Go figure. He called him Caesar. Caesar had been a plow horse in his younger days but now just toted Jimmy around town.

Hearing Mr. Martinez' old truck pull up in front of the house, I lost all composure and headed for the back door of the house.

"Aý, Querido, tienes que ir a la escuela como los otros!"

I had been caught. Jimmy and some of the other kids were already in the back of the truck. I thought they looked just like prisoners being carted off to jail. Jimmy was sitting on the wheel well so he could see us all being transported to execution. Years later I saw this movie about people in Paris, France being hauled off in a cart to get their heads lopped off. It was like one of those "deja vu" things.

There were only six classrooms as I recall, and we immediately spotted some fellow detainees we knew and assumed we were in the same class as them. Jimmy and I raced to a couple of seats by the window and immediately pulled our big wooden desks as close to the window as we could, thinking that just in case air got short, we could still get some.

"You can't move your desk off the X," we suddenly heard as soon as we had got them where we wanted them.

I turned to see a kid pointing at this big chalk X on the floor where my desk had been.

"Why not?"

"Don't know."

We were in trouble and the teacher had not even come into the classroom yet. Jimmy and I looked at each other and knew in a heartbeat that if we had any chance of survival it would be fighting in the open and not trapped within the confines of a school building. Simultaneously, we both looked at the big window which was just a little out of reach, but obtainable if we stood on our desks and jumped. In a flash, I had my desk right up against the wall where I could grab hold of the window sill, pull myself up, and make my escape. I did. To this day I can still see those little hands of Jimmy's trying to reach the window sill. With each jump he would call, "Lariano, Lariano!" I was burdened with guilt as I disappeared into the red willows beyond the playground.

You recall my telling you that Jimmy was a midget. He just couldn't jump high enough. I was abandoning my friend but just couldn't make myself go back and surrender to whatever torture was doled out to escapees. It must have been pretty painful for Jimmy and I guess the disappointment added to his never amounting to much later in life. He became a lawyer and went into politics.

It took a pretty good while to walk the path between the mission school and town. It was about 5 miles. Within a mile of town I saw a man coming up the path horseback and recognized him immediately as Tony Two Hats.

"What are you doing here Tony?" I asked.

"Waiting for you," Tony answered.

We didn't have a phone so I was curious how he knew I would be coming down the path.

"How did you know I was coming home, Tony?"

"Just did."

Tony pulled me up behind him and we rode the last mile at a very slow walk back to the hatchery. When we arrived home, my grandfather was in the orchard picking apples with my grandmothers. Although my early arrival was obvious to everyone, no one seemed to make a big deal of it. My grandfather did ask,

"How was school?"

I just shrugged my shoulders and walked into the house to

my room. He knew as well as me how school was. I'd been gone less than an hour. What I really wanted to do was pick apples but I guess I was feeling a little ashamed and concerned that I had disappointed everyone by not getting an education.

Chapter 7
Returning to the Scene

The quiet at the dinner table that night of my big failure was deafening. We had chile rellenos, my favorite, along with sopapillas. After dinner, Essie produced seven little cups of flan which was always a special treat and a silent message that I was not to be thrown out with the garbage and still had "some" supporters in spite of my pitiful failure as a scholar. It was still pretty quiet though for dinnertime at our house. I felt pretty badly about what I had done, but still no one chastised me or made fun of my cowardice. My biggest regret was that I had abandoned Jimmy.

My grandfather and I were doing the dishes as we usually did. The grandmothers would cook, we would clean. On Friday nights however, "we" would cook AND clean up as a special treat for the ladies. It was fun for all of us. We would start the affair with me going into the yard or field depending on the season and gathering flowers for the table. I loved to do that and it always brought a wonderful response from my grandmothers. My grandfather could build about anything and he had made a little bench called a "banco" for me to use in the kitchen that allowed me to reach the stove, sink and a small pump handle that brought water into our kitchen.

This particular night, the night of my big school disaster was a Monday so we were just finishing the dishes when a knock was heard at the door. This was not unusual and I paid little attention until I heard the voice of a stranger who had come to call.

Turning on my bench, I saw a young man clothed in the brown robes of a Franciscan Priest. This too would have not been extraordinary except for his age. I thought most priests were about a hundred years old. He was young.

The Franciscan introduced himself as Father Bill, and he sported a smile that made you like him right off the bat. He was greeted by all and invited in for coffee and sopapillas. He accepted immediately and sat himself down at the kitchen table. My grandmothers were all smiling like possums and I think it was because this young priest was I guess what you would call real handsome. I remained on the bench and before I could step down, he glanced at me and said in Spanish,

"Algo me dice que tu eres, Lariano."

"Sí," I responded, a little surprised that he apparently spoke our language. He obviously wasn't from here. I was also surprised and more than a little alarmed that he already knew who I was. Above the aroma of the sopapillas frying in the hot grease, I smelled conspiracy.

Unsure whether to jump down and join the group at the table or continue to act like I was washing invisible dishes, the guest made that decision for me.

"Le gustaría juntarnos, Lariano?"

Without a doubt, it was a conspiracy and by the looks of how things were shaping up, I was the "conspiree." It took about half a second for the school issue to come up.

Father Bill informed us that he had just been assigned by the Santa Fe Diocese to work as a Teacher and Counselor at the mission school. In a flash I knew that if I couldn't be taught, I was about to be counseled. I've always had a way of predicting things. I was right again.

It started off with Father Bill's sharing with all of us how interesting it is that some kids just can't wait to get into school each day and how much fun they have there. He really didn't have to go into much of an explanation about those "other" kids who eventually end up liking school and after about a thousand sopapillas, he even had me believing a little of it; not all of it. Some of it. The sopapilla dough was gone, and out of consideration for my grandmothers, I abruptly interjected,

"I'd sure like to come to school tomorrow!"

By saying I would like to come to school, I guessed he would be satisfied and would maybe leave. If he did, the grandmothers would not be compelled to come up with more food for him at this late hour. It's for sure he would have gladly gone through everything they produced and offered him. Priests are funny like that. It's like they don't see good stuff to eat every day. I guess they're too busy praying.

I was up at 6:30 the next morning and greeted by four smiling grandmothers. You'd thought I was going off to Harvard as proud as they looked. Jesus, it was just the first grade at the mission school. After a huge breakfast, like a lamb to the slaughter, I was off to school.

The second day I rode to school with the Silers. Roma never spoke a word. I'm sure to her it was like riding to school with the village idiot.

Like a jet, I was out of the car, in the school building, and racing to a seat by the window. Jimmy didn't speak as I entered, but I could hear this annoying, "tap, tap, tap." Looking toward the front of the room I saw this GIANT nun, pitch black from head to toe and tapping on her desk with a ruler. With her other hand she was pointing this foot long finger directly at me and then to an empty desk about a mile away from the window. She obviously knew exactly who I was. I immediately obeyed as I was alarmed by the silence of all my friends who sat motionless in their desks. Not a single one turned to acknowledge my presence or even make a funny face at me. They stared at the front of the room and acted like I just moved in from a leper colony.

I sat quickly and was totally shocked at what happened next. The giant black plague said very politely,

"Thank you, Lariano and welcome to the first grade!"

"GULP!"

I felt myself relax just a little and then broke into a smile as the familiar face of Father Bill passed by the door. He spotted me immediately and gave me a big "thumbs up" sign.

Father Bill's big smile was as good as a pat on the back, and assured me that surely I could at least make it through the first grade. With a big sigh of relief, I glanced into the hall again hoping to catch another reassuring look from my new friend. He had gone about his business. What I did see, however was a little blond girl with a scrunched face sitting across the hall in the second grade classroom. She had both her thumbs in her ears and was flapping her fingers and sticking her tongue out at me. It was Roma.

Knowing what I do today about education and looking back at how kids started back then, it's amazing anyone ever succeeded at anything. We had books at home, and I was read to from my earliest memories. I loved being read to and even liked the stories that were extracted from the big books. I really liked the ones with colorful pictures.

School has changed a lot since I was a little kid. Back then, you learned to read, write and do arithmetic when you go off to school in the first grade. Nowadays, you start school while you're still sucking on a bottle. I think kids need the opportunity to be kids. I prefer how it used to be. Seems like a lot of us turned out OK even though we didn't start school in diapers.

There were letters all around the classroom and I recognized some of them. There were big ones and little ones. There were also numbers starting with the number zero. This, I thought, might be easier that I had feared it would be.

The teacher, Sister Jean called each of our names, and you had to answer, "Here, Sister Jean."

We were in trouble with the very first kid. Sister Jean called out,

"Alex Abeyta."

"Aqúi, Señora!"

Sister Jean politely responded,

"Alex, we speak English here in school. Let's try that again. "Alex Abeyta."

"Aquí Señora!"

Of course the third try had the same result. It was getting pretty confusing to Alex and everyone else just what we needed to do here to ever get on to the second student, Consuelo Benetez! If it was "English" she was needing from Alex, he was in big trouble. The Abeytas lived very close to us and I had never heard ANYONE in their family speak a word of English. It just crossed my mind that if we ever DO get past Alex, we were headed for a disaster. Consuelo Benetez was Taos Indian and spoke nothing but Tiwa. Sensing this pending crisis, I looked around the room to sum up the severity of the problem. Starting in the first row, first seat, there was Adela Montoya, then Benito Carillo, then Michael Castillo, then Bobby Lujan, then Cecilia Many Goats, then Paca Perez and lastly Domingo Little Crow.

"GULP!" I knew every one of these kids very well and was pretty sure none of them spoke English very well. What we knew we learned from the Saturday matinees at the Taos Theatre and the prospects of Sister Jean saying anything like,

"Put your hands up and hand over that money box!" were just not very good. This second day was looking pretty difficult and I was glad I had missed the first one.

Being very patient and obviously needing and seeking assistance, Sister Jean spied me where I had hoped I was invisible at the back of the room. Looking like a little white boy, she solicited my help,

"Lariano, surely YOU speak English don't you," she said with a little frustrated smirk.

"Sí, Señora, un poco!" I responded and immediately knew I had made a big mistake which would probably result in my having my tongue cut out in front of all my friends. I quickly stammered,

"Yez ma'am." But the damage was already done.

Breaking the horrible silence that fell over the classroom, a small voice was heard from the far side of the room. It was little Cecilia Morningstar, and she was standing up beside her desk which practically dwarfed her. Cecilia politely and proudly said,

"Mebbee we lun Inlice?"

I had seen acts of bravery in my life. I had seen people do things I would never even think about doing. But this! When Cecilia stood up in her little blue homemade flour sack dress and moccasins and spoke to the teacher the way she did, she became my life long hero. We had never seen such an act of heroism. At lunch I offered her a tortilla and she accepted it. I was honored.

"Ayúdame Díos!" She was looking at me again and before I could dodge her gaze, she asked,

"Lariano, do you know your ABC's?"

Feeling relieved that I could finally answer a question and rise to immediate stardom in the eyes of Sister Jean, I responded,

"No Señora, she die long time ago."

Chapter 8
Beyond Education

After that first day which seemed to last about a thousand hours, things got a little better at school. We did manage to get through the first day with the help of Father Bill who was sent for immediately following my failure to give the correct response about what I was soon to learn was called the "alphabet."

I would like to clarify at this point that I did not come from an ignorant family. Nor did Michael Castillo, Paca Perez, Rosa Montoya, Cecilia Many Goats, or Domingo Little Crow. None of us came from "ignorant" families. We simply came from a different world. Our parents were not negligent of our educations. They were commonly united in seeing that we had every opportunity available to us. Due to our geographic location and the absence of "outside" influences, scholastic opportunities for poor children living in Northern New Mexico at that time were limited. Of the things that we had access to and needed in our daily lives, we had complete knowledge and mastery. Adela Montoya's mother and grandmother were both, "Healers." Curanderas they were called and used what nature and common sense had provided to heal us when we were ill. They could walk through the forest and tell you the names of every plant growing there and what medicinal value it offered. Domingo Little Crow's grandfather could tell you the entire history of the Tiwa people since before the Spanish arrived in the 1500's. He knew names, dates, and places, and all without the benefit of a written record. Cecilia Morningstar's entire family had been potters, and had intermarried with the Santa Clara people over three hundred years ago. Their black pottery sold for hundreds of dollars to mostly white collectors. Cordelia Coronado's mother had her own exhibit in what I learned in later years was called the Smithsonian Institution. Cecilia Many Goats father was paid as a consultant by the Harvard School of Archeology. "My" grandfather had completed the fourth grade in school before he went off with his brothers to work on the big cattle ranches in Texas. All the time I lived in his home however, he consulted for the government of our state and sometimes the government people from Washington, DC as he was the only person of any race in the state of New Mexico who was fluent in English, Spanish, French, Athabascan, Tiwa, Towa, Tewa, Ute and Comanche.

The point I wish to make is that while our community of diverse ethnicities had limited exposure to the outside world, we did well with what we had, and managed to survive well until we were essentially displaced by people with money and the desire to purchase the lifestyle that had been given us by birthright.

Things did get better at school and fairly quickly. Realizing that Sister Jean was going to have a very difficult time in a room full of kids she could not speak with, Father Bill came to the rescue of all of us. Sister Jean moved to the 6th grade where lots of kids had learned to speak English. The following Monday, to our surprise, Father Bill strutted into the classroom accompanied by a diminutive nun who was not much bigger than Cecilia Morningstar. Other than her small stature, what caught our attention immediately was this big toothy grin. Without saying a word Father Bill made a sidestepping movement and held out both hands, palms up towards her like he was introducing a movie star. Taking his lead, she gave us a big toothy grin and said,

"Aho…..Bonjour……Buenos días…..Yáh teh!!!!!"

In a matter of seconds she had won us over!! Father Bill was so proud of himself he was grinning like a Cheshire cat! School had now begun in earnest. In no time at all, and to the dismay of our parents, we were developing our own school language. It was a combination of all the languages we had always spoken, but now enriched with a large dose of English.

We learned her name was Sister Bernadette. She was Zuni and had essentially grown up at the Santa Fe Indian School where she learned Tiwa, Tewa, Towa and English too. She already spoke Spanish as most Puebloan people do. She was just what the doctor ordered. We called her "Bernie" and everyone loved her. Bernie lived in the convent at the mission school and she had a yellow bicycle which she brought from her last assignment in Albuquerque. We didn't have bicycles mostly because all our streets were sand. Bernie taught us to ride on the hard rock paths at the mission school. She fished too.

It was sometime in this first year of school that several of us got famous. It must have been in the spring because I don't remember it being cold and the ponies didn't have long hair. I think several of us were at the pond when Michael Castillo came flying up on his black pony. Michael was waving his arms frantically, pointing in the direction of the plaza shouting,

"There's a horse at the store!"

This made little sense at all and Michael was doing little to explain his excitement.

"Es muerto; he's dead!!!"

Now THIS was news, and something of interest to us as we were puzzled at what a dead horse would be doing at the Penney's store. Before we could get horseback, Michael was shouting again.

"Get some money, get some money!"

Now we were not only confused about the dead horse, but perplexed that we needed money to see the thing. Most of us got somewhere in the neighborhood of 25 cents on the weekend for the Saturday matinee but this was late Thursday afternoon and there wasn't a nickel between the six or seven of us. We mounted up and went anyway since this was the most excitement we had encountered since Michael's little sister Lupe had fallen in the toilet hole.

"Unbelievable!" Right there on the front porch of the Penney's store was a man using some tools to secure the final bolts which held this "pony" to a slightly elevated stand. The "pony" was red and white, a little like Scout but he was frozen in this pose like he was running full speed at about a hundred miles an hour. On his back was a black leather saddle covered with shiny brass buttons. It was beautiful and we were mesmerized! Standing on a mount beside the pony was a small box about the size of a cigar box with a slot in it. Under the slot, boldly printed was a mark that read, "5 Cents". We were speechless. I recall there must have been about seven of us by then; Michael Castillo, Bobby Lujan, Domingo Little Crow, Benito Carrillo, Bobby Yazzie, Joey Little Wolf, and me. Not a nickel between us. Not a cent!!

"You boys want a ride?" the big man said, after securing the pony to the porch and giving us a big grin and pointing to the horse. We were not real sure what this English speaking man was saying to us, but the big grin indicated that he wanted to be friends. We were grinning like a bunch of possums. Taking nickels from the big man, we were all nodding and grinning in appreciation. Bobby Lujan was the first to go, mainly because he was the biggest and could beat most of us up when the situation called for it. He had also saved us many times from being murdered by the marauding Questa boys, so he essentially earned his position. We each had our nickels and knew that eventually we would get our turns. Bobby handed me the reins to his horse, and climbed on the imitation one. Inserting his nickel, he was off to the races.

It was pretty amazing riding that thing, and we were all enjoying it enormously until it would suddenly stop still about as abruptly as it started. When your time was up, it was a little disappointing, realizing that it would be a while before another nickel could be spared so frivolously.

Joey Little Wolf was just finishing his ride when a big blue car pulled up to the curb in front of Penney's. Two white ladies stepped out and each carried a black box camera. They were chattering like chipmunks and pointing at us where we stood on the porch around the mechanical horse. We knew from past encounters what was coming next. We had all experienced this at one time or another as visitors came to Taos in the summer. They wanted pictures. At first it struck me as very confusing "why" those white ladies would want pictures of this mechanical horse. Then it dawned on me what they found so photographic. There we were in various assorted attire. Most of us wore jeans and shirts that had been made from flour sacks. None of us had owned a pair of store shoes in our lives as the rubber and leather needed for shoes had all gone to the war effort and hadn't made it back to New Mexico yet. Domingo Little Crow, whose father was Arapaho and married into the Tiwa culture, wore a headband, typical of Plains Indians. Such was the case of Bobby Yazzie, a Navajo who always wore a wide headscarf and a silver necklace of squash blossoms his father had made himself. We all wore moccasins which pretty much was the common bond we shared. They were practical, easy to make, available, and cheap.

I recall feeling a little uncomfortable in thinking that how we looked might be cause for a photograph. Suddenly I realized however, that it was not simply how we looked, but what was going on that caught the white ladies attention. It struck me. Here were seven boys, all obviously from town, taking turns holding each others "real" horses and ponies to take turns spending a nickel to ride a "mechanical" pony. I guess to an outsider that was worthy of a photo.

Bobby Yazzie was always a smart kid. As the ladies approached us, making gestures with their cameras, Bobby responded by rubbing his thumb and finger together in the universal gesture meaning, "coins." This was brilliant! Before we could even hold out our slightly soiled palms, these white ladies were paying us some "serious" money just for taking our pictures. By now, everyone was rubbing their thumbs and fingers together and hauling in the loot. By the time the white ladies got around to posing us all like they wanted, I had seventy-five cents in my jean pocket! It was a "huge" financial windfall that we would repeat with some success in the coming years.

The ladies took our pictures all standing around the mechanical horse while holding onto our real ponies and horses. Of course Bobby Lujan got to sit on the thing while the pictures were being taken. The rest of us just stood there like a bunch of dumb whatever we were. We were now rich however, so we were feeling pretty smart thanks to Bobby Yazzie. About a month later, one of the pictures the ladies had taken was hanging on the front window of the Penney's store. We were not only rich, we were famous.

Chapter 9
Bernie, Father Bill and Me

After our initial year of getting educated at the mission school it seemed like the months, seasons, and finally the years all seemed to blend together. When the first grade class passed to the second, Bernie went with us. We were like a big family of struggling orphans who were slowly but surely assimilating knowledge into a new language. It was happening slowly, but very surely. Father Bill was always there giving us the "thumbs up," and reassuring us that we were the greatest class to ever hit the mission school. We liked that but had our concerns that he might be exaggerating just because he seemed to like our mixed up little band of vagabonds. In actuality we were no different from the other kids who had begun at the mission school. We were just his first and that made us special.

It was late in our second grade year that Father Bill came in one morning and asked us all to pray for our friend Rosa Montoya. Rosa was the first child I ever remembered seeing. Now Rosa had contracted a strange and serious illness called Polio. Rosa was very, very ill. We prayed hard because we all liked Rosa a lot. She and several other kids from the area had all contracted polio and were sent to Albuquerque for treatment. Almost a year later a fifth grade girl named Estrellita Martinez returned, but she was very crippled and did not come to school. Later, we heard that Estrellita had died.

It was around Christmas of our 3rd grade year that Mrs. Montoya came to school and told us the sad news that Rosa, my Rosa, had died also. This was a terrible time for children and people thought that the sunlight made you catch it. I remember this as "the time of darkness; el tiempo de obscuridad," because we didn't play outside as much as we had earlier.

It was following the death of Rosa Montoya that I became very close to Father Bill and Bernie. I was very upset at the loss as she was one of my very first memories. The Montoyas lived in a small adobe just down the road from my Aunt Ruth and Rosa and I spent a lot of time together playing with Aunt Ruth's Cocker Spaniels and picking strawberries from the garden. I was close to the Montoya family and always felt very welcome in their home. Before the death of Rosa, I had not experienced pain. My life in Taos with my grandparents had been wonderfully idyllic and full of love, security and laughter. Beyond the boundaries of our little village there was no outside world, only the magical life of Taos. Now the thought of losing a friend had made me for the first time think about more than Scout, fishing, and playing around the mill pond. Rosa was gone and with her, my innocence.

It was about this time that Bernie asked me about my family. Everyone knew that I lived with my grandparents and that was just the way it was. No one questioned. My family was not some secret that no one talked about at home or at school. It was just accepted that my grandparents were my family. Now, Bernie had asked the question that maybe some had wondered about but no one had asked about. Answering was difficult for me because in actuality I knew very little about them. It was just not a subject that we talked about a lot at home. I don't recall that I ever asked why I was living with my grandparents when I knew that I had a mother, father and sister living in another state. When things were wonderful, why ask? Anyway, Bernie had opened a sealed trunk that sooner or later would have been opened anyway. As we spent hours talking about the loss of Rosa and our other friends, it seemed a door was slowly opening to other questions that I would begin wondering about.

My third grade year was ending and one afternoon Father Bill and Bernie asked if I would like to visit after school. Trusting them that I was not in trouble, I quickly agreed. We sat at a big outdoor table in the church courtyard and it was beautiful that May afternoon I recall. Father Bill began the conversation by telling me that he had been visiting with my grandfather about maybe meeting my family. He went on to say that they had a home in Gunnison, Colorado where they spent the summer each year. Gunnison was not far away. It evolved that my mother had contacted my grandfather asking his opinion on my spending some time with them the coming summer. My grandfather had not mentioned this to me at the time and when he finally did, a long time later, he told me that his fear of losing me had kept him from approaching me with the issue. Instead, he had gone to Father Bill and Bernie to ask for advice. I didn't understand my grandfather's fear as he was, and always would be my "parent," I thought at the time. I don't recall having any feelings at all about a visit one way or the other except for a tugging feeling in my stomach which I could not understand at the time.

Interestingly enough, as I began to consider the possibility of meeting my family, I began feeling fearful. Looking back over these many years I don't know to this date that my memory of fear is actually a composite memory of events which happened later, or if I actually had something like a "premonition" that deviating from the path that had been my life for nine years would change my life so dramatically. I just remember feeling "fearful." The conversation with Bernie and Father Bill ended without resolution.

Later that day I shared this feeling with Tony Two Hats as we rode out towards Twining Canyon in search of turkey feathers. Tony listened very intently, was silent for a while, and then shared something with me that I still hold strongly to until this day. In Tony's quiet, scholarly way he said,

"There is only one thing in life that you can always put your trust in. This "thing" is the feeling you have in your stomach."

Tony's advice that day became the compass that guided my life.

It was unusually quiet at the dinner table that evening. After dinner my grandfather and I went about cleaning the kitchen and washing the dishes as the grandmothers busied themselves with chores. No one sang. No one danced. It was as if everyone had a secret and no one wanted to discuss it. I especially did not want to discuss it because I was already feeling that if I even expressed an interest in going to meet my family it would be like I was betraying the people who had made my life so full of happiness. I think my feelings of fear which I shared with Tony came from the notion that "if" I ever left my home in Taos and the people who raised me, I might never be able to come back. This idea frightened me because I knew I was secure here and very much loved. Taos was my home, my family, my security was here. If ever I needed reminding all I had to do was recall the weeks after the loss of Rosa and how my grandfather for the longest time after that would ask me to sit with him before the big kiva fireplace in the living room. We would just sit and listen to the crackling of the piñon and juniper wood burning in the fireplace, all the while his big, comforting arm holding me near to him. If ever I needed reminding, all I had to do was recall my first look at Scout through that frosted window pane and feel the warmth of his loving hand on my shoulder. This was my home. I could not, would not ever leave it.

Chapter 10
Changes

The school year was about over when Bernie and Father Bill asked me to join them again for another one of those little meetings. It was fine with me as they had both become very special to me and I welcomed any reason to spend time with them both. They knew about places and things the rest of us knew little about. It was fun to hear their stories. Father Bill had been raised in an orphanage called Father Flanagan's. His mother was a very poor woman who could not raise him. He told us he had never met his dad but always wished that he had. Bernie had a big family back in Zuni, New Mexico and she had known since her childhood that she wanted to be a nun. She said she had never questioned that desire ever since she was a little girl at the Santa Fe Indian School.

In no time at all, the subject came up again about a visit to meet my family. Father Bill went into his story about how all his life he had wanted to know his father. He insisted that it didn't have to change anything at all. It was just so that when I got to be a grown-up like him, I would never look back and regret that I had not done that. Bernie just set there nodding "Yes," with her big grin. They did have a point. I guess the truth was that I was a little curious about those people and especially curious about a sister that I had never met. I wondered if she would be anything like Roma. It might even be fun I thought. They confided in me that my mother had called at the suggestion of my grandfather to share with them her desire to know me. I was always what you would call "soft hearted" and when Bernie told me that, I was finding it hard not to give in.

That night at the dinner table I simply blurted out,

"Can I go visit my mom and dad this summer?"

It was like a huge weight had been lifted from all our shoulders. Appearing very relieved that the subject had finally been aired, my grandfather immediately responded,

"Of course you can go, son! You can go any time you like."

For a few seconds it got very quiet again as if no one knew where to go from here. My grandfather began,

"Your dad has a big home up in Gunnison where they go every summer. I hear it's beautiful and there's trout up there as long as your arm. It would be something to see!"

"Sí," chimed in Paca as if she knew a trout from a chipmunk. I guess they were all nervous and so was I. Anyway, the ice was broken and without elaborating at all, it was decided that I would visit my family this coming summer in Colorado.

After dinner, I climbed up on my bench to start the water for washing. My grandfather was gathering dishes from the table and bringing them to where I was pumping water into the sink. It was still pretty quiet and suddenly the question I needed to ask just popped out.

"Grandfather, if I go visit them in Colorado can I still come back home?" I had barely gotten the words out when he bolted to where I was standing on the bench and hugged me like he had never done before. He didn't get an answer out but was nodding,

"Yes, Yes."

I could hear him very softly crying. I think he was remembering Rosa too, and just needed to cry.

And so it was settled. At some point in the summer I would be driven to Gunnison where my parents and sister were vacationing. I would stay as long as I wanted. I think I was actually getting a little excited for the trip. After all, my grandfather had promised me, "There are trout up there as long as your arm!"

School ended on a great note. Contrary to what Sister Jean had told the entire school about failing and having to repeat the same grade over, we all passed again. Next year however, Bernie would stay behind with another group of kids who needed her skills as badly as we did. All the girls cried when Bernie made the announcement to our class. The boys of course were very stoic or at least until we got off somewhere by ourselves. We loved Bernie. We REALLY loved Bernie. She guaranteed us she would be right across the hall and would see us every single day. This was little consolation. A short while later I went into the bathroom and found Domingo Little Crow sitting on the floor crying.

"Why you cryin?" I asked him.

"Somebody hit me," Domingo responded.

"Who hit you?

"I don't remember," Domingo said.

I had known Domingo Little Crow my whole life and I certainly knew him well enough to know that if somebody hit him, he would remember who it was. We ALL moped around for several days after Bernie made her sad announcement.

Suddenly school was out for the summer and in less than a day, we were in trouble. Across from the Taos Inn was the home of a very, very cranky white lady named Mabel. She was rich. People said she got all her money selling cars. We believed this because she drove a big purple car that had her own name spelled out in the front of it and on the back too. In big silver letters it said "DODGE!" She had married someone from New Mexico named Lujan but we didn't know him and never saw him. We saw her A LOT! Every time we passed by her house we couldn't resist jumping up on her wall and running down it. The only time we didn't do this was when we were horseback. Anyway, the wall was made of big rocks and it was about three feet high; about Jimmy's height. It was just wide enough that you could run down it without falling off and it was a lot of fun. Mrs. Lujan was always yelling at us to "Get off my wall!" and "Go away you little animals!" We had just come from a school picnic in Kit Carson Park on the north side of town and were headed back to the plaza to see if anyone wanted to take our pictures. We were all dead broke. We were shocked when we came to the Dodge-Lujan house because there were these men working on the wall with a cement mixer. Two men were mixing cement and the third man was sorting sharp rocks. As the men mixing the cement would dump some on top of the wall, the third man would place a jagged rock in the wet cement. It looked very mean to us and made us feel pretty sad. That wall with the jagged rocks on top remains there today across from the Taos Inn. I guess we were the last kids to ever run down that wall. I never understood why with all her money she had such a problem with us playing on her wall.

Chapter 11
Going to Gunnison

The trip was arranged for some time in late June. We were to drive up in my Aunt Ruth's yellow Jeepster, which was always fun. A trip with Aunt Ruth and Uncle Curtis was always an event as they always filled it with the Cocker Spaniels they raised. They wouldn't leave home without all of them. On this trip however, only Aunt Ruth and my grandfather would join me. I, of course wanted everyone to go but I could tell by all the wriggling and gesturing that for some reason they thought it would be best not to show up with me, my grandfather, four grandmothers, Uncle Curtis, Aunt Ruth, Tony Two Hats and five Cocker Spaniels. I conceded. We did take Rusty however, my favorite.

I didn't have a bag as I had never been anywhere so getting ready was an experience. Tony ended up bringing a little bag from his home which I really liked. It was beautiful tan buckskin with a beaded Thunderbird rosette on the front. It had a big button made of deer horn and a strap which fit nicely over my shoulder. It was perfect I thought for the trip.

That evening, as we finished a dinner of green chile tamales with piñon nuts, I was still bragging about the travel bag Tony had given me. Billie reached under the table and produced a small package. She offered it to me saying,

"Algo para tú, queridito" and at the same time Paca produced a small box and offered it to me with,

"También, para tí, Lariano."

I was shocked that I was getting all this special attention and it wasn't even my birthday or Christmas. I didn't know which to open first but decided on the package. It was a total mystery but something told me it was tortillas or apple empanadas for our trip. That was always one of my favorites and the apples came from our own orchard. Finally I opened it. Unbelievable!! Inside the package was a yellow, striped shirt which I had seen in the window at Penney's. It was beautiful and really soft to feel compared to flour sack shirts which we typically wore. I wanted to put it on right then, but was persuaded to wait until tomorrow to wear it on the trip to Gunnison. In a million years I could never have suspected the contents of the box. As I opened it and looked inside I was stunned. Smelling very new and clean, before my eyes were a pair of black tennis shoes. They were beautiful! This was the first pair of store shoes I had ever owned. As usual, all the grandmothers were crying and hugging each other. I even caught my grandfather wiping away a tear. We were all turning into a bunch of crybabies. When everyone had gone to bed for the night, I put on the new shirt and tennis shoes and slept in them.

The following morning Bernie took my picture with Tony Two Hats standing in front of the hollyhocks that towered over our heads. Tony was smiling as big as me and the photograph still sits on my mantelpiece. While Bernie took pictures of us all, Father Bill feasted on a huge breakfast. Of course when it was initially offered him he responded, "Oh no thanks, I'm fine," which translated into Father Bill language meant, "Somebody feed me, I'm starving!" Anyway Paca made him some huevos rancheros while the rest of us gathered for pictures.

It must have been around 9:00 when Aunt Ruth finally said,

"I guess we should be going."

Turning to Tony for a final look, I noticed that he held a small bow and three arrows. He walked up to me and offered them in his normal quiet way. As I accepted the gift, Aunt Ruth commented,

"I doubt that you will run into anything in Gunnison that might need shooting."

It was more than a little cumbersome holding onto the bow and arrows while attempting to carry my fly rod. The deerskin bag fit nicely over my shoulder. Looking again at Tony and trying to decide whether or not to take the bow along, I knew that he had given me the gift for some reason only known to him. He wanted me to take the bow and arrows. I did. I stuck the arrows into the deerskin bag with the end adorned with turkey feathers sticking out. The bow hung from my shoulder. Fly rod in hand, I climbed into the yellow Jeepster.

Wiping the last of the huevos rancheros from his chin as he exited the house Father Bill commented,

"Jesus, Lariano, you look more like someone going after a killer trout than on a visit!"

As we made the circle drive around our house and headed toward the road I noticed Scout standing in the corner of his little pasture and looking at me as if to say, "Take your time coming back!!" I'm sure he needed the rest.

Turning onto the road that left the hatchery I looked back one last time to wave, "good-bye." Everyone looked a little sad I remember as we made the last turn and headed for the plaza. I'm not sure how I felt. I sat in the back seat behind Aunt Ruth and my grandfather. They didn't speak a lot which was uncharacteristic for Aunt Ruth. We drove past the plaza, past the Taos Inn and around the corner where you turn off to the pueblo. In another five minutes we were driving past Aunt Ruth's house on the Questa highway and headed north to Colorado. Our trip would take us through Questa, north to

Ft. Garland, Colorado, then west to Alamosa and from there I didn't know. I was told we would cross a mountain pass called Buffalo Pass and enter Gunnison from the east. I had gone over this route many times with Bernie. She could have done it blindfolded.

I had made the first portion of this trip twice before as we ran cattle all the way from the Colorado border into the Valle Vidal and finally ending up in the grassy meadows just north of Taos. Twice a year we would haul many horses and helpers from town, mostly Indian, and drive the cattle out of the mountain pastures where they summered. After counting and branding, we would run them back into the mountains until it was time to gather them for the winter. We usually unloaded the horses near a little community named Costilla. I had never been farther north than this but the sight of big mountains in the distance assured me that I was safe. I could never leave the mountains.

I did have one concern. I had been told by Indians from the pueblo that there was "evil" in the big valley north of the New Mexico border. It had always been avoided by them as a place where bad things would happen to them should they linger there too long. Their ancestors had hunted the valley for hundreds of years but never settled there. I wondered if maybe that was why Tony wanted me to have the bow. Maybe he thought I needed protection.

Entering Colorado we were soon in the ancient community of San Luis. Aunt Ruth commented that some of our family, many years past, had moved into this area to ranch and that we had lost contact over the years. They were a part of the "Santisteven" branch. My grandfather added that the area was known for having a large wild horse herd that had roamed free for as long as he could remember. A little further north we entered the community of Ft. Garland. I was told that Kit Carson, a name I knew well had been stationed here during the early days of the fort. I had visited his Taos home many times and had a picture of myself standing beside his grave in Kit Carson Park.

Leaving Ft. Garland, we turned west onto what looked like a never ending valley. I could see the mountains on the far side which I was told were the San Juans. I was glad that we would be going back into the mountains as the vastness of the San Luis Valley was a little frightening. I liked the security of the mountains. Aunt Ruth assured me that before long we would be across the valley and back into the mountains. Reaching the town of Alamosa I remember having my bow at the ready just in case I needed it. Arriving in Alamosa, we crossed the Rio Grande River which was comforting as I knew if things got really bad, I could follow the river all the way back home to Taos. We let Rusty run for a while in a big park beside the river and then we were off again arriving shortly in a town named Monte Vista. I liked Monte Vista because we were again at the foot of the mountains.

From Monte Vista we traveled north to a place named Saguache and then up Buffalo Pass which would deliver us a short distance east of Gunnison, our final destination.

As the town of Gunnison came into view I noticed that all three of us had become very quiet. Even Rusty, my favorite of the Cocker Spaniels sat very quietly on my lap. Feeling the urge to take one of the arrows from my bag and have it ready, Aunt Ruth finally spoke up,

"Well, here we are."

Gunnison looked the same as the other Colorado towns we had passed. It was pretty but decidedly different as it lacked the adobe homes that were common in New Mexico. There were lots of pretty log cabins and some brightly colored wood homes that Aunt Ruth described as "Victorian." They were very pretty and colorful. Some had green grass lawns. I vividly remember when seeing them for the first time, what kept going through my mind was, "white people." My assessment was correct as there seemed to be a shortage of Spanish people and I hadn't seen an Indian since Tony Two

Hats gave me the bow and arrows. Suddenly I felt VERY far away from home. We had driven quite a ways since crossing the Rio Grande and I was hoping I could retrace the trail back to it should it become necessary.

Chapter 12
The First Meeting

A short drive west of town we approached a big sign beside the road which announced, "NEVERSINK RESORT." This was it. Crossing a wooden bridge into the group of cabins, I thought this was a place that looked like a lot of fun. Small streams were everywhere and they all seemed to lead into the big Gunnison River. Lots of cabins made up what was the Neversink Resort and on the far west end were private log homes with big screen porches. The beautiful homes were nestled into a massive grove of cottonwood trees. I liked this place!

Driving slowly through the scattered cabins, and searching for the home we would recognize from a picture, Aunt Ruth said excitedly,

"Look at that girl standing on the bridge! I bet that's Judith!"

On the small bridge in front of one of the bigger cabins was a young girl dressed in pedal pushers and a sweater with a pink poodle on it. She stood there with her hands on her hips looking at us very curiously. Aunt Ruth commented,

"She reminds me a little of Roma."

My grandfather very quietly affirmed, "Uh-huh."

I mentioned that Aunt Ruth had been quiet for most of the trip. Of all things when she finally DID speak up, she had to comment that the girl we presumed to be my sister, reminded her of ROMA! It was Judith. Recognizing a yellow Jeepster, she awkwardly waved us over the bridge. Three of us sat in the Jeepster but her eyes never left ME. I remember wanting to touch the top of my head to see if maybe a buzzard or something had perched itself there unknown to me. Could I possibly look THAT strange?

We drove across the bridge and parked the Jeepster immediately in front of the big cabin. Judith walked alongside never taking her eyes off me. I had a firm grip on my bow and with my free hand located one of the three arrows. Alerted by Rusty's barking, the front door of the cabin suddenly opened. In the doorway stood an attractive lady about the age of Aunt Ruth. She was dark with beautiful black hair and stood motionless in the door.

"Hi, Dorothy!" Aunt Ruth shouted out.

"Hi, Dorothy," added my grandfather.

"It's HIM," followed my sister Judith.

What happened next was disturbing. My mother seemed to get very weak, and the little smile that had been on her face turned into sobbing. Tears ran down her face and she just stood there with her arms half raised. My grandfather quickly jumped from the Jeepster and stepping inside the screen porch, grabbed her as if to keep her from falling. Still sitting in the Jeepster, I didn't know how to react until Aunt Ruth finally turned to me and said very jovially,

"Well climb out of there and let's meet these folks!"

Rusty jumped out before I could get out and ran up to Judith. She seemed to like dogs. Aunt Ruth opened the door to the screen porch and indicated for me to come in. Realizing my presence, my grandfather slowly loosened his grip on the lady and stepped a little to her side,

"Lariano, this beautiful lady is your mother."

It seemed an eternity before she finally reached out her arms to me and grabbing me repeated over and over;

"Larry, Larry, I am so sorry."

I didn't know how to respond because I had no idea what she had done to be so sorry for. Anyway, she seemed to really need to say she was sorry so I just let her say it over and over. My new yellow shirt was drenched with her tears, but I liked her immediately, and felt like she liked me a lot too.

"Where's Eddie?" Ruth asked.

"Fishing," Judith replied. "He'll be back." "What's this bow and arrows for?"

"Shootin stuff."

"What kinda stuff?"

I didn't answer.

Finally my mom's tears turned into a big smile and she said excitedly,

"Get your things, get your things, I'll show you your room!"

I didn't hesitate. I couldn't help but notice my sister who was standing by the Jeepster, looking very suspiciously at my bag. She had on a pair of brown shoes with little slots in the front. In each of the slots was a dime!! It crossed my mind immediately that she could ride the horse at Penney's four times with that much money. I had the feeling that she even had more money than those two dimes. I was getting a little more use to her, but her stare advised me to keep my bow and arrows close at hand.

Climbing into the Jeepster to retrieve my bag, she offered to help. I felt a little better. As she climbed out with my things she looked down and commented,

"Nice shoes!"

I responded, "Thank you, they're new!"

"Nice," she repeated.

I was feeling better all the time and commented,

"Yours too!"

"They're penny loafers," she stated.

"Those are dimes," I advised her.

"Oh, REALLY," she commented a little sarcastically.

I was wishing I hadn't said that.

Part II
Reflections in the Mill Pond

Chapter 13
My Father

For the next half hour or so my sister and I made trips back and forth from the Jeepster taking the few things I had brought and placing them in the room where I would sleep.

My mother, grandfather, and Aunt Ruth sat at the kitchen table drinking coffee and watching us closely. I couldn't help but notice the big smile appear on her face each time we entered the cabin. I also could not help but notice the big smile on my grandfather's face when he would look at the big smile on my mother's face. What really caught my attention is that my grandfather was holding her hand as if he were to let go, she might just float out the window and disappear into the Colorado sky. They both looked very happy. Once my mom got up from the table and gave me a very big hug as I was passing by. She just hugged me, smiled, and sat back down at the table. My grandfather just nodded approvingly.

"What's this bow for," Judith asked again?

"It's from my friend."

"So what's it FOR?" She plied me again.

"Shootin' stuff." I offered. .

"You know how to shoot it," she asked?

"Yep."

"You know who Little Beaver is?" she questioned.

"Of course," I responded.

"You sort of remind me of him," she said.

"Thanks." I said.

"Do you know what a 'compliment' is?" she inquired.

"I think I do."

"Well, that wasn't supposed to be one."

"OK," I answered not really having the slightest inclination where she was going with all that. I personally loved Little Beaver and couldn't think of ANYBODY I'd rather be like unless it was my grandfather, Father Bill, or maybe Roy Rogers.

It didn't take long to get all my things put away in the big pine chest when my sister commented that my things "looked funny." The big chest was a bit of an overkill as I placed my two extra shirts, some underwear, and a few pairs of badly worn socks in a drawer. The chest had about a thousand drawers and my stuff just took up half of one of them.

Watching me like a buzzard, she couldn't help but comment,

"Those shirts are funny."

She had noticed the two flour sack shirts that had been painstakingly scrubbed and neatly pressed before being placed in my travel bag. Why did I just know this was coming?

"Why does this one say, Pillsbury?" she inquired, unfolding one and examining it closely.

"I don't know."

"Where are your OTHER clothes?" she inquired?

"What OTHER clothes?" I responded.

"Well, the ones you usually wear," she probed further.

"I usually wear these."

"But what do you wear to school?" She just couldn't let go of this subject.

"I wear "these" to school," getting a little irritated that she just wouldn't drop the issue of my clothes. I hung my travel bag on the bed post and went into the living room to see if my mom would hug me again. She did.

We had been at the cabin for about an hour when my curiosity got the best of me and I inquired,

"Where's my dad?"

No one seemed real eager to answer but my mom did finally indicate that he had gone off fishing earlier that morning and should be back any time.

"He's been catching a lot of trout," my mom added in an effort to keep the conversation going. No more had she gotten the words out when Rusty barked and ran out the front door of the cabin.

"I bet that's him now," my mom said.

It was my dad. He was driving up in a big blue car with the end of his fly rod sticking out the back window. As he stepped out of the car I noticed that he still wore his hip waders from fishing. He also wore a fancy fly fishing vest that had all kinds of gadgets dangling from it. Seeing us all on the porch of the cabin, he offered a little wave and walked around to the back of the car. Opening the trunk, he took out a stringer of very nice trout. Holding them up and grinning he said,

"Boy, did I stumble onto a great spot!"

"Eddie," my Aunt Ruth spoke. "This is Larry."

"Well darned if it isn't," he responded almost sounding like he wasn't expecting us at all.

"Hello, Son," my grandfather spoke out, offering his hand.

"Hello, Dad," my father responded.

"Hi," I offered, and imitating my grandfather, held out my hand.

"My, you're a big boy, aren't you?" he commented looking at me.

"You should see HIS clothes!" of course my sister had to chime in.

All of a sudden my mom slipped back into the cabin. I think she needed to go to the bathroom.

"Do you want me to clean those fish?" I offered, admiring that they WERE a really nice stringer of trout.

"Well, sure boy!" he answered, offering me the stringer. I had noticed a small run-around near the back of the cabin, and taking the fish I was off to clean them.

As I turned the corner of the cabin I thought I heard Judith ask him,

"Do you want to see his stupid clothes?" I didn't care. These were really nice trout, and I was going to catch some myself!

Returning to the cabin after finishing the task, I held the cleaned fish up proudly for the people sitting at the kitchen table to see.

"Wow, that's a great job!" my mom commented.

"Yep, good job," added my dad.

"You smell like those fish!"

She always had to add her two cents to everything. It crossed my mind to "accidentally" bump into her, and smack her with that stringer of fish right on her pink poodle. I didn't, but it did cross my mind.

Not long after that Aunt Ruth stretched out her arms and said,

"Well, I guess we need to be headed back to New Mexico."

Suddenly it struck me that "we" didn't include "me!" I felt a sudden panic at the thought of staying here without the company of Aunt Ruth and my grandfather. I'm not sure whether it was fear or what that made me very uneasy as I moved closer to Aunt Ruth so that I could actually put my arm around her neck. Suddenly I noticed that I was having a hard time breathing and felt a little sick. I didn't want them to leave, and especially to leave without me. I recall the feeling of tears wanting to pop out when I felt a very warm and re-assuring hand on my shoulder. It was my mother, and she had noticed my anxiety. My mother was a large woman, and I vividly recall her leaning over and kissing the top of my head. Suddenly I was OK. I saw the relief on the faces of my grandfather and Aunt Ruth. It was going to be OK. I might not need the bow and arrows after all.

In no time they were back in the Jeepster waving good-bye to us. I began to feel uneasy again, and I guess my mom was sensing that as she put her arm around my shoulder while waving with the other. I waved, but couldn't get "good-bye" out to save my life. As they turned and slowly drove back over the bridge leading to our cabin it suddenly got very quiet again.

"Why does HE talk so funny?" O,ooo...I knew that one was coming!

"I don't talk funny."

"Yes, you do!"

"No, I don't!"

"Yes, you do!"

This would have continued all day if my mother hadn't interceded and commented, "Larry speaks Spanish. Isn't that wonderful?"

"I think it's stupid!"

If I hadn't been staring straight at her I would have sworn it was Roma hiding in my sister's body. PEAS IN A POD!

"It's about time we were thinking about dinner, isn't it?" my mom suggested.

"Yep. How about going into the Cattlemen's in town for a change?" my dad responded.

"Is "HE" going too?"

"Well of course HE is," my mom retorted. "Do you want to just leave HIM here for the bears?"

Before SHE could answer that question affirmatively, my mom excitedly suggested,

"Let's get going! You kids put on something clean and we're off to town!"

I could tell by the horrified look on her face that "something clean" could mean one of the two shirts in the pine chest. It did.

"Oh my God," was all she said when I came darting out of

the cabin. I was pretty excited about going into the restaurant. My sister told my mother that she was suddenly feeling sick, and asked if she could stay. Giving her a very stern look, my mom informed her,

"You're going! Get in the car!"

She reluctantly obeyed, and quickly placed herself in the front seat along with my dad. I sat in the back directly behind my sister. Before we even got across the bridge, I learned that by putting my foot directly under the seat in front of me where my sister sat pouting, I could give her a little "goose" which was silently infuriating her. Every time she started to turn around and yell at me to stop, my mother would give her a stern look and comment about "how much fun we were going to have this summer." I'm not sure she was convincing anyone.

The restaurant was great! There was everything in the world on the menu, and with a little assistance I was able to read it. I had become a pretty good reader thanks to Bernie and my grandmothers who insisted that I read to them in English every single night. Noticing the prices of the things on the menu, I suddenly got a little worried. I had been given 5 dollars for the trip to Gunnison. Almost anything on the menu would take up at least half of the money I had for the whole trip. Not wanting to run out of money, I commented,

"I don't think I'll eat anything."

"But Larry, you must be starving. I know you haven't eaten since early this morning," my mother commented.

"Just let HIM starve," of course SHE had to comment.

"What sounds best to you from all these things?"

"It all sounds good to me," I responded.

"Then you're going to eat and then we'll have a big piece of coconut pie," she added.

I WAS starving, so reluctantly I pointed to what I was pretty sure was a cheeseburger with french fries. I showed my mom then reached into my pocket and offered her the 5 dollar bill I had stuffed there. Looking shocked, she stated,

"No, you're not paying for anything!" she commented excitedly.

Not certain about what to do next, I put the money back into my jeans pocket and waited for the waitress to return and take our order.

"I'll order for you!"

I was shocked at the sudden assistance my sister was offering. Maybe, I thought, she was starting to like me.

"Just don't say anything," she added, and I suddenly realized that her willingness to help out was not totally based in kindness. As the waitress approached the table, my sister gave me this "look", and put her finger to her lips reminding me not to say anything. I really wanted some green chile to put on my cheeseburger but didn't want to risk a scene by asking for it.

The cheeseburger was great, and the coconut cream pie was almost as good as my grandmothers'. I was stuffed, and really enjoyed our outing. We didn't talk a lot about anything but fishing. That was OK. It seemed like my mom wanted to ask me things but just wasn't going to do it on our first meeting. My sister ordered two tacos but only ate one commenting,

"Yuk, they're too hot!!"

I wanted to take the other one home and indicating with my finger to my mom that I would like it, she asked for a little box to take it with us. I ate it later and it was good. My grandmothers made great tacos.

Chapter 14
Trout Fishing

That first night I went to bed listening to the crackling of a big fire in the rock fireplace in the living room. It was very different from the small kiva fireplace nestled in the corner of my room at home. It was still very comforting, and when my mom came in and gave me a good night kiss on my forehead, I was pretty much at ease with the strangeness of the place, and the company. As she left the room she touched her fingers to her lips and blew me a final kiss,

"I am so happy that you are here with us, Larry." I think she really meant it. As she turned and left I heard from the adjoining bedroom,

"G'night!"

"Good night," I responded half way expecting her to follow it up with something really ugly.

"Sweet dreams," she added.

"Dúerme con los angelitos," I responded in the nicest way I could respond.

"Oh my God!!" I heard her murmur as we both dozed off to sleep.

***

"You gonna sleep all day, boy?" I heard my dad questioning about the time the sun entered my bedroom window.

"No, sir," I responded, wiping the sleep from my eyes and trying to focus on the man standing in my doorway.

"Do you fish?" he asked which I thought was a little strange as everyone in our family fished.

"Yes, sir."

"You wanna go fish, boy?"

"Yes, sir!" I responded jumping out of the warm bed and reaching for my jeans and shirt.

"Yes, sir!" I repeated and grabbed my tennis shoes and little box of trout flies I had placed in the drawer with my clothes. This was the most excited I had been, and I was really looking forward to showing my dad that I indeed, did fish. I had learned from my grandfather and Aunt Ruth who were commonly known as excellent trout fishermen around home. My Uncle Floyd was reported to be the best fly fisherman Taos had ever produced.

"You need something to eat, boy?" he asked as I raced for the front door and my little fly rod which was suspended from nails on the cabin porch.

"No sir! I'm ready!"

Instead of getting in the big car, my dad indicated that we would fish the Gunnison River by the cabin and the little run-arounds that fed into it. I didn't care, I just wanted to fish. Before my dad could slip on his hip waders, I had attached my little manual reel to my bamboo fly rod, tied on a 6x tapered leader, and was digging around in my fly box for some light tippet.

"Aren't you going to tie on a fly, boy?" my dad inquired seeing my small hands perform a perfect nail knot between the leader and fly line then following it up with a surgeon's knot attaching the tippet to the leader.

"I'm going to look at the water first." I responded wanting to see perhaps what the trout might be feeding on this beautiful June morning.

"H,mmm...good idea."

The Gunnison River was big, and as pretty trout water as I had ever seen. Dad opted for a Black Woolly Worm on a #12 hook. The big river was a little high and slightly off color due to heavy run-off. I thought he had made a good decision and decided that he probably knew a lot about trout fishing, choosing the sinking fly over a dry, floating fly. As I watched him however, something caught my eye. I was standing near where one of the run-arounds entered the big river. A little ways from the bank, a large rock protruded. The water coming from the run-around sort of ran up against the big rock, and caused the current to slow considerably between the two. Watching closely I thought I had seen the dorsal fin of what looked to be a fish moving between the rock and the smaller stream. This fish was not looking for nymphs. This fish was looking for the small Caddis flies that still hovered from an earlier hatch around the deep, still water. I always had a Caddis fly, and tying on a #14 to my tippet, I carefully dropped the small imitation into the stream and let it drift towards the big rock.

"Bang!!"

The initial jolt jerked my small fly rod completely from my hand and dragged it into the river. Instinctively, I grabbed at the rod before it was gone and thrust the tip straight up into the air. He was still there my rod reported by bending into a complete arc. The drag on my inexpensive manual reel was singing, and before I could locate the fish, half my fly line was already gone. Knowing that I used only 6x tippet and leader, I quickly realized that I would never in a million years land this monster that had attacked my fly. Watching helplessly, I heard my dad comment,

"Getting a strike there, boy?"

I wasn't "getting a strike!" I was in what seemed to be a life and death struggle with a trout I feared would eat his way up the line and the rod, reel, me, new tennis shoes, and all! After what seemed like an eternity, the fish made a turn out of the deeper water where he had swum for safety, and was hiding behind the big rock. My dad, observing the battle, had come over to where I was playing this monster trout and offered,

"H,mmmm...that's a big fish."

It was a full thirty minutes before I dragged the giant fish onto the rocky bank. It was a German Brown, and using a tape measure my dad carried in his fishing vest, he measured the beast at a fraction over 26 inches.

"Holy smokes, he's as long as your arm," my dad commented, which I thought was funny as this was exactly what my grandfather had said about the big trout in Gunnison. He was, in fact, as long as my arm. My grandfather was always right.

We fished until mid-morning, catching many more beautiful Rainbows, Browns, and an occasional Native. It was a great morning and I enjoyed it. I enjoyed being with my dad. He didn't say much, but on occasion would look over at me and smile. On one of his larger Rainbows, he asked me to help net the fish. I did. He said "thanks" and I was glad I could help him. It made me feel important.

Returning to the cabin before lunch, my mom greeted us at the door.

"My goodness," she commented, eyeing this massive fish I was attempting to carry. Dad was carrying my fly rod as I could not handle both.

"Larry caught that fish on his first cast!" I felt like my dad was almost bragging on me. It felt good.

Standing at the cabin door still in her pajamas, my sister commented,

"Those things stink!"

I was proud of my big fish. It was as big a fish as I had ever seen. I couldn't help but wonder what Bernie would think of this big monster. After a while it crossed my mind that I had to do something with this giant trout. I had been catching trout for as long as I could remember and it never bothered me to bring them home, clean them, and enjoy them at the table. Trout were plentiful when I was a boy. Streams were clean, free running, unspoiled, and full of trout of every kind. Now suddenly, I found myself standing in front of my parent's summer home holding the biggest trout I had ever seen, and wondering what to do with it. The longer I stood there with the fish, the more I regretted taking him from his home. He must have been pretty happy, I thought, swimming around all day looking for Caddis flies. Taking him from his home, I thought, was something that I didn't have the right to do, but without giving it a second thought, I had done it. I had killed the big fish just to make "me" feel good.

My mother, standing on the porch of the cabin, noticed that I was having trouble deciding what to do with the big trout.

"What are you thinking, Larry?"

"I'm sorry I killed this fish."

"There are so many fish in that river I doubt that it really matters," she offered in an attempt to console me.

"I think it matters to this one," I replied suddenly feeling that I had done something very wrong.

"Well let's clean your fish, and we'll celebrate him at dinner tonight," she suggested.

Her comment made me feel a little better, and immediately reminded me of going with Tony the previous winter to hunt deer. We were a long ways up Twining Canyon; almost to timberline. We had seen a lot of deer as we rode along the snow covered road. I had pointed at several bucks as we slowly approached them horseback. Each time Tony had nodded "No." I didn't understand why we had to keep riding and looking when we had passed up so many. It was freezing cold, and the further we rode up the canyon, the farther it would be to ride home. Suddenly, Tony held up his hand just enough that I could see him telling me to stop. Very slowly, Tony pointed into a grove of aspens about 40 yards ahead of us. In the aspen I saw two very large deer. Both had large horns, and both were staring back at Tony and me. Tony just sat there looking for a moment, then very gently drew his old Winchester from the saddle scabbard. I grabbed Scout by the saddle horn and mane knowing that with a shot would come a reaction from my pony.

"Bang!"

One of the large bucks dropped instantly as the other disappeared into the forest. Scout braced, then took a couple of steps back and settled down. Skinny didn't even move after hearing the shot. He had been on lots of hunts.

Riding up to where the deer lay, Tony slid from his horse. Seeing that the large deer was dead, he slipped the rifle back into the scabbard and dropped the reins to Skinny who just stood there looking bored. I rode up beside them and dismounted. I felt very excited, but in a strange sort of way. Tony had not even turned to look at me. He concentrated on the large animal that lay dead before him. Reaching into a small leather bag he carried from his belt, Tony extracted something that looked like ashes and slowly and reverently dusted it over the big deer. I wanted to ask what he was doing but somehow knew that I needed to be quiet. I didn't speak and Tony didn't offer an explanation. I think Tony knew I wasn't ready yet for an explanation. I was glad that he had done it for some reason.

"We have a deer to clean, Lariano."

"We sure do," I added.

It was what happened next that my mother's statement had taken my memory back to. After spending what seemed like hours in the freezing snow, Tony had the big deer skinned and cut into several big pieces.

"How are we going to get all this home," I asked Tony?

"We won't," Tony answered.

"Why not, Tony?"

"He doesn't just belong to us," Tony responded.

"What do you mean, Tony?"

"He belongs to all the beings in the forest. We're just one of the beings who share him."

I decided to stop questioning as I was getting nowhere and understanding less with every answer.

After tying two large portions of the deer on Skinny, and one behind my saddle on Scout, Tony took a cord he had carried in his saddle bag and tied it to the fourth big piece of deer. He threw the cord over a high branch and dragged the big quarter about 8 feet up the aspen tree trunk. By this time I was totally confused but tying off the cord to the tree trunk, Tony seemed satisfied and managed to clamber onto Skinny in spite of the big load behind his saddle. Tony, making a motion with his lower lip towards home, turned Skinny and we were headed back down the canyon. About a hundred yards into our ride, Tony turned to me and asked,

"Why did we do that?"

Feeling too puzzled to even attempt an answer, I just shrugged my shoulders.

"What do you think will happen to that deer?"

Thinking for a minute, I finally blurted out,

"I think a bear will get it!"

"Do you think a bear will get it all?"

"He may drop some of it," I speculated.

"What will happen to the meat he drops?"

"I think the coyotes and birds will get it."

"Will that meat be wasted?"

Suddenly I got the whole thing! When Tony turned in his saddle for my answer, I just smiled a little. Tony smiled back, and in a couple of moments told me,

"This deer has been in the forest a long time. He has made it possible for many young deer to be in the forest. Nothin' lives forever. We are born, we live, and we make way for the young we leave, hopin' we leave somethin' useful behind. This big deer will feed us. He will feed many of the animals of the forest. His hide will keep us warm on cold nights and we will make shoes from his skin. Hopefully these shoes will walk an honorable journey."

Tony didn't speak again all the way down the canyon.

Remembering this experience with Tony, I suddenly was

feeling better about the big trout I had caught. Looking up at my mom, I asked,

"Can we really have this big fish for supper? He's enough for all four of us?"

"Only if you help me cook him," she said flashing a big grin.

"Please let me help, I'm a good helper!"

Thus ended the episode of the big fish. It did indeed feed all four of us and tasted delicious along with the hot corn bread and the potatoes and onions she fried to go along. The big apple pie she made which we covered with vanilla ice cream wasn't bad either. Everyone agreed that it was a great dinner. I felt proud again.

Chapter 15
Home

For the next two weeks we enjoyed a routine of getting up, having a nice breakfast, and going fishing, or sometimes making a drive to a pretty spot in the area. Once we drove east from Gunnison and crossed Monarch Pass. In less than an hour we arrived in the town of Salida. It was pretty and we had a nice dinner in an old hotel. I think it was called the Victoria. After dinner, we returned over the mountain pass and arrived back at the cabin a little before dark. The drives were usually interesting but we didn't talk much. This was so different from home as everyone was always talking away about something. These silent times were beginning to make me uncomfortable.

I had been away from home for a little over two weeks. I had enjoyed being with my mother. I had even enjoyed being with my sister at times, and had learned many techniques I could use at home to get the better of Roma. Dad and I had fished a lot and caught wonderful fish. I don't recall that we ever talked about anything other than fishing.

While the visit had been pleasant I had begun, especially in the second week, to wonder about the people at home. I missed my grandfather and all the grandmothers. I missed all my friends and wondered what they were doing. I especially missed Father Bill and Bernie and wondered if they were missing me as much.

One evening at dinner, I finally asked the question I had wanted to ask for days,

"When do I go home?"

I recall it was one of those evening dinners where hardly anything was said at all but after my question, it got even quieter. I fully expected my sister to answer with something like,

"Tomorrow would be a nice day for a drive," but not even she had a response. My father just sort of shrugged his shoulders. My mother sat motionless just like all the air had been let out of a balloon. I felt like I had been doing pretty good on my visit but at this very moment I felt an urgency to gather all my things and get to the Rio Grande as fast as my legs would carry me. It was the first time in my life that I had experienced panic. I needed to be "home" and I needed to be there as quickly as possible.

After dinner I dried the dishes and helped my mom put them away in the knotty pine cabinets that reminded me a little of home. My mother must have looked at me and smiled a hundred times as we did the dishes, but she hardly spoke. It was terribly quiet, and I was wishing I had said nothing at the dinner table about going home. The only problem was that I wanted to go home very badly. I liked the visit, and I enjoyed my family, but I needed to be home and I needed to be home now!

That night before crawling into my bed I said my prayers. It was the first time I had done so since coming to Gunnison. I had learned from Father Bill and Bernie that you should close each day by giving thanks for the things you have and especially for your family and friends. It was a good way to end the day. That night however, I just couldn't stop praying. I prayed for my grandfather and all the grandmothers, and all my friends, and for Scout. Most of all, I prayed that someone would hear my prayers and come get me. I was desperate to go home.

Evidently "somebody" did hear my prayers because at breakfast the next morning my mom inquired,

"Larry, do you really think you need to go back to Taos?"

"Yes, ma'mm. I know they are needing me to help."

That was a lie, but it was about all I could think of at the time.

"When would you like to go?" she questioned.

"Maybe today," I answered.

"That's so soon," she responded.

"They REALLY need me," I lied again.

"What do you think, Eddie? Could we drive Larry down?"

"Sure" was all he said.

Hearing that we would be leaving within hours, I breathed for the first time in two days. I felt badly again. I think it was guilt or something. I didn't know what to do. I didn't know what "they" wanted me to do. I know my mom probably wanted me to stay longer. Maybe even my sister too, but I knew I HAD to go and I had to go right now. I offered to help with breakfast dishes but my sister said,

"I'll get them."

That made me feel good but didn't do much to sway my need to get home as quickly as possible. Getting up from the table, I went straight to my room and began packing my belongings. Stuffing my shirts and things into my bag felt good but I just couldn't do it fast enough. I was almost trembling with excitement at the thought of arriving back at the old hatchery. I remember it was like I had to hold my breath until we got there.

It seemed like hours, but before long I had all my things sitting on the porch of the big cabin. I must have checked a dozen times to make sure I had everything; bag, fly rod, fly box, bow, arrows, and oh yes, there was the beaded belt. I had spent $1.00 of my trip money on a beaded belt that said,

COLORADO on the back. I couldn't wait to show it to Tony.
I knew it would make him feel good to know that there were
Indians in Korea. I didn't know where Korea was, but it said
right on the back of the belt, "Made in Korea!"

Finally, we were off. We re-traced the trip I had made not
long before with my grandfather and Aunt Ruth. It was very,
very quiet in the big car. I sat in the back seat with my mother.
I didn't even try to goose my sister the whole drive back to
Taos.

Retracing the route we had taken earlier, my heart
pounded with excitement when I saw the big sign which read,
"Bienvenido! Welcome to New Mexico, Land of Enchantment!"
I could hardly conceal my excitement in knowing that we were
headed to Taos, and in a matter of minutes now we would
climb the west mesa and approach the beautiful adobe home
of Aunt Ruth and Uncle Curtis. We must have still been a
good ten miles west of town but I was straining my eyes to see
the big house which would assure me that I was home again.

Suddenly there it was looming in the distance. I must have
been babbling like a chipmunk, telling everyone about how
Aunt Ruth raised strawberries, and how Rosa and I used to
pick them, and how Rosa had gotten sick and died of Polio,
and how the Indians hunted rabbits from horseback in the
fall, and how Tony had shot the deer and left the meat for
the forest animals, and how we hunted turkeys in Twining
Canyon for Thanksgiving. All of a sudden, I could breathe
again and I needed all the air I could get to tell my stories to
my parents.

Pulling into the circle drive at Aunt Ruth's, we were
greeted by a pack of Cocker Spaniels. Rusty led the charge,
and before my sister could get out of the car, she was mobbed
by this unruly band of tail waggers and tongue flappers. They
were happy to see people, and I know they were excited to
see me. My sister thought they were funny, and I think she
actually laughed when a couple of the dogs began barking at
the others because they weren't getting enough attention.

Exiting through the kitchen door, Aunt Ruth and Uncle Curt greeted us with open arms. Uncle Curtis sported a huge smile, and Aunt Ruth wore an old white apron that told us she was cooking. In the air I could smell roasting chilies and maybe even a peach pie. I bounced around like one of the Cocker Spaniels. I don't recall ever being so happy to be anywhere in my life.

While the grown ups visited, I took my sister for a ride on my Uncle Curt's tractor. It wasn't real big and I had learned to drive it well when we plowed the gardens in the spring. I sat in the big seat, and my sister stood just behind me holding on for dear life. I drove my sister down the road behind Aunt Ruth's house to the small adobe where the Montoya's lived. Hearing the tractor, the Montoya family ran out to greet us.

"Esta es mi hermana! Se llama Judy!"

"Mucho gusto," Mrs. Montoya responded with a big smile.

"My sister smiled back at her and the seven Montoya children that were all grinning like possums. Driving back to Aunt Ruth's, I reminded my sister that this was Rosa's family. I had told them about Rosa.

"Does everyone here wear those same shirts?" she inquired, obviously noticing that the Montoya kids wore shirts very similar to mine. This time however, she didn't seem to be making fun of us as much as just curious. I was relieved that she didn't comment on the shirts while we were visiting with them. My sister was very pretty, and I almost felt proud that she was my sister.

Back at Aunt Ruth's we were welcomed with peach pie and ice cream. It was wonderful, and I ate as fast as I could, knowing that when we finished we would be going to the hatchery. While my sister and I waited for the grownups to finish, I showed her the peach orchard where I helped pick the peaches each year. She wanted to pick some but I told her they were not ready yet. I remember telling her,

"Maybe you can come back in the fall when we pick them?"

All she said was, "I doubt it."

After what seemed like an eternity, we loaded up and headed off to town. Aunt Ruth rode in the big car with my parents so that Judy and I could ride in the Jeepster with the 5 Cocker Spaniels. Uncle Curt drove and the dogs licked our faces the whole way into town as they could smell the hint of peach pie and ice cream that we hadn't quite wiped clean. Passing the liquor store in El Prado, Uncle Curt honked the horn as he always did. I never understood why he did that, but he always did. Maybe it was to re-assure the owner that he was in town and would probably be in very soon.

Nearing the plaza, I showed Judy the wall at Mrs. Lujan's house and explained the jagged rocks on the top. She seemed moderately impressed and even less so when I pointed out the mechanical horse at the Penney's store.

Making the final turn into the hatchery, I recall it looking like a fiesta. Aunt Ruth had a telephone, and she had called the Silers to tell my grandfather that we were coming. It was a grand homecoming with everyone smiling, laughing, hugging, and crying. I felt like I had been away for months instead of just a couple of weeks. My mother was laughing and grinning right along with them, but I remember my father and sister just looking on in amazement. My sister didn't say it, but I knew she was thinking,

"Oh Dear God!"

"Lariano" Paca shouted, "You just missed Father Bill and Bernie!" They came for lunch, and to see if we had heard from you!"

I was sorry I had missed them, but knew I would go visit them later as they would have a million questions about my visit.

"Where's Tony?" I inquired of my grandfather.

"I think he went up to Blue Lake for a ceremony. He'll be back before long."

I wanted to see everybody, and be assured that nothing had changed since my departure. It was very good to be home.

Noticing the excitement and the strangers at our house,

Roma came out to investigate. Aunt Ruth introduced Judy to Roma, and they immediately became friendly and talkative.

"Hey, Judy!" I shouted. "Come look at my horse!" I implored her.

"Yeah, he's great," she responded, and immediately returned her attention back to Roma.

"I bet you missed me, didn't you Scout?" I plied him, rubbing his forelock excitedly. He didn't respond, and just kept swishing his tail at flies. I wanted to jump on him and head out for the Mission School, but knew that would have to wait a while. Noticing that my sister and Roma were headed around the house towards the pond, I decided to join them. In a moment, we were all standing by the pond on that late June day. The sun was bright, and the big willow tree was as motionless as the water. There we were like I remembered so many times before, but for the first time, with my sister. We stood there gazing at our reflections; Roma, my sister, and me. It was nice.

Looking over my shoulder, I noticed my mom approaching us.

"Your dad says we have to be leaving for home now."

No more had she said it than she began to cry. I gave her a big hug, and told her that it was a pretty drive, and if you stop in Cimarron Canyon, you can get water from the Drinking Log. It had been there forever, and we always stopped when we were in the canyon. That didn't seem to make much difference to her, and she kept crying. She was holding me pretty tight and I just really didn't know what to do.

My grandfather, Paca and Essie soon appeared where we stood by the pond and joined mom in the sobbing. Before they could really get into it, they were joined by the rest of the grandmothers and Aunt Ruth. It was quite a scene; everybody standing there at the pond crying. It was a picture I remembered a long time looking into the water and seeing everyone's image reflected there; all holding on to each other and all sobbing away. I was too happy to be home to feel like crying. I just sort of patted everyone on the back and slipped around to the front of the house where dad was waiting in the car. Soon we were joined by all the mourners. It was an unhappy scene, and I just wanted it to be over with.

"Good bye."

"Good bye, sister," I answered.

"Good bye, son," Mom said, trying to hold back her tears.

"Good bye, Mom, good bye Dad," I said waving as they got into the big car.

"Thanks for all the food and stuff," I reminded them.

"We love you," my mother said lowering herself into the car.

Everybody waved and in a second, they were gone. For the longest time, we all just stood there.

The silence was finally broken by the sound of a familiar "whinny" behind us.

"Somebody dead?" was the first thing out of Tony's mouth as he rode upon the somber scene.

"No," was the only response given. It was my grandfather turning to Tony, assuring him all was well.

"Everyone is fine, Tony."

"Looks like somebody died," was all he responded.

With this, all the grandmothers started crying again. It was a terrible scene and seemed it would last forever had the silence not been broken by Rusty barking at the approaching car.

"Got anything to eat???"

It was Father Bill and Bernie coming up the drive. Father Bill was yelling out the car window like he was starving or something.

"Hi Bernie!" I shouted at the top of my voice, "I'm home!"

Before she could even climb out of the car, BERNIE started crying, and then the grandmothers all started up again. How could everyone be so sad when I was so happy?

"Dear Lord," Father Bill, exclaimed, "This looks more like a wake than a homecoming."

With that, everyone began to laugh, and the sad scene turned into the kind of happy gathering that I remembered and loved so much.

"Got any white man food?" Tony asked turning towards the little house. "That Indin stuff we eat up at Blue Lake jus' makes me hungry. No wonder all the Indins is dying out!"

"Yeah," chimed in Father Bill!" "Let's whip up some white man food!"

Everyone's tears turned to laughter, and we all headed for the house.

Noticing my bag still contained all the arrows I had left with, Tony commented,

"Have to shoot anything up there in Colorado?"

"Almost," I said giving Tony a big grin.

Chapter 16
The Homecoming

Before we could all get into the big kitchen which was the main meeting place in our home, the questions began coming at me like hailstones. Everyone was asking all at once what my visit had been like, and what we did, and what my favorite thing was, and what my sister was like. The inquiries were coming so fast I didn't know how to start. Finally I said,

"It was Ok. I caught a big fish." Looking across the table at my grandfather, I added, "It was as long as my arm."

"Tell us all about it!" just kept coming from everyone, but I just couldn't find a way to tell them what it was really like. I tried again,

"It was very quiet."

"What do you mean, QUIET?" was uniformly plied.

"We didn't talk much."

"You're gone over two weeks and didn't talk much," they kept probing.

"We just didn't talk much."

"About anything?"

"No, not about anything?"

Everyone looked puzzled that I had so little to report to

them. They were very curious and I was doing very little to stem their curiosity.

"We just didn't talk much," I re-iterated. "We just didn't talk much."

Feeling very uncomfortable for the very first time with these people, I asked to be excused to go to the bathroom. As I was leaving the kitchen, Bernie sort of intercepted me as I was leaving and said,

"I'm sorry, Lariano. It's going to be OK. I am so glad you're back."

"Bernie," I said. "I don't think it's going to be OK."

"What do you mean, Lariano?" she asked.

"It's just not OK, Bernie. I'm not OK. Something is wrong with me."

"Oh, no!" she assured me. "You're fine. You're just fine."

"No, I'm not, Bernie. I'm not just fine!"

I had no idea of how to explain to Bernie how I felt about the visit. All I knew was that if I hadn't come home today, I don't think I could have ever come home at all. I didn't know how to tell her that "I couldn't breathe." Bernie just stood looking at me, wanting to make things better, but temporarily at a loss for words. When I came back into the kitchen, she was talking quietly with Father Bill. I knew they were talking about me.

Father Bill winked at me as I entered the kitchen. He gave me his usual "thumbs up" as I walked over to the big kitchen table and sat down beside one of the grandmothers. I had barely sat down before someone asked,

"What's wrong, Lariano?"

"He must be tired," I heard another say.

"Are you OK, son?" my grandfather asked.

"I'm fine," I lied, and then asked if I could be excused.

Feeling that it would be good to swing on the big swing over the pond, I made my way around the house. The swing looked inviting, and I jumped onto the wooden seat and started kicking my legs so that it would begin to swing back and forth over the pond. With each big arc, I took a deep breath and took in all the air I could possibly hold. I was breathing again, but still wasn't completely comfortable. As the swing came to a standstill, I looked into the pond and saw my reflection. It was still me that I saw, but somehow I was different. The image in the water looked like me, but it wasn't. Something had changed, and suddenly I feared that I would never be the way I was before the visit to Colorado. I felt like running, but suddenly noticed that I was having a hard time breathing again. It was just like the day before but this time I was home. I was safe.

Perhaps a half hour later I heard Skinny begin to let out a little snort. He always did that when Tony approached. Seeing me still sitting on the swing, Tony walked over.

"Hard time, huh boy?"

"Yes, Tony."

"Wanna go ride a little?"

"Sure Tony, let me go tell them I'm going!"

Running from the house, I grabbed my bridle without ever slowing down and raced to the corner of the pasture where Scout was standing observing me. He didn't run away, but stood nicely while I bridled him and jumped on bareback. Using his bottom lip to point, in typical Indian fashion, Tony indicated that we ride a small lane going west towards Taos Creek. I was happy to be horseback with Tony and Scout, and noticed I was breathing much easier.

"What happened up there," Tony inquired?

"Nothin', Tony, nothin' happened at all."

"Did someone say something that made you feel bad?"

"Not really, Tony, nobody said nothin' at all!"

Tony was very quiet for a little bit and then began,

"You know boy, there's different kinds of quiet. There's the kind of quiet when you sit by a fire just listening to it and nothin' else is makin' a sound. That's a good quiet. There's the kind of quiet when you've done somethin' real good, and you know you did somethin' real good, but you don't brag about it. That's a good quiet, too. Then there's a quiet when there NEEDS to be noise. Sometimes people need to speak up and make noise so that others know what they're thinkin'. If they don't speak up, and say what they're thinkin', it makes you suspicious that what they're thinkin' is not good. That's a hurtful kind of quiet, and it's not good for anybody."

"Do you like old Tony," he suddenly asked me?

Surprised by his question, I immediately answered,

"You KNOW I like you Tony!"

"I know you like me too," he responded, "but if I didn't know you so well, and you never told me you like me, I might think that you didn't."

"I don't understand."

"Does your mama like you, boy?"

"Yep!"

"How you know?"

"She told me a million times!"

"Does your daddy like you?"

"I dunno."

"Did he ever tell you he did?"

"No."

"Maybe he shudda. His kind of quiet was not what you needed. All your life you've been surrounded by people who tell you, AND they show you how much they like you. Not everybody is that way you will learn."

"It made me feel real bad, Tony."

"I know, boy."

No more had Tony got the last word out before a huge buck jumped up right in front of us where he had been watering in the creek. Skinny just stood there, but Scout jumped high enough that I lost my seat and went tumbling into Taos Creek. Tony was laughing out loud at me sitting in the running stream and then I began laughing too. We were laughing so hard I could hardly catch my breath. I noticed at that moment however, that I had been breathing very normally while visiting with Tony.

"You gonna sit dere all day, boy, or we gonna ride?"

Laughing, I crawled out of the stream and finding a tree stump was able to jump back aboard Scout. I still remember we were giggling like schoolgirls as we continued up the creek trail. I remember thinking how I wanted our ride to last forever, and for nothing else to ever change the way things were at this very time in my life.

By the time Tony and I got back to the hatchery, Father Bill and Bernie had gone back to the mission. The Jeepster was gone with Aunt Ruth, Uncle Curtis, and Rusty. The grandmothers were nowhere to be seen but my grandfather was standing in the apple orchard like he was checking unripened apples. Tony offered a quiet, "Aho," and indicated he was headed to the pueblo. I rode over to where my grandfather was standing and as I approached he gave me a big smile.

"I'm really glad you're home, boy. We missed you very, very much."

"I missed you too, grandfather. I don't think I'll ever go anyplace again."

With a gentle laugh, he nodded and said,

"Let's you and I go see what the ladies are up to."

With that, I sunk my heels into Scout's fat sides and ran him back across the hatchery yard to his little pasture. Jumping down, I grabbed the bridle and raced towards the house. It was good to be home. It would be some time before the questions ceased about the trip. Finally I think everyone came to the conclusion that I just didn't want to talk about it. I continued telling them "It was fine" and the truth was, "It was just OK."

It would be a long, long while before I was mature enough to understand the implications of that first visit. I didn't understand myself just why I had been so uncomfortable. All I knew at the time was that it was past, and I would go on with my life the way it had always been. While this seemed easy to do however, I was having a difficult time understanding why

I felt so sad about my mother. I felt I had disappointed her by wanting to go home to Taos. As time went by, I felt more and more guilty.

Chapter 17
Moving On

The rest of that summer passed very quickly, and in no time at all we were back at the mission school. I attended the first day without incident making the second year in a row that I had started school and made no attempt to escape. I think I was accepting my fate, and would attend school for however long it took for me to get an education, whether I wanted to or not.

My visit to Colorado was nothing more than a distant memory except that I had received several letters from my mother. They lived in Dallas, Texas and as we were studying all the states in school, I made it a point to show all my friends the little postmark on the envelopes indicating that it came from another state. I remember Bobby Yazzie being confused that there were "white people" living in Texas. I recall him saying,

"I thought the Mexicans killed them all at the Alamo!"

History WAS a confusing subject to most of us as the little book we had talked about how the white people came to early New Mexico and civilized it. This account conflicted totally with what we had learned from our parents and grandparents.

Cordie Coronado told us there was a big stone wall behind her grandmother's house with names and dates of her family that was living there before the pilgrims ever landed on that rock. Of course we all had seen the carved and painted pictures that appeared all over the place telling about Indians who lived here many, many years before the Spanish ever came to New Mexico. My grandfather and I spent many wonderful days exploring the kivas, caves, and cliff dwellings where the Indian people had lived for thousands of years before "America was discovered." When we questioned Father Bill about all this he simply replied,

"It's all a matter of perspective," which of course meant absolutely nothing to any of us. We had learned that when the teachers had no explanation for something, they simply said,

"It's all a matter of perspective."

This was one of the more useful lessons we had learned at school, and we used it frequently at home. I recall when Domingo Little Crow and I got caught smoking my grandfather's pipe. He had asked us,

"Do you boys think that taking my pipe and hiding in the woodshed to smoke it was an honorable thing to do?"

Domingo simply spoke up and said,

"It's all a matter of PERPLEXIVE!"

School began as usual and we liked our new teacher. She was older than Bernie, but very nice. She too, spoke the many languages that were heard in our community, and got along very well with our own unique language which was a mix of all of them. Her name was Sister Anna Maria and we called her "Sister Anna." She didn't have a bicycle, but returning to school on a Monday morning in September she surprised us with "yo-yo's" she had brought back from a weekend trip to Albuquerque. In no time, we all learned how to "yo-yo" and except for one chipped tooth, we mastered them without incident.

Not long before the Christmas holidays, as Father Bill sat with us at dinner one evening, he brought up the subject of my becoming an altar boy at the mission. I liked this idea as I really enjoyed going to mass with all the grandmothers every Sunday and holidays.

Being a part of the mass would be great. My grandfather was never very involved in the church, but always supported the rest of us and encouraged us to participate. He used to say,

"Tony and I have our own religion," which they never talked about much, but we knew included a few drinks of peach brandy that they made from the left over peaches from our orchard.

Anyway, that fall I became an altar boy at the old mission church. I loved helping out and enjoyed the beautiful ceremonial aspect of it all. The mass was said in Latin but I still understood most of it. It was during the mass, that I felt the most at peace and secure. Watching Father Bill perform various ceremonies and always seeing Bernie right there in the front row smiling gave me re-assurance that I was truly OK, which I had temporarily doubted.

Before Christmas, I received a package in the mail. It was postmarked Dallas, Texas and I knew without opening it that there would be something good inside. I had written my mother earlier in the fall and told her about turkey hunting with Uncle Curtis and Tony. I also told her that I was an altar boy now and I was sure she was proud of me.

Opening the package on Christmas morning, I found that indeed it was full of good things. There were two beautiful shirts, two pairs of new jeans and to my surprise a picture of my mom standing next to my grandfather. I really liked the picture, and it made me feel very good to know that my mother and grandfather were good friends. I liked my mother a lot and still fretted from time to time that I had disappointed her so much. In the big package was a smaller package which to my surprise concealed a pair of gloves and a Christmas card from my sister. The card said,

"Hope you are catching a lot of fish, Love Judith."

This came as a real surprise and I immediately wanted to reciprocate and send my sister something in return. Unable to come up with anything appropriate, I finally decided to send her the picture Bernie had taken of me and Tony on the morning I left for Colorado. She obviously liked the picture because she kept it her whole life, and then passed it back to me.

My third grade year flew by, and in May I got another letter from my mom in Dallas. This time the letter included pictures of their home, and a huge lake that was right in front of the big house. The house looked like pictures I had seen of the house where the president of the United States lived. The house was so big I could hardly make out my sister and mother who sat on the front steps. They looked like ants on a log, but at the bottom of the steps a bicycle was parked on a stand. Somehow I knew it was my sisters. The big lake was called White Rock Lake, and looked like the ocean from the pictures. I wondered if it was good trout fishing. There was another picture of my sister and a large black lady wearing an apron. A note on the back of the picture said, "Judy and Old Bea, the maid." I had seen a black lady in Albuquerque once on a visit, and she was big and wore an apron too. I decided that all black ladies must be identical. In the letter my mom asked "when" I wanted to come to Colorado to visit this summer. It seemed like so long ago that I barely remember the visit except for the big fish I caught. I did remember that when I came home I worried about the visit for a while, and even told my grandfather that I didn't want to go back. That was so long ago and the thought of going back there, and catching another big fish, and eating in the restaurants was actually sounding pretty good. I do recall wondering if it would hurt my grandparent's feelings if I asked to go visit. I likewise remember worrying that "it would hurt my mother's feelings" if I didn't. I decided that I needed to talk with Father Bill and Bernie.

The next day I asked Father Bill if we could have "one

of our little talks." Of course he agreed and that afternoon following school we met at the big picnic table in the church yard. I told them about the invitation and to my surprise, they didn't seem as excited as I thought they would be. Bernie asked me,

"Do you want to go, Lariano?"

"I dunno. I kind of do and I kind of don't."

"What do you mean, by that, Lariano," Father Bill asked?

"I'm afraid."

"Afraid of what," they both asked simultaneously?

"Afraid I can't breathe," I said almost embarrassed. "And I'm afraid I'll hurt my grandfather's feelings if I go," I added.

"What will happen if you "don't" go?"

"I'll hurt my mother's feelings," I said dropping my head and feeling like I just wanted to disappear. Father Bill and Bernie looked up at each other and sort of sighed. It was not an easy problem to fix. Finally, Father Bill suggested that we go inside and pray for an answer. That sounded good to me as it was pretty obvious we were getting nowhere. Inside the church, the three of us knelt at the front altar. Father Bill was on my left and Bernie on my right. At that time, there was no place in the world I would rather have been. We prayed and prayed and prayed. After what seemed like hours, Father Bill nudged me with his elbow and said,

"That's about all my bony knees can handle for one prayer."

I smiled and we ended our prayer and left the mission. As the three of us walked through the massive wooden doors that had hung there for hundreds of years, Bernie turned towards me and asked the strangest question.

"Lariano, what do you want to do when you are grown up?"

Without hesitation, and without even thinking, I responded,

"I want to be just like you and Father Bill, Bernie. I want to live here and be just like you and Father Bill."

It was like at that moment a great light came on and there was not a single doubt in my mind that I would ever consider doing anything other than be just like Bernie and Father Bill. I loved them. They were my best friends, my guides, my heroes. I wanted nothing more in my life than to be just like them and live my life at the mission.

Father Bill and Bernie drove me into town as it was nearing dinner time and Father Bill had asked me "If I had any idea what was for dinner?" Bernie commented dryly,

"Since when does the menu matter to you?"

We all laughed and drove on into town. I remember when the three of us were walking up to the house, you could clearly smell hot enchiladas fresh out of the oven. There was also the smell of hot peach cobbler. Glancing over at Father Bill, I noticed him make the sign of the cross, obviously giving thanks for his good timing. Bernie just shook her head in acceptance of his questionable manners.

"Staying for dinner?" Paca invited graciously.

"Oh, we really can't," Father Bill responded as one of the grandmothers without hesitation set two extra plates at the table knowing he had no intention of leaving. They stayed. It was good.

Part III
Reflections in the Mill Pond

Chapter 18
The Gift

Much later in my life I became familiar with the expression, "Perfect Clarity." As a boy, I had no idea of the meaning. Standing in the mission doorway with Father Bill and Bernie that spring day, I had experienced "Perfect Clarity" and had no idea that I had. I doubt that either of them had realized the full meaning of what I had disclosed to them. My revelation had not been one that I had given much previous thought to. What I did know however, was that standing there in the doorway of that old mission with the faint smell of piñon and antiquity, I had made a discovery within myself that I not only wanted to be around my friends, Father Bill and Bernie, but I wanted my life to be like theirs—just like theirs. They were happy, contented people who spent most of their time trying to make our lives better. They were present when we learned right from wrong. They were there when we learned to read, when we wrote our little stories. They were there at our parties, and they were there when we said our "good-byes" to Rosa. And yes, they were always there when we were upset, frightened, or puzzled about what to do. They were always there. I wanted to be there to help someone, too. Even as a child, not yet 9 years old, that feeling could not have been clearer to me. It was like I had walked from darkness into the light, and I was no longer afraid of anything. I could even go back to Colorado for a visit, and afterwards return home and find it just like I had left it.

At dinner I asked if I could visit my family in Colorado this summer. The answer was simply,

"De claro, of course you can!"

The same three of us left on June 20th for Gunnison, Colorado. The trip was much the same as I recalled from the previous year, except I didn't feel that taking my bow was necessary. I did, however use my deerskin bag and pack it just like the year before; except for including the shirts and jeans I had received as gifts at Christmas.

The second summer I remained three weeks. Not much was different except that I spent more time with my mother, and a little less time fishing. I had taken a book with me to practice, and found that it was very nice reading it to my mother. The book was named My Friend Flicka, and it was about a boy and his horse. I loved reading that story to my mom. I think she already knew the story, but never let on that she did.

My sister was nice to me some of the time. We would take walks and she would tell me about her school. Her school was named Highland Park, and she told me there were about two thousand kids there. When I told her I attended St. Francis Mission School, she said that it sounded "funny." When she asked how many kids attended St Francis Mission School, I lied and said I didn't know. I wasn't sure how many two thousand was, but I was sure it was more than fifty!

A couple of days before I left for home, my mother asked me if I would like to come visit them in Dallas some time. She followed that question with a, "You know, it's your home, too." I didn't feel like it was my home at all, but I was a little curious about it. I told her again, just like the previous year, that the grandparents really needed me, and I didn't think I could make a trip that far. While I had felt pretty good on this trip, the thought of going all the way to Dallas, Texas sort of made me short of breath again. I was ready to go home and the very next morning, I did.

The following year swept past more quickly than the previous. It was much the same as the others with our days spent in school and our afternoons and weekends horseback or fishing. I spent as much time as possible with Father Bill and Bernie. I asked questions incessantly about how they chose the careers they did, and what they did to accomplish them. By now they had realized that I was very serious about the disclosure I had made to them the previous year. I had shared my hopes with all the grandparents and while they may have doubted my ability to stay with such a difficult plan, they never doubted my sincerity. Even my grandfather noted my tenacity and commented one evening before dinner as I began grace, which had become my custom to do.

"Can you hold it down to about fifteen minutes? I'm starving to death!"

Being the righteous and dutiful grandson, I did. "Thank God," I heard him mumble to himself.

Chapter 19
Changing Directions

It seems the older you get, the faster time goes by. I barely recall the days, months, years between my youth and my teenage years. They were good years. School had become an acceptable necessity, and I looked forward to learning about the world outside of Taos, New Mexico. Learning made our little village seem like such a small part of it all.

In the summers it seems that more and more people were coming to town to vacation. The little sandy streets that led to the plaza now clamored with traffic and at times, the dust from their cars made our ponies choke. One day, as several of us were riding into town, a car of vacationers pulled up behind us, and started honking its horn so that we would move out of the way. The loud horn caused Bobby Yazzie's horse to jump sideways and Bobby fell off and broke his arm. The car didn't even stop to see if he was OK.

Not long after that incident, I returned home one day from fishing and found my grandfather and several of the other men from town sitting around the kitchen table talking. I could tell they were very upset about something so I just stood in the doorway and listened. It seemed that Mr. Lujan had overheard some state men talking who were staying at the Sagebrush Inn. The men evidently worked for the highway department and were surveying the road coming into town from the south. After all the surveying was complete, they planned to pave the road all the way from south of the Sagebrush Inn to the Plaza.

"What can we do?" I remember Mr. Benetez asking.

"Let's shoot 'em," Jimmy's dad, Mr. Martinez suggested. This was his solution for about everything. Tony was very quiet during the arguing and just sort of sat there with his head lowered. Noticing me standing in the doorway, he motioned with his bottom lip to the door, and I knew that meant to meet him. Walking around to the pond, he said very little. I climbed up on the swing and just sitting there, I asked him,

"Tony, what do you think about this road?" Thinking to himself for a long moment, he replied,

"This not a bad thing for old Tony. It don't matter how many people drive up and down this road. Tony has a roof over his head at the Pueblo and a bed to sleep on. It's been dat way in my family for a long, long time. No one can take Tony's house and bed. It's not for sale. This mebbe is a bad thing for Lariano and all your friends. YOU own the houses you live in. You can live in dem, you can sell dem. It's your house to do whatever. Somebody offer you lot of money for your house, you take the money and now it's their house. You don't have a house no more. You gotta hand full of money. Lariano, if you have a hand full of money, what you gonna do with it?"

"I dunno."

"That's the problem," Tony said. "You gonna go buy you another one with a fish pond out back like dis one?"

"There's not another one like this one Tony. You know that."

"That's just what I'm tellin' you. Once DIS one is gone, it's gone forever. You can't have dis one with the pond anymore.

"We'll just keep our houses, Tony."

"No," Tony responded. "When he hand out enough money, all the houses be for sale."

There were times when talking with Tony could be pretty depressing. I thought he was wrong about selling all our houses until a few days later Bobby Lujan told us at school that he was having to get rid of his horse because his dad had sold the little pasture where he kept him to the state men to park their road making equipment. We were all upset by this as the thought of ANYONE parting with his horse was unthinkable. Bobby went on to say that his dad, "was buying a truck with the money he got," but that didn't seem to console Bobby in the least. This new development was more than a little disturbing. Once again, Tony had shared something that would indeed come to pass. I was just thankful that my family would never be affected by new people coming, and that Aunt Ruth would always have her beautiful home on the Questa Highway, and even though I might live at the church like Father Bill and Bernie, we would always have my home at the hatchery, and the mill pond. Nothing would ever change that, I assured myself.

The next three years brought little change to me and my family. I attended school regularly, helped out at the mission church, and spent countless hours with friends; riding, fishing, hiking, playing. I was also getting more involved with Father Bill and Bernie so that when I was old enough, I could attend the seminary and return to northern New Mexico. I would spend my entire life doing the things I had learned from my beloved mentors, and all the while living in the only place in the world where I could be content.

The changes in our community over those three years were a little more than significant. It started with the road. In spite of all the protesting, which even included an armed confrontation by my grandfather and many of the people from town, the road came. With the road came a lot of workers. They came from all over and sort of flooded our little town. At night, many of the workers would come to the cantinas and drink until they became loud and discourteous. My grandmothers and some of the other ladies from town quit dancing at the La Fonda because the people we not so politely referred to as "fueras," were rude to them and treated them with little respect. Of course when this issue came up in discussion at our house one evening, Mr. Martinez, in his customary way, suggested, "Let's shoot them!"

None of the "fueras" were shot, and some of our friends even commented that their little businesses were doing better with all the new people in town. Miguel Molina, who owned the El Prado liquor store commented, "It was like having 300 Uncle Curtis'." While no one was ever shot, there was a sense of danger in town now as the streets were filled with big equipment and men shouting, "Get out of the way, stupid Indian!" and things like that. We had never experienced anything like this, and it was not good.

With all the new workers and visitors in town, Aunt Ruth decided to buy a small building on the east side of the plaza and open a restaurant. She called it, "The Little Pig," modeled after one she had seen in Albuquerque. She sold bar-b-que which was a new treat, and had become very popular in cities. Her business did so well she was persuaded to invest some of her money in a mining venture over in Questa. Many of the people in town, even though their assets were limited, borrowed money using their homes as collateral and invested in the mine. As soon as we were all rich, no one would even think about selling their homes any more.

No one got rich in the mine over in Questa. After a while, they didn't find what they were mining for, and the mine closed down. Aunt Ruth had put up her land, which included the large strawberry field and The Little Pig as collateral when she invested in the mine. It was a terrible time. Aunt Ruth and Uncle Curtis both went to work for the new public school. They operated the cafeteria which must have been good for the kids, but sad for Aunt Ruth and Uncle Curtis. They had always worked just for themselves and were free to travel, fish, hunt, and roam any time they wanted. Now they worked in the school cafeteria just to save their home.

I don't recall a single one of my friends whose family didn't lose either their home or their land in the mine disaster. People whose families had farmed or ranched the pretty lowlands around town were now working in the restaurants, motels, and souvenir shops. Several of my friends moved away. I guess we were lucky. My grandfather rationalized that no one in their right mind would want a big block of land with old adobe homes a hundred yards or so from the old plaza. Besides, it would be mine to own when I got old enough and they were gone.

With each summer visit to Colorado, I became closer to my mother and sister. It was fine being with my dad, and we always caught a lot of fish. The summers following my fifth and sixth grade years, my mother's brother and his family spent their vacation in the summer home with us. My uncle's name was "Toad," and I always thought that was funny. I liked him a lot and his beautiful young wife, June was the love of my life. She was not only lovely; she was the nicest lady I had ever met. Her warm smile and kind heart always reminded me of Bernie, and I just couldn't spend enough time with Uncle Toad and Aunt June.

It was fun being a cousin to Cindy and Scotty. He was much younger, but still cute and entertaining. Cindy was fascinating. She was always laughing and ready to play about anything you wanted to play. I remember she had this pony tail that always bounced when she ran. Cindy and Scotty's dad, Toad, was my mother's youngest brother. She had three and eventually I met and liked them all. I really liked my new family and it was sad when their vacations ended and they returned to Oklahoma. Before leaving, Cindy asked me to come visit them and I could meet "all" the cousins. She told me they were all fun and we would have a great time. I remember thinking that I would like to do that.

All the places where my "other" family lived seemed so far

away. I recall them saying they drove for two days to get to Colorado. It only took two "hours" to get there from Taos and that was very comforting; especially in those times when I needed to get home immediately. Still the lure of those faraway places haunted me a little, and my curiosity of seeing what their homes were like with the cars, bicycles, friends, stayed pretty constant in my mind throughout those school years.

It was the day that my cousins left for home after their second year of visiting us in Gunnison that the question finally came up. Mom and I were sitting on the porch swing at the cabin. I was getting ready to go home to Taos the next morning. We were talking about all the fun things we had done during the visit. In my mother's normal, quiet way, she asked,

"Have you ever thought about coming to live with us?"

I vividly recall not being able to answer her question right away. I do recall thinking that it had crossed my mind about what it might be like going to the big city, and living in the big house on White Rock Lake. I remember thinking I could probably have a bicycle. I had already asked my sister if most of the streets in Dallas were paved. I could see all my cousins. I would be with my mother every day. After these fantasies passed the reality always came back to me that I could never leave my home in Taos. In a million years I could never leave my grandparents, my friends, Father Bill, Bernie, Scout and my plans to work at the mission church. Living in Dallas was an exciting thought. It just wasn't one that would, or could, ever be possible. My life in Taos was as good as any boy had ever dreamed.

I was ending my fourth summer visit when the conversation with my mom took place about coming to live with them in Dallas.

The next morning I was packed and ready early to return home. After breakfast, we loaded up and headed south for New Mexico. After dropping me off, my parents would drive home to Dallas. I recall looking back at the cabin which I had learned to love, and thinking about all the fun we would have next summer when I again, came to visit. As we pulled onto the highway leading into town, I looked back at the cabin one last time. I had no way of knowing that none of us would ever see the cabin at Neversink again.

We arrived in Taos before noon. Roma and some of my friends were fishing in the pond, so my sister and I ran around the house to join them. It was a beautiful August day, and as they all greeted us, we stood there grinning and laughing, I noticed the image this scene made on the surface of the water, and remember thinking I would like to have a picture to keep of all our reflections in the mill pond.

As we played around the pond, the adults sat at the kitchen table talking. They visited longer than they usually did, and when they finally came outside, I noticed that my mom, my grandmothers, and maybe even my grandfather appeared as if they had been crying. This was discomforting to me, and I didn't inquire at the time. We said our "good byes," and in an instant they were gone. I took a deep breath and felt relieved that while it had been a good summer visit, it was over and I could get back to my real life. Turning back towards the pond where the kids were waiting, I heard a car approaching up the drive. Turning to see, I spotted the old black mission car with arms waving out both sides and a voice yelling,

"What's for lunch?"

Laughing at this funny scene, I knew I was really home and ran to greet them. Bernie always gave me a big hug, and Father Bill would sort of get me in a headlock and rub his knuckles over my crew cut head. We would laugh and giggle like schoolgirls! It was a scene that had been re-enacted many times before, but each time was as good as the very first.

"Prisa, prisa!" I could hear from the kitchen, and knew the grandmothers were going full speed to get lunch ready for the obviously starving young Franciscan. Their giggling almost drowned out the sound of hooves chattering on the stony drive and Tony's shouting out to us,

"Aho, mus' be time to eat!"

Sitting at the kitchen table that day, feasting on tacos, chicken mole, fry bread and flan, I looked around the table at the faces of the people who had made my life so wonderful. I looked at every single face and said a little prayer of thanks that they were such a big part of my life. As if he knew exactly what I was thinking, Father Bill grinned at me and gave me a little, "thumbs up." It was almost like in some mysterious way, he knew we were enacting a scene we would never play again. In his silence, he was giving me permission to go to Dallas.

Chapter 20
Never Say Good-Bye

The following weeks passed very quickly. I remember feeling like I was caught up in the current of a large, swift river, and could not manage to swim out. I couldn't ever slow down as the day came closer and closer to when we would meet my parents in Shamrock, Texas, and I would continue on with them to my new home in Dallas.

During this time, it seemed that everyone had lost their voices. Hardly anyone spoke at all; much less did we speak about my moving to Texas. It was like if we didn't talk about it, it just wouldn't happen. I learned that my new family practiced this technique very well. Now, we were doing it at home in Taos. If you just don't talk about things, they're not real. I had to learn to do this too, and I admit it was much easier than sitting down with my grandparents and talking about my leaving. That would have been difficult. We avoided the subject, and simply exchanged "half smiles" and winks when we were together. I remember those last days as being deadly silent, and thinking that when the day arrived, we would simply drive away without saying good bye to anyone or anything. When the day came, we did just that. We simply drove away. The grandmothers busied themselves with small talk, and acted like they didn't even see us get into the yellow Jeepster. Scout stood in the corner of his pasture just looking at us. He didn't even swish his tail. Catching my eye, Tony made a gesture with his lower lip which I knew carried many different messages. Roma gave a brief wave from her window. In minutes the sight of the adobe house at the old hatchery, and the early aroma of piñon burning in the kiva fireplace were gone.

Our drive took us through Taos Canyon to Eagle's Nest Lake where we had spent many fun times camped on its shores, listening for the small turkey bells attached to the fishing rods, telling us a trout was sampling our bait. Leaving the basin, we entered Cimarron Canyon and stopped once more at the Drinking Log. Leaving the canyon, I turned and watched the towering peaks of the Sangre de Cristos fade into the distance. As the last peak disappeared, I recall thinking it looked like a candle, flickering, blinking, then disappearing. I turned away thinking that we were driving towards the edge of the world, and eventually, we would just drop off. It was a terrible, lonely feeling.

In mid afternoon, we arrived in Shamrock, Texas. Aunt Ruth commented at the welcome sign promising "Good Luck!" I remembered the shamrock tucked away in my bag between the pictures of Bernie and Father Bill. They gave me the pictures and the good luck token before I left.

Pulling up to a small motel, my grandfather continued his newly acquired silence. As my mother exited the door of the small cabin type motel, I did see him flash a large smile. He turned and shared that smile with me and I suddenly felt a little better.

Putting her hands to her mouth, my mother walked quickly to where we were pulling up in front of the cabin. The tears were flowing already, and she hugged and hugged me. My grandfather was sort of rubbing her back in his very loving way. He never spoke, just kept nodding his head, "yes," in his way signaling that everything would be OK.

My sister and dad exited the cabin, and the first thing my sister said was, "Wanna watch TV?" Never having seen a television, I was pretty curious, and entered the room to investigate.

Before long, Aunt Ruth stuck her head in the room and informed us that it was time to go.

"Lariano, your father," suddenly she corrected herself and said,

"Your "grandfather" and I have to be heading back."

Only then did it strike me that I was not "heading back." I was going in the opposite direction, to a place I knew only from pictures. My breath left my body in a sudden "swoosh!" I knew this feeling all too well. I didn't say anything, just stood there nodding, "Yes," and thinking,

"Don't say good bye, don't say good bye, please don't anyone say good bye. Everything would be just fine if we just don't say 'good bye.'"

In less than five minutes, the yellow Jeepster was gone. I was standing on the porch of the motel, holding my little deerskin bag, and thinking that all my insides had just vanished with that yellow Jeepster.

"Come in, come in," my mom was insisting, but all I could do was stand on that little porch and stare down the road where the little yellow car had gone. In my mind, I could see a very long cord, one end attached to the vanishing car, and the other to my heart. Each second the cord was getting tighter and tighter and in a matter of seconds the cord would break loose from me and be dragged off behind the yellow car until car, Aunt Ruth, my grandfather, and the cord would disappear into the west where my beloved mountains lay beyond the faraway horizon.

Dallas, Texas was a very long ways off. I had never been in a car that long, and in spite of all the things my mother told me about how much fun it would be to live in the big city, I was not excited. I was a little curious however, about a turtle that she said lived in a big aquarium at the fairgrounds in Dallas. She said, "It was as big as a dining room table."

"Bigger!" my sister added.

I was also very excited about seeing another television set like the one in the motel. That was pretty interesting, and in between programs a thing called "test pattern" would come on the screen, and you turned knobs until the picture was clear. The picture was the head of an Indian, and I wondered if Tony knew him.

My sister said that when we got home, we were going to the Ice Capades to see Sonja Henie skate. I was completely shocked hearing the news that people this far away from Roma even knew about Sonja Henie. Her knowledge had spread a long way.

Part IV
Reflections in the Mill Pond

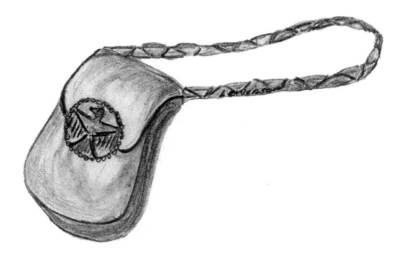

Chapter 21
Moving

The decision was made that I would not attend school in the fall. I would move to Dallas in September, and spend the fall with a private English tutor who would prepare me for going to the big school in the spring. This was my father's idea, and a condition he imposed on my coming to live with them. He had made the comment more than once that "If you speak any language other than English, you were probably washing other people's clothes, or cleaning their houses." I wasn't sure what he meant by that, but it was agreed that before I would start school, I would be tutored at home until my mastery of the English language was complete.

We were up early the next morning and driving southeast on what seemed like an endless journey. I kept straining my eyes to see if mountains might appear in some direction. They never did. What I did see in every direction were armadillos. I had never seen one before, and I thought they must be the stupidest animals I had ever come across to try and cross the highways with all these cars. Their smashed carcasses lined the roads.

In the middle of the afternoon we finally came within sight

of Dallas, Texas. It was enormous. I had visited Albuquerque several times but it was nothing like Dallas, Texas. A long time before we even arrived you could see the tall buildings that looked a little like the towering rocks near Tierra Amarilla where we used to picnic and climb. Even after seeing the outline of the tall buildings we drove for what seemed like hours getting to what was called, "North Dallas." I was sure that when we got closer to home we would begin to see mountains as my sister's school was called Highland Park. If it was a "highland," it surely had mountains. I thought we must still be very far away as I saw no mountains. I did see cars, and cars, and cars; giant trucks of every kind, buses of every color, and one had a place on top where people could sit up high and see out through big glass windows. I thought that would be a lot of fun to ride one back home through the forest. Here in Dallas, I didn't see a lot they could be interested in seeing. It wasn't very pretty I thought, and we hadn't seen a single deer, antelope, or elk the entire trip. Since we had come into the city, the armadillos had even vanished. I couldn't help but wonder what Tony would think of these big buses with the glass tops. At the same time I was thinking that he might look pretty funny riding one of these with all these white people. The more I thought about it, the less I imagined that he would even want to ride one anyway.

It was almost an hour after sighting the outline of the big city before my sister said,

"There's White Rock Lake!"

I remembered the picture of the big white house and how it sat back a ways from the lake. Suddenly there it was, just like the picture and "yes" it still looked like the one the president of the United States lived in. What was more exciting was the size of the lake. It was huge and I was sure it must be full of trout. Pulling into the circle drive, I jumped from the car and ran down to the lake to look for signs of feeding fish. Approaching the massive body of water I noticed a sign and ran over to it. I suspected it told the regulations for fishing, and informed you about how many trout you could have in possession. It didn't. What the sign said was,

"NO BOATING, NO SWIMMING, NO FISHING!

My room was on the second level. An enormous black lady wrestled my deerskin bag from my arm. Thinking it impolite to put up much resistance, I let her have it. I was sure now that all black people were identical as she was a mirror image of the black lady I had seen in Albuquerque the year before.

"You mus' be HIM!" she offered, in a more or less annoyed way. "Sho wish dey puts you down hea on de groun flo so I's not runnin' ups and down dese stayuhs pickin' up yo trash."

I was stunned. I wasn't exactly positive what she had said, but by her tone and the look from those tortilla sized eyes, she wasn't happy to see me. In a desperate effort to protect myself from an all out assault, I said,

"I'm a REEELY good boy, Señora!"

"ALMIGHTY JESUS, LAND O' GOSHIN!! WHEA DEY FINE DIS OFUN CHILE OUT DERE IN DAT NEW MESCO WIT ALL DEM MESSCANS! Yo cum own chile, yous got sum lunnin up to do."

To my complete amazement this frightening ebony figure suddenly reached out and put an enormous black arm around my probably trembling shoulder.

"Mone now boy, ain't gots all dey be messin' wichu!"

Putting my little bag on the bed and pointing towards a large chest of drawers, she shot me a quick glance and winked.

"Wen yous done chile, mone down de kichin. Old Bea gos sum hot cookies ans I tinks one o two dem gots yo name on 'em." "Mone now!" she said and departed.

This last exchange I understood clearly, and before she was half way down the big staircase, I caught up with her. I had noticed in the seconds it took me to put my possessions away that there were lots of new store clothes already in the drawers. I guessed they might be mine, but was more interested in following "Old Bea" to the kitchen and investigating those hot cookies she had told me about. As scary as Old Bea was, I felt like maybe I had made an ally who could help me get started in my new home. The house was so big I didn't even hear my mom, sister or father. I had no idea where they had vanished to but was confident that Old Bea would keep me from getting lost. The chocolate chip cookies were wonderful and I had milk that came from a bottle with a picture of a cow on it. It was cold and good. Old Bea winked at me after I finished the second cookie and pointed to the stove top where the others were still cooling.

"Mo dese?" she asked nodding her scarf wrapped head towards the stove top.

"Please, señora." I responded.

"Land o Goshen, Almighty Heavenly Jesus de Lawd: if you aint's de pecurist ting eva cum down de rode!"

"Si, señora," I responded not having the slightest notion what she was talking about.

It was about the fifth cookie that I heard my mother yelling for me. Her call had a little fear in it as she might have suspected that I slipped out and was escaping back to New Mexico.

"HE in hea!"

My mother came through the door looking a little relieved and smiling at me.

"Would you like to walk through the house with me," she asked?

Thinking to myself that if I could sound a little like Old Bea, my mother would think I'm fitting in quickly.

"Sho I wuds!" I responded in my newly acquired jargon.

From behind the closed swinging door to the kitchen I heard a voice that could only have been my sister.

"Oh Dear God in Heaven!"

The big house was pretty amazing and it took a while to see it all. On one end was a big garage with room for four more cars. On the wall leading into the garage were buttons and if you push them, the garage doors went up and down.

Over in one corner, I spotted a bicycle I guessed belonged to my sister. I was hoping she would let me ride it sometime. Behind the big house and a little distance away was a much smaller house. A brick walkway led from the back door of the big house out to the little house.

"What's that?" I inquired thinking that I much preferred the idea of living in the small house instead of the giant house with a room at the top of the stairway.

"That's where Old Bea stays when she works too late to go home."

It reminded me a little of Bernie and Father Bill who lived at the mission. It was convenient as they worked almost all the time. I imagined that this worked out pretty well for Old Bea except that there must be times when she didn't go home to her family. Thinking this about Old Bea, I had my very first thought of "going home to my family," and felt a tug in my stomach. I asked if I could see inside Old Bea's little house but my mom told me that was up to Old Bea. I settled for that.

All the new clothes I found in my room were indeed for me. There were almost as many new clothes as at the Penney's store and I didn't see any way I could wear them all. I remember thinking how I would like to send some of them to Father Bill so that he could give them to the kids whose families had very little. I would have to talk with Father Bill and my mother about this. I tried not to think of home much because every time I did, I got a little sad thinking about how they all must be missing me. I was missing them too. I imagined Scout standing in the corner of his little pasture waiting for me to return from the mission school. I thought about my grandfather and all the grandmothers, and all my friends, and even Roma. I worried that Father Bill had replaced me with another boy to help with the Eucharist and that Father Bill and Bernie were maybe sorry that they had ever brought up the idea of meeting my parents. The more I thought about it, the sadder I got and before long I found myself stretched out on my new bed with my face in the pillow.

"Whas de matta you boy?" I heard in the unmistakable

voice of Old Bea. This time, however, it was much softer than
before. With a loud "creak" Old Bea sat down next to me on
my bed and sort of rubbed my back. Again she inquired in a
low tone,

"Whas de matta witchu, boy. Yo dun gots yo feelins hurt
cause yo be so diffunt?"

I couldn't answer, and tried to muffle my sobbing in the
pillow.

"You be a good boy, Mistuh Larry, and you an Old Bea's
get down dis rode as bes we kin. It's terrible hard sumtimes
and you wundas if you ever make it dea to whea dat rainbow
be hidin.' You jus' keep travlin' dat rode and one days you be
finding dat pot uh gold. You jus' keep travlin' dat rode. Good
Lord gotchu by de han, boy, and he not gonna let go til he
gotchu whea dat rainbow end."

I must have begun to understand Old Bea a little as her
words made me feel a little better. She kept rubbing my back
until I could breathe a little and the tears slowed down.
Mustering my strength and without turning my face from the
pillow, I said,

"Grácias."

"Land o' Goshen!" she softly replied.

Chapter 22
Old Bea and the Tutor

His name was Mr. Cunningham. He came from London, England and made me spell funny. Old Bea didn't like him from the beginning.

The plan was for Mr. Cunningham to come to our house every school day and teach me to talk like him. We also would study Math, Science, Social Studies and History.

I was a little anxious at first as he was nothing at all like the teachers at the mission school. In an attempt to impress him with my knowledge of history, I chattered away about how the Spanish people had come from Spain a long time ago looking for gold, and instead they only found Indians. I told him they must have been pretty angry at not finding much gold so they got mad and killed most of the Indians they found and claimed the new land for themselves, even though it didn't have much gold. I told him that the Spanish were doing pretty well living with what was left of the Indians until one day white people showed up and told everybody that "because they were smarter than everyone else," God wanted them to have all the land whether it belonged to the Indians or the Spanish settlers. They said it was "God's Will," and I guess it was because they were not finished yet, but well on the way to getting all the land. I was in the middle of telling him about Bobby Lujan's dad selling his pasture to the white men when Mr. Cunningham abruptly interrupted me with a "Thank you that will do."

I was learning a little math, and catching on to some of the science lessons too. His history lessons were quite a lot different from what I had learned. He seemed to take a lot of pride in how the Texans drove the Mexicans out of Texas. The Mexicans did sound pretty terrible in his account, but I just never quite understood why they had to give up their farms and homes just because they were Mexicans. I read in my history book that before the Mexicans even came to Texas, the Indians lived there too just like in New Mexico. I decided that the Mexicans had been very thorough in getting rid of the Indians in Texas because I had now been in Dallas for several weeks and not seen a single Indian.

Learning to talk like Mr. Cunningham was very difficult. He knew words I had never heard and learning to pronounce them perfectly, much less spell them correctly, was almost impossible. The "talking" lessons were going pretty slow and when I suggested that Old Bea join in the lessons it was not well received. I was thinking that if "anybody" had trouble talking correctly, it was surely Old Bea and not me. Old Bea never joined us on the long afternoons of reading, writing, spelling, math, science. She did pass the door of my father's study from time to time and roll her eyes like she thought Mr. Cunningham was maybe wasting his time and maybe even mine too. I did hear her chuckle one time when she was passing the study and heard me ask Mr. Cunningham where, "Land o' Goshen" was.

By the time Thanksgiving holiday came around, I was doing "pretty well" according to Mr. Cunningham. He had commented to my mother that "I was a bright boy, but very easily distracted." It WAS a constant struggle, his trying to keep me on task, when if the truth were known, I didn't want to be there at all. Mr. Cunningham was OK as a teacher but he was nothing like Bernie. I missed Bernie and the Mission School. I missed them all. One day Mr. Cunningham said that we would begin to study French in the spring. I told him that I would prefer to study Latin as the Mass was in Latin and I wanted to be ready when I went to school to be a Franciscan. Mr. Cunningham only laughed a little and said, "You'll get that silly notion out of your head soon enough," then went on with his lecture. I didn't understand at all what he meant by that, but decided not to make a big deal of it.

We didn't attend the Catholic Church in Dallas. My parents were Methodists. I missed being an altar boy for Father Bill but the Methodist knew some good songs and sang a bunch of them every Sunday morning, so I was somewhat content to go along. My English was really good by the second year and I just sang up a storm. I liked the one about "Gathering at the River," but it always made me think of fishing for trout back home and I'd get a little homesick.

Chapter 23
The Holidays

On every holiday we visited family in Oklahoma. All of my mother's relatives lived there, and I had lots of cousins whom I liked immediately. They were great fun, and we stayed at the small home of my mother's parents. We called them Mama and Papa Pat. They lived far out in the country, and being around all the cousins and playing in the country was the happiest I had been since moving away from home. On the first Thanksgiving visit, Mama Pat caught two big chickens and spun them around by their necks until their heads popped off. My sister and cousins, Sue Ann and Cindy ran off behind the house when the chickens started jumping around without their heads. Me and my two cousins, Donald Paul and Mike just sort of stood there in awe.

Those fun holidays with my mother's family in Oklahoma were always high spots of my year. I loved the short trips from Dallas to southern Oklahoma as I knew it meant days of playing with my cousins whom I had grown to love and looked forward to seeing. I also loved being with my mother. My sister Judy and I still fought frequently but the battles were less fierce and sometimes followed by laughing. Though my father was always present, I don't recall spending much time with him. He always seemed like his mind was faraway, and the only times he spoke were to correct me for something I had done. I just tried to stay away and out of his sight as much as possible.

It was during the Christmas visit of my third year of living with my family that one of the strangest things in my life happened. During the holidays, all of my mother's brothers would get together and dig a new hole for my grandparent's outhouse. With the new hole completed, the uncles began the job of moving the outhouse to the new hole for the coming year. It had rained a lot the past year and the uncles struggled to get the outhouse free from its footing. With one big tug, the small building broke free and was loosened from its resting spot. It came loose so quickly that my Uncle Jack, who was on one side pushing, lost his balance and fell into the hole, head first! I remember him standing in that hole from the previous year with his arms uplifted, pleading for his brothers to lift him out. They didn't. They just stood there beside the hole, pointing at my Uncle Jack and laughing so hard they were crying. It wasn't nearly that funny to my Uncle Jack. In years past, I had heard my grandfather on occasion, say words that made my grandmothers blush a little, and sometimes cover their mouths and giggle. Uncle Jack knew some of those same words and a lot more that I had NEVER heard. He was calling the other uncles all kinds of names and the louder he yelled the names, the harder they laughed at him. Finally, my Uncle Toad put a long ladder into the hole where Uncle Jack was standing. As soon as the ladder was in place, all the uncles ran off before he could climb out of the hole. Once at the matinee in Taos, there had been a movie called Curse of the Vampire. It had a mummy in it, and the mummy was all wrapped up in something white like rags or paper. Seeing Uncle Jack climb up that ladder, all covered with that white paper reminded me of that mummy.

For three straight summers after moving to Dallas, we were

unable to make the summer trip to Gunnison. Always it had something to do with my father's business and that he was just too busy to take the summers off and go the mountains. Each spring when the news was shared that again we would not be going, I felt very sad. It had now been three years since I had returned home to see my grandfather and grandmothers. I had received letters from Father Bill and Bernie but even the letters were beginning to be fewer and farther between. The letters from my grandfather were usually very short and didn't have a lot to say.

In a letter I received from him not long after Christmas of my third year away, he told me he had some bad news. He told me that Tony's old horse Skinny had not "fattened up" for the harsh mountain winter, and with the first heavy snow, Skinny had died. This made me very sad to learn this as Skinny was the only horse I had ever known Tony to have. They went back long before I was born I was thinking as I began reading the rest of the letter. My grandfather told me in the next line that he would rather "cut off his arm" than tell me the rest of the bad news. Now prepared for the worst, I read on. My grandfather said that the whole family had shared Christmas dinner at the house and Father Bill and Bernie had joined them. Later in the evening, Father Bill and Bernie, along with all the grandmothers, went off to the late Christmas Mass. Aunt Ruth had asked Tony if she could drive him home to the pueblo but he refused, saying he wanted to walk the mile and a half home even though a light snow was falling. The following morning, Domingo Little Crow's father arrived at the house around 9:00AM and told my grandfather that Tony had been found alongside the road not far from the pueblo. He had apparently had a heart attack and froze to death by the side of the road. Tony Two Hats was gone.

Following this terrible news, my grandfather added one more line. All it said was, "We love you, boy."

All the rest of that winter and spring, I just sort of moped around thinking that finally this coming summer we would get to go to the mountains. I was finally getting to go home. Now Tony Two Hats was gone and I would never see him again. Even when the Easter vacation came around and we made the trip to Oklahoma to visit my cousins, I just couldn't find happiness. Even though I had come to love my Oklahoma family, Tony was a part of me that these people didn't know and could never understand. I grieved for Tony Two Hats, and wished I had never left my home in Taos. When I stopped eating and showing interest in anything at all, Old Bea began following me around asking the same question over and over again.

"Whas de matta chu boy?"

Her incessant questioning was only equaled by the same question from my mother, just phrased in better English.

"Is something troubling you, son"

There was indeed something troubling me. For three years I had been living with a family I barely knew. For three years I had attended school with kids who made fun of me. For three years I had lived in a house with a man whose only interest in me was to make sure that I would not embarrass him.

I wanted to go home and thankfully with summer approaching, I could not only return to the mountains for the summer, I would return home for good.

Just the thought of it made my heart race. My only regret was that I didn't get home in time to tell Tony goodbye. I had made a terrible mistake in leaving home. Tony had known that from the very first visit. Now, three years later, I had learned who I was, and where I belonged. Unfortunately, it had taken Tony's death to wake me up and show me very clearly where my heart was. Even though it would be several weeks before we made the trip to the mountains, I secretly began packing my old deerskin bag in preparation. I shared my secret with Old Bea, but didn't tell anyone else that I would not be returning with them at the end of the summer visit.

Part V
Reflections in the Mill Pond

Chapter 24
The Sky Is Falling

The school year was coming to an end, and with it would come the end of my time in the big school in Dallas, Texas. The experience had not been terribly bad except that it had reminded me repeatedly that I was "different" from nearly all of the other kids who attended the big school in the "right" part of town. Old Bea and I had become very close over the past three years, and while she didn't want to see me leave the big house, she assured me that, "You gotsta follow yo' hawt, no mattas whea it leeds ya."

MY heart was at home in Taos with my grandfather, the grandmothers, Father Bill, Bernie and all my friends. It was time to go home. The move would be difficult as I had truly learned to love my mother and sister. I was sure they would understand, and maybe even support me in this decision. I would bring it up as we prepared to make the trip to Gunnison.

We were all very busy packing and preparing the final days before the departure. It had been three years since I had seen my home and all the people I loved. A full week before our departure I had secretly managed to get all my things I was planning to take with me stuffed into little boxes and bags so that I would leave nothing of value behind. I wanted to take all my store clothes with me, but couldn't as there would not be enough room in the car along with everyone else's things for the summer.

I vividly recall my mother looking very tired the days before we were scheduled to leave, and I imagined she had worn herself out getting ready. She loved the summer home as much as everyone else and had worked hard preparing to go. Two days before we were scheduled to leave she told me that she was going into the doctor for a checkup as we would be away for almost three months. My father drove her into town and it was almost supper time when they returned. Old Bea had made fried chicken and mashed potatoes, and my sister and I were already at the dining room table when our parents came in through the front door.

Without their saying a word, we knew something was wrong. Mom gave us a little smile and said, "Umm, smells good!" but even the tone of her voice told us that she was upset. Old Bea took mom's sweater and very kindly said,

"Mone ova heah and sits down, Miz Wood. Old Bea dun fried up sum chickin jus de way you likes it."

Even Old Bea knew something was wrong. Old Bea was so much like Tony Two Hats in that way. They always seemed to know stuff before it was ever said. As mom sat down between Judy and me at the table, our father entered the room and took his normal place. Old Bea just stood there instead of going into the kitchen to bring out the dinner. It was like she knew there were things to be said, and would not move until it was done. Then Old Bea did the strangest thing. She walked around the table to where my mother was sitting and patted her very warmly on the shoulder. In a soft voice, Old Bea said,

"Miz Wood, yous a fine lady. You be walkin in the shadow of de Lawd. You always been so kind to everones and de good Lawd he be with you right dis minute and give you de strength of all his angels."

Hearing this, my mom turned in her chair and gave Old Bea a big hug. Judy and I sat motionless in our chairs waiting for the sky to fall.

Mom began by telling us that she had gone in to see Dr. Taylor today because she had not been feeling good and wanted to be well for our trip. She had hoped it might be something simple, and would be feeling good in no time. She went on to say that during the exam, Dr. Taylor had found a lump in her stomach that surprisingly was pretty large and needed further examination. At this point she began apologizing that the further examination was scheduled for the following Monday and this would keep us from leaving for a few more days. Of course this news was met with sighs from my sister and me, and we were more concerned with getting to the summer home than doing a further examination which we knew would result in something simple and fixable.

I remember feeling almost angry at my mom for going to the doctor in the first place. Whatever was wrong with her couldn't be anything much but it was keeping us from going to the mountains for a few more days. It was a Thursday that she had gone in, and now we had to wait until the following Monday to do the examination.

I was further disappointed the next Monday when my parents returned from the hospital and announced that it would now be Wednesday before the results of the examination were available. Again, I went to my room and pouted over the delay.

It was about 10:00 in the morning on the following Wednesday that I heard a car drive up and I was shocked to see all three of my mother's brothers climbing out. They had driven down to Dallas from Oklahoma. I was happy to see them but thought they looked very serious for three men who typically would be laughing and joking with each other. Hearing my shouts that they were here, my mom came from her room and met them at the door. They all four hugged like I had seen them do many times on the holidays. It was a familiar scene except that no one was laughing.

This time my mom and dad and all three uncles left for the hospital. They returned around 4:00 in the afternoon and after a little nervous small talk, my Uncle Paul asked if sis and I would sit down at the dining room table with them.

It began with, "How would you two feel about moving to Oklahoma?" My initial response was one of shock as nothing like this had ever been discussed. Many times following a holiday visit, the cousins had made comments that they wished we all lived together. Those were just kid's dreams as we always had fun. This was different. Uncle Paul was actually bringing up the idea of a move to Oklahoma where my mom's family and all our cousins lived. They were actually asking us "if" we wanted to move to Oklahoma to live.

I recall both Judy and I not responding immediately. By this time she had a boyfriend, and of course this would not be good for her. It would mean moving away from him. Judy had just graduated from Highland Park High School, and planned on attending Southern Methodist University which was not far from our home in Dallas. I, of course could not make the move to Oklahoma as I had made up my mind to return home to my family in Taos. I had just not told anyone yet. With this news about a possible move to Oklahoma, I didn't know how to bring it up.

After a few more moments of silence, my sister asked, "Why are we moving to Oklahoma?"

At that time, my Uncle Paul began to tell us the story we already knew about Mom's not feeling well, and about the checkup, and how she would feel better if she were living close around her family. Judy and I both agreed that moving to Oklahoma was a pretty drastic step just to make Mom feel better. Still, we sat quietly and waited for the opportunity to visit with Mom alone so she could explain this mystery to us. I imagined that I would take that opportunity to share with her my plans to return to New Mexico. She would understand.

It was the following day before the opportunity presented itself. Sis and I found our mother sitting alone in her rose garden behind the big house. She smiled when she noticed us approaching but we immediately noticed that she had been crying. Initially Mom apologized for "causing" us all this trouble and acknowledged her concern that we were leaving our home and friends. Again, we listened quietly until Judy finally inquired,

"Mom, what's wrong with you?"

Her explanation was unclear to me as she used words that I was unfamiliar with. I had learned English very well over the past three years but still was unfamiliar with the word, "cancer." Mom's explanation was so simplistic and un-alarming that I didn't even ask "when she would be well again." As badly as I wanted to tell her of my decision, something told me to just keep quiet. A week later the moving men took my boxes and bags, and put them into a big green truck along with all our other possessions. I was moving away as I had planned earlier to do. I just wasn't going home.

Old Bea stood on the porch of the big house as the truck pulled away with the contents of our house and our lives. I watched her for the longest time, waiting for her to go back in and do the final cleaning. She just stood there. As I watched, I thought I could see her head very faintly moving from side to side as if she were denying that this was happening to all of us. She just stood there. As I watched her, I remembered all the times over the past years that I had talked with her, laughed with her, cried with her.

Old Bea took me on my first bus ride, explaining to me that we could not sit together, as she must sit in the back, and I must sit in the front. I remember her stern look when I refused to sit away from her and seated myself right beside her in the very last row. I recall how the first time we had ridden the bus downtown to the Neiman-Marcus store to purchase some things for the house, and how badly I wanted to ride the elevator. When I learned that Old Bea would have to walk up the stairs while "I" rode the elevator, I refused, and went with her up four flights of stairs to where they sold the linens we were shopping for. I remembered seeing Old Bea drink from the fountain which was labeled, "COLORED," and wondered which fountain Tony would drink from.

As I watched her standing on that porch I thought that everything I had learned in my young life that had any real meaning at all, I had either learned from Old Bea or Tony Two Hats. The idea of having neither of them suddenly made my chest feel tight like it did years before when I became afraid of something. Like an old nightmare from my past, I began to feel panic. I needed to go home, and I needed to go home now. It had been years since I had felt that if I didn't get home immediately, I would stop breathing and die. This time, I was a long, long ways from home and didn't know how to get there. I had no river to follow. I needed to see my grandfather, Bernie, Father Bill and my little room in the small adobe house at the hatchery. I needed to go home, and it had to happen immediately. For the first time in years, I could not breathe. Seeing me looking uneasy, Old Bea walked down the stairs of the big porch, and came to where I was standing beside a large oak tree.

"Whas de matta, you boy?"

I wanted to talk with Old Bea, but just couldn't get any words to come out. Finally, I asked her a question I had wondered about for three years.

"Old Bea, why can't we fish in this big lake?"

Old Bea was silent for a moment, and then began to answer my question.

"Mista Larry, if de white peoples let evabody fish in dis lake, de nigga kids be out heah fishin' n swimmin' and nest thing you knows, dey be stealin' de white kids bicycles 'n stuff."

"Do you believe that, Old Bea.?" "Do you believe those kids would be stealing all the bicycles?"

"No, Mista Larry, I don'ts, but I figgas it de way de white man thinks to keep de niggas out."

"I don't think like that, Old Bea."

"I knows you don't chile, and cause you believin' lots of

things diffunt from lots of peoples, you be gonna have a hawd time fittin' in and livin' in dis white man's world. You be walkin' to de beat of a diffunt drumma, and you gotta be reel careful that you don't gets out o step wit de people you be tryin 'walk wif. You a diffunt kind 'o chile. Shouldn't nevuh pulled you out dat New Messco, and livin' with dat grandpa dere. I knows bout dat man, and I knows from yo mama, dat dis is a fine man what raised you up, and dat drumma dat he be marchin' wit ain't got no rhythm 'tall. God willin' you gets yosef back dere purty soon and gets yosef in step wit dat man what raised you up 'n undustans ya."

"I will, Old Bea, I will, just as soon as I get the chance, I'll go home."

Later the same evening, we loaded into the car, and drove to our new home in Oklahoma. The trip seemed long, but it was actually just a little over three hours. It was quiet. My mom attempted conversation, but mostly just kept apologizing for our moving to Oklahoma. My sister pouted most of the way because she was moving away from her boyfriend. My father didn't speak at all during the trip, which was normal for him. I sat in the back seat with my mom, thinking every mile of the way that I would stop breathing and die if I didn't get home pretty soon.

The house in Oklahoma was nothing at all like the big house in Dallas. It was in a neighborhood where the houses were pretty close together. The inside of the house was nice, and mom was doing her best to show us all the nice things about it. No one was impressed. Within an hour the big green truck arrived, and men began moving furniture in. The house was so much smaller, only a little bit of the furniture fit. Mom just kept going from room to room assuring everyone how nice it would be when all the furniture was in place. Sis was still pouting. I found a lawn chair which had been unloaded, and put it in the back yard which faced the west. In the distance, I thought I could see a mountain. Finding me sitting in the yard, my mom asked,

"What are you looking at son?"

"I think I see the mountains!"

"Well, actually you do." "You see the mountains over by Ft. Sill. The biggest one is called Mt. Scott."

"Then those mountains are not the Sangre de Cristos?"

"No, son, those are not the Sangre de Cristos." "The Sangre de Cristos are a long, long way from here."

Hearing this bad news, I felt like dying. Surely, I thought, our drive had brought us close enough that I could see New Mexico in the distance, and in seeing the mountains, surely I could find my way back home. I thought about my first trip to Colorado what seemed like ages ago, and how I knew that if things got bad, I could follow the Rio Grande River all the way back home. Now, I had no idea where the river was. The mountains in the distance were not "my" mountains. There wasn't a pine or aspen tree in sight. I would learn the next day that my bow and arrows had been lost in the move. Worst of all, there was no Tony Two Hats to make me another. Old Bea's words were pounding in my head, and I knew I had to find a way to temporarily survive in this world that I didn't fit in. I had to get by until I could find a way back home. It was that very night, my first night in Oklahoma that I found my way to survive. It came in the form of a bottle.

Chapter 25
Storm Clouds

Later that first afternoon, some kids from school stopped by to meet my sis and me. In a small town, new kids moving in were a big deal. The word had already preceded me that I was a very talented athlete, and played guitar very well, something that I had learned at an early age back home. When you could play guitar in the late fifties, you were immediately popular and in demand. I did play well for a 14 year old kid, and when I was asked to play, I performed a little Chuck Berry on my recently acquired Gibson Les Paul electric, which I had been given by my mom to lessen the shock of the move. The kids were very impressed, and asked if I could go with them later to another kid's house for a party. Mom agreed immediately as it looked like a great opportunity to get acquainted with everyone. Sis, feeling too old, as she had already graduated from high school, chose not to go.

After dinner, I heard the horn of a car honking out front. It was a little exciting as I had never actually been out with a group of kids, and especially not in a car driven by a kid. I grabbed my guitar and amplifier and was out the door in a flash. Mom waved as we circled the black Ford convertible and flew down the street. There were five other kids in the car and it belonged to a kid named Jay. As soon as we were out of sight, Jay reached into his pocket and pulled out a pack of cigarettes. He passed them around and everyone, including me, took one. In a flash, everyone had lit up using Jay's Zippo lighter, and we were racing towards town all puffing away. I had never smoked a cigarette. Roma had made me puff on a grapevine once, and it just hurt my lips because it was so hard to puff on. Cigarettes were easy to puff on. I didn't really like smoking it, but everyone else was, so there was no way I could not.

As we zipped up one street and down another, the kids were yelling at other kids to "Come on!!" "We're going to Jay's house!"

Jay's house was big. It was nice too. It wasn't nearly as big as our house in Dallas but it was obvious that Jay's family had some money. I was a little surprised to learn that his family wasn't home, so I wouldn't get to meet them. By this time there were about a dozen kids all filing into the basement that they referred to as "the party room." The basement of Jay's house was real nice. It had a pool table, a ping pong table, a shuffleboard table, which I had never seen before, and covering one whole end of the giant room was a long bar with as many different bottles as the bar at the La Fonda. Entering the big party room, Jay turned and shouted,

"Ladies and gentlemen; name your poison!"

I had never heard that expression, but found out very quickly what it meant. Kids were lining up along the bar asking for all kinds of things with funny names. It looked like fun, but not wanting to look stupid, I sort of stood back. In less than a minute, a really cute girl holding a drink in her hand that looked like lemonade, walked over to me and said,

"How 'bout you, new boy? Can't make up your mind?"

I felt stupid that I didn't know any of the names of the things the other kids were asking for.

"Can I have one like yours," I asked?

"Well aren't you the shy one!"

Giving me her drink, she walked back to the bar and got another. Walking back to where I was standing holding the drink, she said,

"They tell me you play just like Chuck Berry."

"I play OK."

"Well play the damn thing!" she said, taking me by the arm and looking for an electrical outlet for my amplifier. As I took the cherry red guitar from the case, and began "warming it up" a little, the kids were stunned. They gathered quickly as I began playing one of my favorites, "Sweet Little Sixteen." Several of the kids were dancing already, and it looked like my playing and singing rock and roll songs had ignited a fire. After the second song, a Buddy Holly favorite, I took a big drink from the glass I had been given. It sort of made me gasp for breath, and then suddenly made me feel pretty good, and I broke into Johnny B. Goode. The kids were really going nuts with the music and drinking. I was liking it, too. I was liking it a lot. I had become instantly popular in the new town, and felt, at least as long as I was playing and enjoying the drinks, this might not be so bad.

It was pretty late when one of my new friends said that we needed to leave. Jay's parents were expected back around midnight and we needed to be gone. I was sort of sprawled out on a big couch with the girl who had brought me the first drink. The cigarette had been OK. The drinking was pretty good, too. When the girl took my hand and put it on her breast, I was changed forever!

I didn't get home until after midnight. My mom was up waiting for me and knew immediately that I had been drinking. I didn't know how to respond to her concerned look. I offered a "Hi Mom," but it was pretty weak and emotionless. She was struggling for something to say. She was not angry at my behavior but began apologizing again for causing the family to move to Oklahoma. I told her repeatedly that it wasn't her fault. It wasn't. I had found myself in a situation I was unfamiliar with, and did nothing to avoid the decisions I made. While I felt guilty that I had hurt my mom's feelings, I actually didn't feel any remorse. In fact, I was glad I had gone and was wondering how soon I could do it again. There was something about the feel I got from the drinking and the excitement I got from touching the girl that took me away from my constant yearning to go home to New Mexico. For just a few hours, moments, I forgot about all the sadness I felt. Mom asked,

"Are you OK, son?"

I responded, "I'm great, Mom," and walked past her into my bedroom.

The following night, the same group of boys picked me up after dinner, and this time we went to the house of the girl whom I had met. Her parents were gone for the evening, and we essentially repeated the scene from the previous party. We drank, I played, I followed the girl into her bedroom, and learned first hand all the things the nuns had spent so much time and effort warning us about back at the Mission School. The second night when I returned home late, no one was up to meet me; I just went to bed and hoped the next party would come along pretty soon.

The week following our move to Oklahoma, fall football practice began. Word of my athletic skills had preceded me to the new school, and family and friends assumed that with the beginning of school and participating in football, I would settle down and get control of my behavior. To everyone's dismay, I lasted less than a week in pre-school football practice. I simply had no interest in putting forth the effort it took to participate. I was more interested in seeking out friends who had similar interests and motivation as I did. I had met an older boy from town who played guitar well and together we formed a little band. We called ourselves the "Rockin' R's." The "R" stood for "rummies," but that was our little secret. Because of a scarcity of rock bands in the late 50's and early 60's, we were in big demand; sometimes playing dances three nights a week. All the boys in the band were older than I and they had cars. They also had false ID's which made the acquisition of alcohol pretty easy.

At home, very little had changed. Instead of college, my sister had taken a job at a local bank. My dad and I rarely spoke. My mother asked me daily how I was getting along, and my daily response was, "just fine." I was 15 years old and sometimes gone overnight twice a week, driving to and from dances. I knew my mother was aware of what I was doing, but continued to struggle with her feelings that she was responsible for my behavior because we had left our home in Dallas. In addition to her own guilt, I noticed that frequently my father would complain to her about my behavior as if it really was her fault which it wasn't. I would have done the same thing had we stayed in Dallas as soon as I had the opportunity. In spite of my sadness of seeing my mother hurt, I obviously didn't care enough to stop doing what I was doing.

It didn't take long for my girlfriend's parents to hear about "the new boy's reputation" and they forbade her to see me any more. Nothing like that had ever happened to me, and the thought of adults "protecting" their kids from "me" really struck hard. For the first time in weeks, I sat down for a moment and looked at what was happening. I remember sitting on the patio of the new house, and looking towards the west where far in the distance, the Sangre de Cristos lay hidden from my view. In my mind, I envisioned all those people out there in New Mexico, looking at me in amazement and shaking their heads. The idea of what Father Bill and Bernie might think of me now was very unsettling. I had heard from my grandfather and grandmothers very little in the past year. They wouldn't even know me I thought. If only I could take a ride with Tony and talk about what was happening, I imagined that he could get me out of the mess I was making of my life. Tony was gone forever, and I couldn't even find Old Bea.

After what seemed like an eternity of just sitting there rummaging through sad thoughts, I went into my room, closed the door and slept for hours. Later that afternoon, I met up with friends and we went out partying.

For the next few months very little changed. Football season came and went. While a part of me regretted that I was not playing on the team, a larger part of me just didn't care. The games always gave me an excuse to get out of the house, and there were always kids ready to party following the games. In December of that first year in Oklahoma, it seemed like things might turn around a little for me, and I did make the varsity basketball team. I cleaned up my habits and tried to work hard. My mom seemed to be getting sicker instead of better but I assumed it was just a temporary setback and she would be fine in the spring.

Playing on a team had given me the opportunity to feel good about myself again except that I had continual problems with the basketball coach. He accused me almost daily of "not following training rules" and "being a bad influence on other players." This really hurt as I was doing everything I could do at that time to stay away from trouble and keep myself fit. While I was trying my best to do the right things, he was absorbed in accusing me of doing all the wrong things. He even commented once that I was a "loser."

This really hurt, and I never forgave him, or got over that accusation. That coach lived fairly close to our house, and on occasion would visit with my father. I overhead them talking once and both seemed to agree that I was a loser. As the basketball season progressed, and he accused me more and more frequently, I lost interest in trying and began running around with my old friends again. I finished the season, and lettered my sophomore year, but made the decision I would never play on his team again.

I looked forward to the spring, anticipating that with the end of the school year, I would again bring up the subject of going home to live. The old desire to return to Taos, and live with and around the people I had grown up with was still there. I knew I had changed a lot, but I thought if I could just get back home, everything would be like it had been in the years before I left. I spent a lot of time wondering if anything had changed back home and if the people there would somehow know of the things I had done. I felt pretty ashamed. While my reputation was on the mend, there were many who still knew me as the "new boy from Dallas who was nothing but trouble." I had earned that reputation, and was having a hard time getting past it.

My sister had become more and more distant. She had a new boyfriend she was serious about, and didn't spend much time around home. Mom looked weaker and weaker as the winter wore on. When I asked her how she was feeling, she always answered with the same thing, "I'm feeling much better." My father and I rarely talked, nor did I talk much with aunts and uncles. It was like no one had anything to say. Even at Christmas when we met at my mom's parent's house far out in the country, no one seemed to talk much. All the cousins played together, and we had fun but without the constant laughter coming from all the aunts and uncles, it just wasn't the same. It was almost like something was dying.

Chapter 26
Beyond Darkness

That first winter in our new home seemed to drag on forever. As I lost interest in playing basketball, I began to think more and more of returning home. I felt like the past months had left a wound on me that would be a long time healing, but by returning home I would again be surrounded by people who liked and accepted me and in no time I would be back in the routine of things. It had been three years now, and the anticipation of returning home was growing each day.

It was my mom's birthday, March 27th, and I was very surprised to see my Uncle Paul standing in the doorway of my history class at school. Coach Lowry who taught the class, visited briefly with my uncle, then signaled for me to come to the hallway. I immediately thought that there was going to be a surprise birthday party for my mother, and I must be needed at home to prepare. Coach Lowry, our baseball coach, and a person whom I really liked, patted me on the shoulder as I left with Uncle Paul. I was excited at the notion of a surprise party even though mom had been feeling very poorly, and rarely left her bed.

Driving away from school, I excitedly asked my uncle what the plan for the party was. Uncle Paul paused for what seemed like the longest time and then, taking a very deep breath, he said,

"Let's talk about that when we get home."

I was surprised to see that we were driving to his house, the home of my cousin Sue and Don instead of my house. I was more surprised to see the cars of all the aunts and uncles already parked at the little house on 14th Street where they lived. I remember thinking how I hoped I was not late for the party.

Entering the crowded little house, my heart sank and I knew immediately that something was terribly wrong. All my uncles sat around the living room, and all my aunts were sobbing uncontrollably.

Everyone just stared at me but no one would talk. Finally, my Uncle Paul put his hands on my shoulders and said,

"Larry, your mom has died."

It's funny how you sometimes do the strangest things when you learn very shocking information. I remember when I learned that Tony Two Hats had frozen to death walking home to the pueblo, how I raced to my room and searched frantically for the bow he had made me even though I knew it had been lost in the move from Dallas. Hearing this news from my Uncle Paul, I ran into my cousin Sue's room, and climbed into her walk- in closet. It was very full of clothes, and I remember how I had to struggle to get to the very back of the closet where it was the darkest. I noticed that I was having trouble breathing, but just had to be in the darkest part of that closet. Struggling for breath, I felt my uncles, and my beloved Aunt June pulling me out of that closet. Finally, as they extracted me, I shoved them away and ran out the front door of the house.

A couple of blocks away from my Uncle Paul's house was the city park. I went there often because it was full of big trees, mostly pecans and oaks. Right in the middle of the heavily wooded park though was a very large pine tree. It had always attracted me because it reminded me of the big pine trees back home in the mountains. I raced down 14th street as fast as I could and headed straight for the pine tree. I was completely winded by the time I made it to the base of the giant tree, but immediately fell to my knees, and finding a sharp stick, I started digging away at the base of that tree. Why, I was digging at the base of that big tree, I've never understood, but for some reason, I felt like if I could dig deep enough, I would eventually come out back home. No one came to the park. I dug for what seemed like hours, but never made much of a hole. Exhausted, I fell asleep at the foot of that big tree, and slept for several hours. It was getting dark by the time I woke up. No one had followed me. I sat there at the base of the big pine thinking that maybe it had all been a bad dream. Not wanting to return home, I walked a few blocks to the home of one of my friends who played in the band. His mom, who had always been a good friend, welcomed me, and I spent the rest of the evening with them. We were scheduled to play a dance that evening, and acting as if nothing had happened, I played the dance at a local VFW hall. Several of the kids at the dance had heard about the death of my mom, but like myself, just went on. My music had become my best friend, and gave me an escape from things I chose not to deal with. After the dance, my old girlfriend who was forbidden to see me, followed me out to a friend's car, and we spent some time together before she had to leave for home. It was good being with her again, and the following day, I wrote a song about our breakup. The song became the trademark for our little band, and I sold the song to an attorney who later sold it to Mercury Records. It was a sad song, and pretty much reflected the way I felt about life in general.

I spent the night of my mom's birthday and death at my friend's house. Years later, an aunt told me they "thought it best just to let me work things out my own way." This was the pattern in my mother's family; you just don't talk about things, and maybe they'll go away. The next day was a Saturday, and I spent most of that weekend with friends. Thinking back, I don't recall any feelings at all. I was just numb, somewhere between trying to understand what had happened, but most of all just wanting to go home to New Mexico. In my mind, I could see the Sangre de Cristos. I could see everyone sitting around the table at my grandfather's, laughing and joking as Father Bill emptied plate after plate of wonderful treats. I could see Tony, high above somewhere, peering down on all of us and smiling. I could hear the music playing as my grandmothers danced to the flamenco guitar. I saw Scout, patiently standing in the corner of his little pasture, and I smelled the piñon smoke from the many fireplaces around town. I thought about the mill pond, and how I would love to see all our reflections reminding us that we were all together again, and the world was right. The only thing I couldn't see was a way leading back to where I wanted and needed to be. It was like the wind had covered up the path, leaving no trace of the trail back home. There was no sign pointing the direction, and no river to follow. My only hope was that my grandfather would return for the funeral and I would return home with him.

The funeral took place on the following Tuesday. I don't recall a lot happening between the weekend and the day of the funeral. An uncle advised me that we would ride together to the large Methodist Church where the service was to be. I don't recall seeing my sister at all the days before the service. In fact, I don't recall anything before leaving my Uncle Paul's house en route to the church. Looking back, I would guess that I was in shock, and totally insulated from the craziness of the world around me. I do recall asking if my grandfather would be there, and my uncle responded that he didn't know. He indicated there would be a very large crowd, and maybe he would be there.

As we approached the big church, I saw, indeed, what was a very large crowd. I had not attended a funeral since

Rosa died, and had certainly not expected anything like this at all. I searched all over for a yellow Jeepster, but didn't see one anywhere around as we entered the large front door of the Methodist Church. The church was filled with people, some I knew, many I did not, and more flowers than I had ever seen. At the very front of the church, covered in flowers was a large, silver coffin. We made our way to the front seats where all of my mother's family had already been seated. The closer we got to the front, the weaker I felt, and at the same time realized that I was having trouble breathing. My knees were buckling, and I grabbed for my Uncle Paul's arm to keep from falling down in the aisle. After what seemed like an eternity, we found seats next to my aunts, uncles, and cousins. My sister was there, seated next to her boyfriend. She was crying, and barely noticed me moving into the row of seats. I felt like everyone was looking at me, and if I hadn't felt so weak, I think I would have run back up the aisle and out of the church. After what seemed like hours, the organ began to play, and the preacher walked up to a big wooden podium. He asked if everyone would bow their heads in a prayer, and as quickly as everyone had done so, I took the opportunity to look around for my grandfather. He was nowhere to be found. Seated again, the minister began the service with something about, "I shall look into the hills from whence commeth my strength." I couldn't believe that "he" felt just like I did. I, too, needed those hills for strength and they were nowhere in sight. Years before, I had been taught about heaven and hell. I was sure that this was hell, and more than anything in the world, at that moment, I wanted to get my mom out of that box, and the two of us escape to the safety of the Sangre de Cristos. It just went on and on, and it kept getting harder and harder to breathe. Everyone was crying, but all I could do was gasp for air. I felt like my throat was closing, and I remember wanting to stick my finger down my throat to make sure it wouldn't close completely and suffocate me. I was dying, and all I could think about was, I don't want to die here in Oklahoma. If I had to die, at least let me go home to do it.

By the time the minister asked everyone to stand for a final prayer for my mother, I was gasping, thinking each breath would be my last. Suddenly my attention was drawn to two men who had gotten up from their seats, and walked to the casket where they removed the flowers and opened the top of it. For the first time in days, I saw my mother. Now she looked all white and pasty, not like the dark, pretty woman I had known. Her eyes were closed like she was supposed to be sleeping, but she wasn't sleeping. She was dead. She was stone cold dead, and all the flowers, and all the singing, and all the prayers in Oklahoma couldn't change that. Suddenly, my uncle said,

"It's time to go say good-bye to your mother."

"Hell no, it's not!" I yelled, breaking away from him, and running the few feet to where she lay in the casket. In seconds I had grabbed her in an attempt to pull her from the box that held her prisoner. Before anyone could restrain me, I pulled so hard that she broke free, and both of us, along with the casket tumbled over onto the floor of the church. To the muffled gasps of all in attendance, several men, family, and friends managed to pull her out of my grasp. As they dragged me up the aisle, I could hear men shouting instructions about how to get her back into the box. Suddenly, I heard nothing, and remember nothing until the next morning when I woke up in the Duncan Memorial Hospital.

My sister married her boyfriend the week following our mother's funeral. They moved to Albuquerque, New Mexico the very next day.

Before she left, my sister came to the hospital where I was still "recovering," and told me that she loved me. That was the first time she had ever done that, and I knew in that moment, that I had grown to love my sister too. She was my sister, and I loved her, and I would miss her terribly. I wanted so badly to leave with her, and go to New Mexico. I almost asked before she left my room, if I could go with them. I didn't. I should have.

I had been in the hospital a little more than a week when one afternoon, my Uncle Paul and my father came to take me home. I hadn't given much thought to going home from the hospital, and actually had enjoyed the peace and quiet. Had they let me stay longer, I would have. The nurses were friendly, and right outside my window was a large pine tree. During my stay, I had visited daily with a doctor who talked on and on about my mom and my plans after leaving the hospital. Every other sentence, he would ask,

"How do you feel about that?" to which I would reply,

"I don't feel anything about anything."

For the first time in my life, I "didn't" feel anything about anything. I just didn't care. I didn't care where I went, what I would do, who I would see. I didn't care. I didn't care. I didn't care. I would gladly have spent my life in that hospital room just looking at that pine tree.

Part VI
Reflections in the Mill Pond

Chapter 27
Another Beginning

I don't recall anyone saying a word as we drove from Duncan Memorial Hospital to our home. It was uncomfortably quiet for everyone. Uncle Paul drove us in his car, and my father sat in the front seat. I sat in the back with my small plastic bag of things I had been given in the hospital: tooth brush, tooth paste, comb, and a small bar of unwrapped soap. I wore the same clothes home I had worn at my mother's funeral. I felt pretty strange leaving the hospital in my dress clothes, but it obviously had not crossed anyone's mind to bring different clothes from home.

The morning before leaving the hospital, I had a long visit with the doctor who had asked so many questions; mainly, "How do you feel about that?" He had advised me about "adjustments" that were needed in order to get along with my father. In hearing about my need to "make adjustments," I was certain that the doctor had been advised of my bad behavior. Regardless, now it would just be my father and I, as Judy had married and moved away immediately following the death of our mother. The thought of living alone in the house with my father was a little alarming. First of all, I felt like I hardly knew him as we had spoken relatively little during the years since I moved from New Mexico. Secondly, I felt that he had always been very quick to criticize me to the other family members even though he and I had never discussed anything at all about my habits; good, bad, or otherwise. My mother had simply advised me to, "Stay away from your dad, and you'll be OK." I had practiced this for a number of years now with varying success. It would be more difficult now.

We were headed home, and the only occupants would be my father; a person I hardly knew and sometimes frightened me, and myself. My apprehension was growing by the minute, and escalated greatly as we turned onto Pine Street where our home lay ahead. I never understood why it was called Pine Street. There were no trees at all, much less a pine tree. My mind began to wander a little as we approached the house. I imagined what I would do if "I" had a car of my own, and just kept driving past the house, straight out of town, out of Oklahoma, and far to the west until I reached New Mexico. Surely, I thought, I could recognize something along the way that would lead me home to Taos. My daydreaming was interrupted as Uncle Paul pulled the car into the driveway.

"Here we are, boys!" Uncle Paul offered cheerfully.

"Why don't you boys join us for dinner this evening?"

Assured that I didn't want to be home alone all evening in the empty house, I quickly responded, "I'd like that, Uncle Paul. How about you, dad?" Nodding affirmatively, we closed the doors to his car, and walked towards the house. Inside, I immediately went to my room, closed the door, and began to play my guitar. I spent the entire afternoon in my room until my dad tapped on the door and said,

"Guess we need to get over to dinner."

"Yes sir," I responded, and in a quick move, I left my room and was headed for the car which sat in the driveway. Dad joined me, and we drove the short distance to the house on 14th Street where my Aunt Blanch and Uncle Paul lived. I hoped my cousin Sue would be home. She and I were close, and could sit under their giant willow tree and talk.

It was late March, and school had not changed much since I last attended prior to my mom's passing. I approached school with minimal interest. I regarded everything with minimal interest. I continued to play a lot of music, and had joined another group of older boys who played well. We played several dances a month, and I earned enough money that I rarely had to ask my dad for anything. I had learned that asking for something usually led to problems between him and me, so I just attempted to avoid that problem. During this time, I became closer to my aunts who always seemed curious about how things were progressing at home with my father. Everyone knew of the obvious conflicts that persisted between us; specifically, that he had no patience at all for young people, and I seemed to top the list of offenders. Nevertheless, we shared the home on Pine Street, spending most evenings together staring blankly at the television set. I had managed to pass my driver's test and had a license to drive a car. My dad had two cars, but asking to use either always brought up the subject of my irresponsibility and poor behavior. As the summer of 1959 wore on, things at home became increasingly tense, but we did little to ease the tension, and day by day, the tenuous relationship deteriorated. By the end of the summer, I had begun staying out more, knowing that it would make things worse at home, but deciding that it made little difference what I did, or didn't do. The result was always the same.

Following one of the summer dances we played, a girl from school approached me and commented on how well we had played. I thanked her and was flattered as she was one of the most popular girls in our school, and a year older than I. I had noticed this girl many times at school, but would never have considered asking her for a date, as my reputation and her being a year older had prevented my giving it any thought. Her name was Patti, and she had approached me seemingly a little interested. Patti asked if I had a car, and embarrassed, I said, "No." She asked how I was getting home from the dance, and I told her I would catch a ride with some of the boys. To my amazement, she asked if I would like a ride home. Stunned, not only by her interest, but by her boldness, I awkwardly accepted.

Leaving my guitar and amp with the other guys in the band, I left with Patti. My best friend and one of the other band members winked at me, and gave this big, "thumbs up" sign when he realized that I was leaving the dance with Patti. For a split second, it reminded me of the many times Father Bill had done the same when he sought to encourage or congratulate me. Winking back at my friend, I smiled and she and I left the building.

As soon as we were in Patti's car, she started the engine, and turning to face me said,

"We've got to run by my house to tell my mom that we're going out for a coke. I also want you to meet my mom. Hearing this, I was immediately shocked, as I knew as soon as her mom realized who I was, she would be instructed to "Take him home, and don't bring him back." Wanting to spend more time with Patti, I took the risk, and rode with her to her house.

"Mom, I'm home!' Patti announced as we walked through the front door. Surprised that her mother would still be up at this late hour, Mrs. McGuire responded,

"Be there in a second, sweetie!"

I was getting more and more anxious, anticipating that this would be my first and last visit to the McGuire home. In seconds, Mrs. McGuire entered the room smiling. Her look was disarming, but I anticipated that would quickly change following introductions.

"Mom, this is Lar........." She hadn't finished the introduction when Mrs. Mrs. McGuire interrupted with,

"Oh, Patti, I know who Larry is. Larry's mother and I were old friends long before she married and moved away to Texas!"

"Larry," she continued, "I am SO sorry about your mom. I was at your mom's service and know how terribly hard her loss must be for you."

I was shocked beyond belief now that Mrs. McGuire not only knew who I was but, had seen me at my worst. Still, she made me feel welcome in her home. I wasn't sure how to respond, and would have probably stood there speechless for hours had the silence not been broken by her giving me this big hug, and instructing Patti to go make hot chocolate for us all. Still feeling the surprise of the unexpected greeting, I stood motionless. Suddenly, I felt tears welling up in my eyes, and felt for a brief second that I had somehow magically been transported home. In some strange way, I even thought for a moment that I smelled the faraway scent of piñon smoke.

It was past 2:00AM in the morning, when Mrs. McGuire said,

"It's late, and you kids need to get to bed! Larry, can you come back tomorrow for dinner?"

Too shocked to respond, I just nodded, "Yes!"

I remember being very quiet as we drove the short distance from Patti's house to mine. I finally said,

"Patti, I really enjoyed coming over and meeting your mom."

"We enjoyed having you over," she responded.

"Patti, do you "know" about me?"

"Sure," she responded.

"Why did you ask me over after the dance?"

"I like you, " she said.

We didn't speak the rest of the way to my house. Arriving home, I opened the door to the small Renault, and giving Patti a quick smile, I closed the door and walked into the house. I lay awake in my bed the remainder of the night. I felt good about being with Patti and her mother. It was the first time that I had felt good about anything in a long time.

Chapter 28
Recovery

For the next several weeks, I spent all the time I possibly could with Patti and her mom. Patti had lost her dad to a heart attack some years before, and we spent a lot of time talking about the things that had happened in our young lives. Often our conversations lasted long into the night, and it seemed the more we shared, the more we wanted to share. We were like little kids that had a desparate need to tell our stories, share our feelings, and finally had found an opportunity to do it. At times, Mrs. McGuire would join in our conversations, and help us work through more difficult topics. For the first time since leaving Old Bea in Dallas, I talked about what my life had been before I came to live with my parents. I talked endlessly about Father Bill and Bernie, and how I wanted to be a priest when I was grown, and how I wanted to return to New Mexico to live with my grandfather and grandmothers. I told them all about my friends, and Scout, and Roma, and how I missed the smell of the piñon smoke. Three years of pent up memories spilled out to my new friends, and sharing these wonderful memories made them feel real again, and not just some fantasy that lived in my imagination. Sharing the stories of my younger years with Patti and her mom made me feel that going home, after all these years might be a possibility. Mrs. McGuire and even Patti pledged to help me. When we talked together about the possibility of going home, it was like I could actually "hear" the voices of all those people I missed so much, and if I closed my eyes and tried real hard, I could see all of us together again, with our reflections smiling back at us from the mill pond.

The following weeks were exciting as school was beginning, and I started a new school year with a much improved attitude. I looked forward to playing football, and even going to classes. We continued to play dances almost every weekend, and while I did spend a lot of time traveling around with the older members of the band, I was drinking a lot less, and worked hard to stay in shape for football. Patti was a school cheerleader, and wanting to please her, kept me on the "straight and narrow." Things at school continued to get better, but unfortunately, things at home continued to deteriorate at a faster and faster pace. At the suggestion of Patti's mom, I was spending more time in the evenings at home with my dad. I attempted conversation, and worked hard at becoming a little better student. I made it a point to ask my dad for help when I didn't understand something. I learned quickly that this was not a good idea, and my asking for help usually led to a dissertation about how I never pay attention, and how I never get the instructions correct, and basically how I could be so dumb. I felt dumb, and thinking that I was not very bright led to my continuing to struggle at school in spite of my newly acquired interest and desire to do better.

It was at this time that something happened at school that again took me back to things that Old Bea had predicted about having a hard time in a place where I was different. The event took place not long into my second year at school when things were going pretty well for me. I was trying to learn and I was playing ball very well which made me feel good about myself. All of the teachers had commented about my improvement, and that I was finally adjusting to the new school, and possibly even to the loss of my mother.

One morning, all of the students were called into the gymnasium for an unexpected assembly. When we were all seated in the seats of the gym, the principal walked into the center of the big floor. He was holding a microphone, and had a stern look on his face. My first thought was that I had done something wrong and it was about to be told to the entire school. I had developed this feeling of guilt over the past year when it had seemed that if something went bad, it was probably my fault. My father had been very instrumental in my feeling this way. In my mind, I had been conditioned to think that I was at the center of anything and everything that was wrong or bad. As the students settled down, I looked at Patti who was sitting next to me and braced myself for the worst. Raising the microphone to his mouth, he began,

"Well, students, today the niggers are coming and there's nothing in the world we can do to stop them."

Hearing this cold, cruel statement coming from the lips of our school principal, I gasped and felt my heart sink. He went on to explain that that a thing called "segregation" had ended, and from now on, the black kids, who had previously attended their own school in a part of town most people referred to simply as "Niggertown," would be coming to "our" school. I quickly looked at Patti in disbelief, and noticed that his comments made her uncomfortable also. I had shared with her my love for Old Bea, and how she had made my life bearable before moving to Oklahoma. Patti knew how his comments had struck me like a knife in my heart. I didn't know any of the black kids in town, none of us did as they stayed in their part of town, went to their own school and never ventured into our part of town. What upset me was that his comments obviously condemned all black people of any age, and in doing that, he had categorized Old Bea as something less than the significant person I knew her to be. Suddenly

I was struggling to breathe, and all of the things that had troubled me from my very first venture away from my home in Taos came racing back. My mind was fighting with notions that if "Old Bea" was a person of lesser status in the world, what about Tony Two Hats, what about Bernie, what about all my friends at home, what about ALL my grandmothers, what about me? I felt trapped inside the body of someone who looked like the people around me, but felt like someone totally different! I hated sitting there, and I hated the principal for what he had said, and most of all I hated me for ever leaving home to try and be something I was not. I was trapped. I looked like something, someone I was not! Again, just like the day I was told my mother was dead; I felt like running. I did. I jumped from my seat in the gym, and pushing kids and teachers out of the way, ran out of the building. I ran all the way back to the park, and again sat at the base of the big pine tree. I could faintly make out the small hole I had begun the year before. I wanted to begin digging again, but knew it was useless. For the second time, no one followed me. No one came I thought until about a half hour later when I saw the familiar Renault drive into the parking lot of the park. I had come to this spot with Patti before, and she guessed that I might be here. She and her mom exited the small sports car, and walked to where I sat at the base of the big pine tree. They didn't speak; just sat down beside me and puts their arms around my shoulders. We stayed for quite a while until Patti's mom, interrupting the silence said,

"Kids, let's go home."

The three of us squeezed into the small car, and drove to their house. I overheard Mrs. McGuire talking on the phone to my dad and explaining that if the school called, which they had done many times before, I would be at her house and everything would be fine. I spent the night with the McGuire's, sleeping in Patti's little brother's room. I lay awake all night thinking about how I hated my life in spite of making a recent turn for the better. For the very first time that I recall, instead of wanting to return to my home in Taos, it crossed my mind to go into the bathroom at Patti's house, find a razor blade, and bring to an end a life which I felt could never fit the body I was trapped in. Unable to find the courage, and not wanting to upset my good friends, I just sat on the edge of the bathtub, razor in hand, until the sun came up the next morning.

"Rise and shine!" I heard as Mrs. McGuire had come from her bedroom, preparing for what she hoped would be a better day. Putting the razor back into the cabinet, I walked into the kitchen, and was greeted with a smile and big hug. It was what I needed to start another day.

Patti drove me home where I showered and put on clean clothes. Saying very little, we made the short drive to Duncan High School. Patti gave me a "peck" on the cheek, and with a quiet, "I love you," gave me a soft push towards my first class.

The black kids had come! There were lots of them, and they moved quietly up and down the halls, finding places in the back of each classroom where they sat quietly looking very much like the people I recalled in the back seats of the big Dallas buses. I made my way to an empty back seat, and sat down next to a black girl with a terrificd look on her face.

"Larry, I think your seat is up here, isn't it?" I heard coming from the English teacher.

"No ma'am, it isn't, "I responded.

Chapter 29
Kaleidoscope

Integration marked yet another turning point in my life. Even though I had returned to school after making my dramatic exodus from the gym, it was like returning to the scene of a crime. I just wasn't sure what the crime was, or who committed it. I attempted to make friends with the black girl I had sat next to my first day back. Her name was Ernestine, and seemed afraid to even talk to me. I wanted to be her friend, but it just wasn't to be, given the nature of things at the time. She didn't trust me, or any of the white kids who made a point of making the new kids feel unwanted at school. I became even more uncomfortable when one of the black kids joined the football team and was treated terribly by the other players. He was "allowed" to play because he was the only kid on the team who had athletic abilities comparable to mine. Back at school, he was just another "nigger." For the second year in a row, I quit the team. Patti felt horrible about my decision to do this, but respected my disapproval and supported me. Now, we were both outcasts.

By the Christmas holidays, things were terrible at home and at school. The only words exchanged between me and my father were hostile and stopped just short of violence. My family constantly encouraged me to accept my father as everyone knew that he too was "different." Between his differences, and my differences, we were a desperate pair. Everyone saw it coming, and it was just a matter of time before a violent episode erupted. It was obvious, predictable, and as unavoidable as an oncoming train. The crash occurred the day of the Christmas Dance.

For weeks I had prepared for the Christmas Dance at school. While I rarely asked my father for the use one of the two cars, this was a special occasion and I wanted very much to drive Patti to the dance in "my" car. We had typically gone everywhere in her little Renault as her mom, Patti, and I had long before agreed that asking for the car was a request that historically led to a disastrous confrontation between my father and myself. Determined to drive Patti to the dance, I began preparing my father weeks before the big event. I had saved my own money from playing dances, and never asked for an allowance of any kind. I had rented a tuxedo, bought flowers for Patti, and as custom, bought myself a small boutonnière to wear on my white tuxedo jacket. With the help of Patti and her mom, I had rehearsed over and over again how I would request the keys to the car on the night of the big dance.

The night finally came. I remember being so nervous in anticipation of making the request that I struggled once again to breathe. Finally, after having gained the courage, dressing in my tux, and attaching the small flower to my jacket, I entered the living room where my father sat watching TV. My knees were trembling as I approached him. He knew I had spent hours in my room preparing for the huge event. Now, I stood there in the living room bracing myself for what I prayed would be a quick and uneventful presentation of the car keys.

"Dad, it's about time to pick up Patti; may I have the keys?"

For what seemed like an eternity, he didn't answer; just kept watching the TV screen. After several seconds, I repeated my rehearsed request. Looking towards the window, he finally responded,

"Which car?"

"Either one is fine, dad, either one is fine," I responded, really hoping he would give me the key to the new Buick Roadmaster which was beautiful and pretty impressive. The other car was a beautiful, almost new Pontiac which rarely left the garage. I would gladly have taken either, but was getting more and more agitated at his making me go through this scene after having prepared him for weeks to respond positively to my request. Again looking towards the large window in the front of the living room, he responded,

"Looks like it might snow to me. I don't think I want the cars out tonight."

Snow was impossible as the weather had been beautiful all week, and the chances of any bad weather were non-existent.

"Dad," I began. "I have been talking about the car for several weeks now. I promise to be careful. I have never asked for anything. I just want to drive Patti to the dance. Please dad?"

"I don't think so."

Shaking and struggling to breathe, I turned back towards my room and tried to take a step. I was praying that I could keep myself together long enough to call Patti and have her pick me up. We would go to the dance and have a wonderful time.

There had been times in my life when I just seemed to lose control and run from scenes which I could not deal with. I wish this had been one of those times. It wasn't. I didn't run. I couldn't run, and all the anger, disappointment, frustration that had hidden away inside me surfaced. It surfaced with a vengeance as I spun around to face my father.

"You miserable bastard!"

I had never called my father a name; even in the worst

of our previous confrontations. I had never called anyone a name. Suddenly, the words jumped from my mouth, and before the shock of my verbal attack struck home, I hit him. I hit him several times, and he fought back furiously. We were like wild beasts fighting for our lives. While I denied it later, I wanted to kill him. I was trying to kill him. I was trying to kill my father, and the more we fought, the more I wanted to kill him. One of us might have died that night had he not been able to grab a large lamp and break it over my head. His attempt to subdue me was successful, and I fell to the floor unconscious.

It was quite a while later. I don't know exactly when as I could not see my watch beneath the confines of the restraint jacket I was wearing over my white tuxedo coat. I remember thinking the boutonnière looked a little out of place sticking out from the top of the restraint jacket. Blood had trickled onto the lapels, and I was attempting to recall what had happened. I could hear the voice of Mrs. McGuire demanding that I be released. I could also hear Patti crying in the background. Strangest of all, far away in the distance, I could hear the music coming from the Christmas Dance at the Duncan High School gymnasium. I would later learn that I was being held for the attempted murder of my father. I didn't see Patti that night. It would be a very long time before I saw her again.

On the small bench in my cell, someone had left a kaleidoscope of all things. I wanted to pick it up and look through it at all the pretty, colorful pictures. Unable to do so as I was inextricably tied up in the restraint jacket, I thought for a moment that in my fifteen years of living, my life had been very much like a kaleidoscope. Looking through, you see many beautiful pictures. I had many beautiful pictures in "my" kaleidoscope. Unfortunately, with the slightest movement, all the pieces fall apart. Before too long, the many colorful pieces form yet another beautiful picture. My mind was brimming with beautiful pictures; home, family, Father Bill, Bernie, Tony Two Hats, and always, always, always....

Old Bea. In the unhappiness of this small jail cell, listening to the music of the Christmas Dance, I could see all the people I loved in my mind's kaleidoscope. They would just be beginning to smile at me when the beautiful pieces would fall, then disappear. They just disappeared, and in my mind's kaleidoscope, I could not find them again. I would never find a single one of them ever again.

Part VII
Reflections in the Mill Pond

Chapter 30
The Lost Year

I was sitting in the back seat of my Uncle David's car when I saw the sign that read, "Oklahoma State Line 25 Miles." I don't remember getting in the car. In the front seat were my Uncle David and Aunt Bea, my mother's only sister. They were facing the front, and not talking. Looking through the window of the big Buick, I could see large sunflowers all along the road. Wildflowers bloomed everywhere, and the grass was green. The trees were covered with leaves which were just beginning to turn golden. I guessed it was early fall, maybe September. Aunt Bea turned to me and smiled. I smiled back, but didn't speak. On the seat beside me was something I remembered from an earlier experience. It was the usual "going home" kit you are giving when leaving a hospital. It contained the usual things you are given when you leave except that there was a small sticker attached with a brief note saying, "Good luck out there, Larry!" I had no idea where it came from, and very little interest in knowing. I didn't inquire, and simply didn't care.

I remember seeing a movie once where the people were walking through a cloud. They could see everything around them except for their feet. Their feet were hidden in the clouds. They just walked on and on. I felt a little like that movie. I didn't know where we were going, didn't know where I had been. We just kept going. I didn't ask because I guess I just didn't care. In a while we crossed the bridge over the Red River, and entered Oklahoma. I remembered Oklahoma. I had lived in Oklahoma. I moved there from Dallas, Texas. I didn't feel like I was coming home. I didn't feel anything at all. I wasn't happy. I wasn't sad. I wasn't anything. I was just sitting in the backseat of a car driving down a highway.

Driving all the way through Duncan, we turned to the east. As we were leaving town, Aunt Bea turned to me and said,

"Larry, you're coming to live with us."

"OK."

In an hour or so, we arrived at a row of company owned houses I recognized as Amerada Oil Camp. I remembered that my Uncle David was the superintendent of the oil company, and that my cousins, Mindy and Mike lived there. I had been there many times before. Turning again in her seat and smiling, Aunt Bea asked,

"Larry, would you like to go to school with Mike and Mindy?"

"OK."

Pulling into their drive, I saw Mike and Mindy sitting on the porch of the company house. They appeared happy to see me, and ran to the car. They were smiling and waving. I waved back.

"You're going to be my biggest brother," Mindy said as they swung open the door of the big car.

"OK."

I liked Mike and Mindy. I remembered that we had a lot of fun on holidays. Pulling me out of the car, Mindy dragged me into the little house, and pointing to a tiny room just off the kitchen, she said excitedly,

"This is going to be YOUR room!"

"Thank you."

Walking into the room, I saw my guitar propped against the wall. In the closet, I noticed some clothes I recognized as mine. My letter jacket hung with them in the closet. On the wall was a picture of the entire family which was taken earlier at a Christmas gathering. My mother was sitting beside Aunt Bea right in the middle of the picture. They were all there. I looked at the picture for a while, then sat down on a little couch that I knew folded out into a bed. I had been there before, but it seemed like a long time ago. Mike and Mindy had a little brown dog they called Cocoa, and Cocoa jumped onto my lap. The little dog licked me on the face, and it made me laugh a little. Aunt Bea sat down beside me and said,

"Larry, we love you. It's going to be OK."

"OK," I responded.

My Aunt Bea was a wonderful cook, and that first night we had chicken fried steak and mashed potatoes. It tasted good. We didn't talk a lot, but it was pleasant. They were very nice people and I didn't mind being there with them at all. After dinner, we watched TV for a while, but I felt very tired, and before long asked if I could go to bed. Aunt Bea helped me fold out the little bed, and giving me a kiss on the cheek said,

"We are so happy that you're here, Larry. We're going to have a lot of fun."

Aunt Bea walked into the kitchen, and shortly returned with a glass of water and some pills.

"You need to take these, sugar," she said, offering me the pills and water.

"OK," I responded. I took the pills, drank the water and went to sleep.

It must have been some time in the middle of the night that I woke up. Something in the night had terrified me, and I woke up gasping for air. From the moisture on my pillow, I knew I had been sweating or crying. I didn't know which. I remembered that I was in my aunt's house, but couldn't hear or see any of them. I was certain that "something" in the house was coming to get me, and I was so afraid that I was having trouble breathing. Not daring to leave the little room and go for help, I took the blankets from my bed, and climbed into the closet. The closet had a sliding door, and I managed to slide it closed behind me. Not hearing anything, and feeling like I was hidden from whatever it was that was coming for me, I finally drifted back to sleep. I probably would have slept all the next day except that I was awakened early the next morning by my aunt's screaming,

"He's gone, he's gone! Call the police, he's gone!"

I remember the look of terror, and possibly relief on my aunt's face when I slid he door of the closet open, and stuck my head out a little.

"What in the world are you doing in there?" she pleaded.

"I don't know." I wanted to tell her that something was coming to get me during the night, but just couldn't get an explanation out.

"Larry, please don't ever scare me again like that," she pleaded as she grabbed me and hugged me.

"OK."

The next night we tried leaving the lights on in the little room. Not being in complete darkness felt a little familiar, and I managed to sleep most of the night.

The next day, Aunt Bea drove me into the little town where Mike and Mindy attended school. It was a pretty school, much smaller than the schools I remembered, but friendly looking. Walking into the main building, we were met by a man who held out his hand and welcomed us. I felt a little uneasy when he introduced himself as the principal. His title alarmed me, but I didn't know why it should as he seemed very nice, and greeted me warmly. In an enthusiastic sort of way, he said,

"I understand that you are quite a ball player. We could sure use you on our football team; WE STINK!" I thought that was funny and answered back, "OK."

Something about this nice man, and the kids who walked past us smiling, made me feel pretty good about being in the new school. Putting his hand on my shoulder, he walked me into every single classroom, and introduced me to every teacher, coach, and student. It didn't take too long because it was a very small school. I liked the little school immediately, even though every face I saw was new. Everyone smiled, and welcomed me. Stopping in the history class which was taught by the football coach, he welcomed me into the room, and after introducing me to every student, stated,

"I plan on seeing you in the locker room after school to check out equipment!"

All the kids in the room were smiling, and giggling, and all I could say was,

"OK."

Noticing that I was a little nervous about the new school and meeting all these new people, Aunt Bea asked,

"Would you like to go home with me now and maybe come back in the morning, or would you just like to start right now and join the other kids in class?"

Answering her question was difficult I recall, and I just stood there for a moment hoping the answer would just come out. It didn't. Finally, Mr. Vandiver, the nice principal, said,

"I think we're having a special "back to school" lunch today in the cafeteria. They're cooking turkey and dressing, and these ladies can cook! "

Hearing his words, I vaguely pictured a lady cooking in a school cafeteria. She was short, a little heavy, but was grinning from ear to ear as kids filed into her cafeteria. I knew this woman I thought. I just couldn't exactly remember how or when.

A minute or two must have passed before Mr. Vandiver broke the silence with,

"Why don't you stay, Larry, we'll have a great day!"

"OK," I answered, and thus began my first day back at school. I had been gone from schools for a long time. I didn't know why, but I knew it had been a long time.

Chapter 31
Returning to Life

That afternoon after school, I went with Mike and the other players to the locker room to check out football equipment. Mike was more excited than I was, and I could see him boasting that I was his cousin, and that I had received an award the last year I attended Dallas schools naming me, "Athlete of the Year." Considering the size of Dallas, Texas, it was a pretty amazing accomplishment given my extraordinary circumstances. I did recall a very large statue given to me at the end of my 9th grade year. It had my name engraved on it, and probably remains today in the junior high school I attended. Recalling that made me feel good, and I enthusiastically put on the football pads and joined the other kids on the practice field.

On the field, I felt a little awkward at first. I almost felt like I was running in cement, and even though I wanted to run a little faster, it was taking a little time. By the end of the practice, I was getting my speed back, and felt like I had been freed from invisible chains. Instead of getting tired out from my first practice on that hot Oklahoma day, I felt like I was getting stronger. When the practice finally came to an end,

I was still smiling like a possum. It was time to finish up with wind sprints, which routinely came after every practice. I was exhausted, but as we lined up on the goal line of the practice field to run at full speed, my heart was racing as fast as my body. I felt like I was flying, and I guess compared to the other kids, I was. After the sprints ended and everyone was gasping for breath, a boy named Rooster walked up to me and said,

"You run like a goddamned nigger!" It was actually a compliment; probably as big a compliment as he, in his mid 20th century way of thinking could pay me. Uncertain how to respond to his comment, I just sort of stood there. It was troubling and made me uncomfortable, but as the seconds passed, I remember the thought passing through my mind that,

"I could run like a goddamned nigger." Still feeling a little stupefied, I offered a little silent prayer,

"Thank you God, for letting me run like a goddamned nigger!"

I was so happy at that moment, I felt like my heart would burst. I didn't want to end practice, and asked Coach Martin if I could run some more.

"Sure, boy!" he responded, and seeing me take off running to the far end of the practice field, the other players who were dragging themselves back to the locker room, all shouted in unison,

"Let's go Comets!"

In a flash, they all joined me, and we ran for another twenty or thirty minutes. We were laughing, and running and shoving each other, and the more we ran, the faster the pace became. Suddenly, out of nowhere, a boy shouted,

"Let's win state!!"

This was funny I learned, as they had not had a winning season in over ten years. Suddenly we were all running and shouting,

"State, State, State!"

The coaches even joined us back on the practice field and in seconds, they were shoving their fists in the air, screaming,

"State, State, State!!!"

This scene, with all my new friends running together on that practice field, and pledging to win, was one of the happiest moments of my life. I recall it vividly today, and the memory brings tears to my eyes. Whenever I'm feeling a little down, I recall that moment and hear the shouts of those boys. We were champions! We just didn't know it until maybe that day.

Even ending our 10-1 season, and losing in the state finals did not diminish our pride. We were champions, and I was a champion, even though from time to time, I had nagging thoughts that I was somehow a real loser. I was not a loser, and decided that I would show everyone for the rest of my life that, I was not a loser.

At the Christmas school banquet, our coach proudly announced to the attendees, that Larry Wood had been named First Team All-State. I didn't know until then, but it was suspicioned that I might be honored, as I was the second leading scorer in the state. There were a couple of ironies accompanying the award. Initially, I was second in scoring only to a black kid named James Long. James played for a large school in Oklahoma City, and his accomplishments were remarkable. Secondly, there had only been two other previous students from this little school who ever received All-State honors. They were my Uncle Toad and my mother, both outstanding basketball players. I was proud. I didn't remember my mother, but I was proud. Two years later, my cousin Mike would become the fourth.

School remained difficult for me. The teachers and all my new friends helped out, and with their constant encouragement, and promise that, "You'll catch up!" I worked very hard. Letters from colleges were arriving weekly and my supporters assured me that I would graduate and go on to play college ball. Some of the larger schools, specifically Notre Dame, my favorite, requested my transcripts but wrote back apologetically that my grades were too low. Undaunted by several rejections, I knew I could play somewhere, and kept working. By the end of the school year, I had narrowed my choices down to the University of Oklahoma, and North Texas State. In spite of many rejections, I was going on to college. I felt good. As far as having any thoughts at all about what I wanted to study in college, I was going to play ball and could care less about a course of study. I would play football in college, and thousands of people would cheer for me. I was a champion.

In the spring of the year, some of my old friends from Duncan began to come visit me. On occasion, I would go back into town with them and talk about old times. It was so strange that I remembered little about earlier times in Duncan. I recalled attending school there for a while, and even remembered that I had a girlfriend there once. I inquired on one of those visits about a girl I vaguely remembered. Her name was Patti.

"Where is Patti?" I asked on my second visit.

Patti, I was told was gone. She was attending the University of Oklahoma in Norman, where my sister, Judy was now living with her husband. Patti's mother had also moved to Norman to be closer to her daughter while she attended college. One of the boys said that Patti had a hard time after I went away. I didn't understand what he meant by that statement, but chose to just let it go.

Judy had come to my aunt and uncle's house for an Easter visit. We were very happy to see each other, but didn't really talk about much at all except how well I was doing, and how happy she was for me. When she returned home to Norman, I remember thinking how happy I was to have her for my sister. I loved Judy.

As the school year was coming to an end, preparations were being made for my graduation from high school. While I understood perfectly what was going on, and understood what graduation from high school meant, I was still confused about a lot of things. I had been asked throughout the year about things that happened before my coming to the little community. These nagging mysteries came to light following the preparation for the graduation banquet which was being held in the school cafeteria. One of the ladies preparing the banquet tables confronted me as I stood watching the preparations. Her son had been the only kid in school who I felt like didn't like me. He was the only kid in town whose family was known to have a lot of money, and when I came to school, he was just "one" of the big fishes in the little pond instead of the big fish. Regardless, his mother was approaching me curiously, and I knew she was about to ask me something. She did.

"Larry, will your parents be attending the banquet?"

I wasn't sure what she was wanting from me. She knew that my mom's parents, my grandparents, attended everything I was involved in. In spite of their advanced ages, they were among my biggest fans.

"What about your father?" she continued.

I still didn't know what she was talking about, but her questions were making me uneasy. I wanted to just walk away, but had been taught that it was impolite, to walk away from an adult who is speaking to you.

"That was so terrible about your other grandparents. It must have been a terrible shock."

With this last question, I was squirming and started to leave. Instead of leaving, I made the terrible mistake of asking,

"What are you talking about, Mrs. Anderson," I asked politely.

"Well there was that wreck and all...so sad, so sad."

"What are you talking about, Mrs. Anderson?"

"Why, the "wreck," sugar, the wreck that killed your grandfather."

This time I forgot politeness. Nodding a puzzled affirmation, I turned and walked out of the cafeteria.

My ride home picked me up in a few minutes and drove me to Amerada Camp. I had stayed with the English teacher after school to practice a little speech I was giving at the banquet. My speech was a "Thank you," to all the kids, teachers, and parents who had made my senior year at the little school successful. Riding back home I didn't speak. One of my friends asked,

"Cat got your tongue?" I nodded affirmatively.

Chapter 32
Pandora's Box

That evening I was cutting potatoes for Aunt Bea, and feeling curious about comments which had been said earlier, I asked,

"Aunt Bea, where are my grandparents?"

"Why sugar, there's just right up the road at their house in County Line."

"No, Aunt Bea. Where are my "other" grandparents?"

It was obvious immediately that I had just opened the latch to a tightly sealed trunk.

"Why, what do you mean, sugar"

"I mean, where are they?"

Seeing that I was not content to drop the subject, she put down the rag she had been washing dishes with, and very reluctantly, nodded to the kitchen table.

"Oh sugar, I know it was pretty stupid of me to think that this subject would never come up. I guess we had just hoped and prayed that it wouldn't. Larry, do you think this has been a happy year for you living here with us?"

"Of course it has, Aunt Bea! It's been a wonderful year."

"Well, since everything is going so well, why do we have to bring all that up?"

"All what up, Aunt Bea?"

"Oh, all that stuff that happened that we can't do a single thing about. It's over, it's done. You're here, you're doing well, and we love you. Why would we want to go back and drag out things that are over and done. Let's just be happy we're here today. OK?"

"OK," I reluctantly consented.

My aunt patted me on the hand, then got up from the kitchen table and went back to her dishes. I walked outside. I sat on the porch of the little house and petted Cocoa for what seemed like a very long time. Late spring storm clouds were gathering far to the west along the southern Oklahoma horizon. They were beautiful, and watching them I thought they looked like mountains. They were far away and looming on the distant western horizon. There are mountains out there I imagined. They are a long ways from here, but there are mountains out there. I watched the clouds until the sun finally disappeared forming a beautiful Oklahoma sunset. Before long, darkness came, and none of my questions had been answered.

I graduated from high school the following week. My grades were pretty awful, but I had managed to acquire a full athletic scholarship to North Texas State University in Denton, Texas. It was a NCAA Division I college, and miraculously enough, I would play major college football. I was excited. When people asked me what I wanted to be, thinking I would reply with doctor, lawyer, teacher; I would respond with "defensive back." It was that simple. I had no other interest.

It was arranged that I would move shortly after graduation to Oklahoma City where I would live with my Aunt June, Uncle Toad, and cousins, Cindy and Scotty. I was excited. Like my Uncle David, Uncle Toad had made a lot of money in the oil business and he was giving me a job for the summer. Their home was large and beautiful. I had my own room with a regular bed and I was very excited the day I moved to Oklahoma City to live with them. My Aunt June was a

wonderful lady, and I looked forward to living with them.
Aunt June was always ready to visit with me, and there were
things I wanted to ask her.

While Aunt Bea and Uncle Dave were Baptists, Aunt June
and Uncle Toad were Methodists. I moved into my room
without hesitation, and looked forward to the summer. Being
with Cindy and Scotty was icing on the cake that was getting
better all the time. My job at Uncle Toad's work was good, and
I showed them immediately that I was a good worker. After
work each day, I would return home with Uncle Toad, and
putting on my shorts and running shoes, take off running
through the beautiful neighborhood. As people began
to recognize me, they would wave and shout encouraging
things. They all seemed to know me, and actually some did
from press clippings that appeared in the Daily Oklahoman
the previous year. Living in the affluent neighborhood and
being recognized, made me feel very good.

Not far from our home and tucked away in a grove of
beautiful Oak and Pecan trees was a pretty church. I had
noticed it every day as I ran past it. One day as I was running,
I noticed a priest who was busy tending the flowers that
bloomed abundantly in the beds that circled the little church.
He waved at me and smiled. I liked him immediately and
decided to stop. His name was Father John, and he invited
me in for a visit. Entering the chapel, I involuntarily reached
out to the bowl of water that stood sentinel at the door of the
chapel. Dipping my fingers into the bowl, and making the
sign of the cross on my sweaty chest, Father John smiled at me
and said in an Irish brogue,

"Ah, thank God, a good Catholic boy!"

Father John asked about my home. I didn't know exactly
how to respond, and didn't really want to go into a long
story, so I told him very little except that I had to get back to
my training. As I walked out of the chapel, the aging priest
asked,

"Will I see you at the Mass on Sunday, Mr. Wood?"

Not sure how to respond, I looked at him and said, "Maybe so."

The following Sunday morning, I rose early, and without saying anything, cleaned up, left the house, and walked the five blocks to Sacred Heart Catholic Church. Walking into the chapel filled with unfamiliar faces, I took a seat at the back of the church. As the Mass began, I realized that I knew every single prayer and procedure. Even though the Mass was still conducted in Latin in 1961, it was completely understood, familiar, and beautiful. I could not take my eyes off the young boys that assisted Father John who served the Eucharist to the small gathering of praying people. I participated in the communion, and then walked straight out through the back door of the church. For a brief moment, I could not remember the way back to my relative's home. I had run this course every day for two weeks, but now was confused momentarily about the directions. I recall not being sure where I was going, but more upsetting than that, I wasn't certain who I was.

The rest of that Sunday was spent at home with Cindy and Scotty. Scotty would rather watch me play guitar than eat. Even at the age of 12, he was a guitar addict. It was fun showing him a few chords, and in no time, he was playing them. He was a natural. Cindy was gorgeous. She was a cheerleader at the most prestigious high school in Oklahoma City. The name even sounded prestigious. It was called NW Classen High school and was huge. I loved Cindy, and somehow felt like I had known her before. It was so strange. She was happy, lively, always singing or playing like she was giving a cheer for some invisible team. One of the best parts of living with her was the steady stream of beautiful young city girls who came in and out of our house hourly. Like Cindy, they were beautiful, vivacious, and obviously all had cars and money. The girls all flirted with me as I was a little older and had already graduated from high school. The fact that I would be going to college in the fall to play football didn't hurt. I liked the girls, but would never have asked for a date. They were obviously from a different world than I. It didn't help much that I wasn't too sure exactly what world I was from. I did feel like I didn't belong with them. That feeling was pretty painful for me, and especially when one girl in particular was making a habit of paying a lot of attention to me. Her name was Kip, and I had never seen a girl as pretty as her. Seeing her walk up the drive, almost every day took my breath away. From the very beginning, I wanted to spend time with Kip, but that nagging feeling of being from different worlds never seemed to let me be free to explore relationships beyond a superficial level. She and I became friends over the summer, and although I wanted to be more that just friends, that invisible barrier remained in the way.

It must have been about the third week of my summer that the topic of my Sunday morning outings came up. We were sitting at the dinner table on Sunday evening chatting about how much fun we were having, and how the summer was flying by when my aunt's curiosity got the best of her and she asked,

"Where have you been going all dressed up on these Sunday mornings?"

Feeling no need to hide my activities, and actually a little proud of my new found interest in church, I responded,

"I've been going to church. It really makes me feel good and gives me an opportunity to give thanks for my family and your willingness to give me such a nice place to live for the summer."

I felt good about my statement as I was, very grateful that I had these wonderful people who would give me a job and take me into their home. My aunt inquired about where I had been going to church as it obviously was not far from home. When I responded that I had been attending Mass at Sacred Heart, a few blocks away, the friendly atmosphere at the table immediately changed. My aunt quickly glanced next to her where my uncle was seated, and took a quick, uneasy breath. It was like she knew what his response would be and dreaded seeing it. His response came quickly,

"No one is going to live under this roof and go to a Catholic Church!"

We all sat there shocked. My cousins were as surprised and stunned as I was, hearing this obvious condemnation of the church. In seconds, my favorite uncle had taken an activity where I felt comfortable, safe, content, and turned it into something so abominable that the very thought of its presence in his home was intolerable. I didn't understand. All I knew was that again, I had done something pretty terrible and that whatever that difference was that dwelled inside me; it was completely unacceptable in my family. In seconds, he pushed his chair away from the table, and excused himself. The remaining four of us sat speechless. I guess we would have sat there for hours had my Aunt June not reached over and patted me lovingly on the hand. She winked and motioned towards the sink, indicating that we might as well wash the dishes as dinner was definitely over. As we rose to clear the table, I was surprised when Scotty and Cindy both came to where I stood and hugged me. It was like they knew I had just fallen from grace, and didn't want me to be thrown away. Aunt June joined in with a big hug. No one spoke. We washed the dishes, and with a shared smile all went our separate ways into our rooms. There were many words that needed to be said. I also recalled at that moment, a conversation that had taken place somewhere, sometime in my past. Someone was telling me about, "Quiet." I knew that I needed to understand why this uncle, who had essentially become my hero, could so completely condemn my attending the "wrong" church. I was upset, confused, frustrated. Knowing that the next morning I would be riding to work with him, it crossed my mind to just get a few of my personal belongings and leave. I thought that if I went to the church and found Father John, he could help me get home. Then suddenly a terrible realization hit me that I didn't know where home was. Home wasn't the little room with the fold up bed back with my Aunt Bea. Home, home...I kept thinking like it was a place that I could almost see, almost feel, but it was hiding behind a cloud just out of reach...just out of sight. I was feeling a little panicked, and short of breath when I heard a "tap, tap," at the door of my bedroom. Turning, I could see the gently smiling face of my Aunt June peaking inside as if she wanted to visit. When she realized that I had begun putting clothes into a suitcase I had received for graduation, she stepped inside the room and motioned for me to sit down. With her arm around my shoulder, the two of us sat side by side on the bed.

Reflecting back on this scene, as I approach the far end of life's journey, I can clearly see the two of us, sitting quietly on the little twin bed; her arm around my shoulder. In her other hand, I imagine her holding a large key which obviously fit an elaborately adorned chest sitting on the floor before us. Starring at the box, then turning to face me, while offering the key, Aunt June softly stated,

"I think it's time someone gave you your life back."

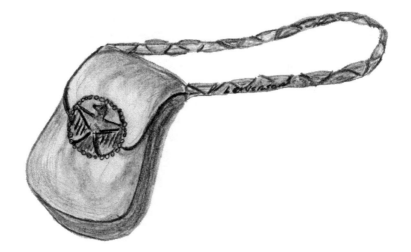

Chapter 33
The Story

Her story began with a vacation trip they had taken to Colorado eight years before. They had come to Colorado to visit my uncle's sister and her family at their summer home in Gunnison. I listened quietly for the remainder of the night as she told me each detail of the visit and the wonderful times we shared. I vividly recall her asking me,

"Do you recall the little girl with the pony tail that bounced when she ran, and the other girl who liked to tease me even though she liked me a lot? " She told me about my mother, and how she loved me so much that she couldn't talk about me, or see me without tears coming to her eyes. She told me about fishing with my father, and how he loved me, but just had difficulty being around young people. She told me about my visits and why I just visited with my family, and didn't live with them at the time. As she shared the details of the story, a picture was slowly taking shape in my mind. The picture was cloudy, but I could see us all there. I was just a little boy, but I could see me there. I could see a small boy, fly rod in hand, wearing black tennis shoes, and going to the river to fish with my father. It was like a very large, somewhat worn picture puzzle that was taking shape before my eyes. As the picture became clearer and clearer, I stopped her and said,

"I think I lived near there. I think I lived in the mountains in a small house with an old man I called grandfather.

"Yes," she responded. "You lived in New Mexico with your grandfather. The little town was called Taos."

"I remember Taos," I told her. "I remember my grandfather, and a house full of grandmothers. I remember going to school there and playing with lots of kids. I remember a pony. That was "my" pony I told her. I think his name was Scout, and my grandfather gave him to me for my birthday."

I was getting more and more excited as she told the story, and I began to remember more and more.

As the story continued, I remember thinking that I "did" have a home, and as soon as I knew the entire story, I could go there. It was the thing I needed the most. I needed a home to go home to. The faster she told the story, the faster my questions came. It was all taking shape, and I wanted to jump up and finish packing so I could finally go home! It was all there, jumping out of the big box, right in front of my eyes. I could hardly sit still on the bed when my aunt interrupted my excitement and said,

"Larry, there's a lot more to the story."

Trying to be patient, I continued listening even though I wanted to jump up and start packing. I told her I wanted to go as quickly as possible to see my grandfather and pick up right where I left off years ago. Suddenly, I noticed my aunt being hesitant. I wanted the story to continue, but she obviously did not want to tell the next part of her story. When I told her I was going to Taos to be with my grandfather, she began to cry.

"It's OK, Aunt June; I'll come back here to visit. I just have to go home for a while. I'll be back to visit."

The next part of the story took away all the excitement that was exploding within me.

"Larry," she began, "Do you remember living with your father?"

"Not really," I told her. I thought I could vaguely remember him, but it was very cloudy and even uncomfortable trying to recall this missing link in the story.

"Your Dad," she continued, "was a very nice man. He was different, but a nice man. You and he had difficulties as he had never learned about being a dad."

She explained how and why I was raised by my grandfather, and that I had gone to live with him, and my mother and sister when I moved away from Taos. She told me the terrible account of my mother's illness, and the tragedy that followed. As she told this part, she became more and more reluctant. Encouraging her, and thanking her for telling me, she continued.

"After the loss of your mother, your father and you had a very hard time. Within a year, you and he were unable to live together, and an incident happened."

She told me that following the incident, I was placed in a clinic with professional people who could help me get over the loss of my mother. With a thousand questions remaining, I asked her the one she dreaded the most.

"Why didn't my grandfather just come take me home?"

"Well," she continued, "He did. At least, he tried."

"Are you sure you want to hear "all" of the story right now?"

"Of course, I want to hear "all" of the story!"

Aunt June took a very deep breath, and continued.

"When your grandfather heard that you were going to a "clinic," he got your Aunt Ruth and a young priest from Taos to come get you and take you home with them. Are you sure you want to talk about this right now?"

"Yes, every single bit!"

"They left the next morning in a yellow Jeepster, the three of them and a black Cocker Spaniel named Mandy. Somewhere near Shamrock, Texas, a truck pulled into their lane and hit them head on. No one survived. Larry, I'm so sorry."

The excitement of hearing the story, faded as we sat on the bed watching the sun rise through the eastern window of my bedroom. I felt like a balloon that had been inflated, then popped. I had questions remaining that I wanted to ask, but somehow they just didn't seem to matter any more. I inquired about the grandmothers in hopes that maybe I could return to Taos and live with them, but was told that following the death of my grandfather, they all just disappeared. It was thought they might have returned to Mexico.

There have been times in my life when I felt like going on required energy that I just didn't have, and when my uncle found us sitting on the little bed, looking like deflated balloons, he entered, gave me a little pat on the shoulder, and suggested,

"Why don't you take a day off? You're doing a good job at work, and deserve another day of weekend."

"Thanks uncle," I responded, and felt myself sink into the big box that had held my secrets for many years. I remember thinking how I would like to just get into the box, close the lid, and never come out again. Later in the morning, I walked the few blocks to Sacred Heart Church, and spent the remainder of the day praying for my loved ones who had gone, and left me behind. Later that evening, I left my uncles house on a small motorcycle I had purchased with my earnings, and deliberately pulled in front of an oncoming car. I was wedged under the large car, and my bike was on fire. I remember yelling at the men who were desperately trying to pull me and the burning motorcycle from underneath the car to "Leave me alone!" They didn't, and I spent the next week in the hospital recovering from cuts and burns. I was angry that my attempt to join my mother, Father Bill, and my grandfather had failed. Again, I felt like a total failure. In spite of doing so well the previous year, old demons crept up inside me, and told me rather convincingly that, I was a loser.

Part VIII
Reflections in the Mill Pond

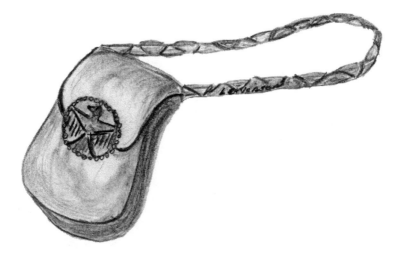

Chapter 34
On the Road Again

The remainder of the summer of 1961 was un-eventful. I continued working for my uncle, and lived in their home. I frequented the little church on 61st Street, but did so in secrecy. My injuries healed, and I began working out again in preparation for my first year of college and football. The burn scars to my arms and legs were my reminders of the night I spent with my beloved Aunt June who had the courage and love to return my life to me. I looked at that knowledge as a gift. While I knew that my family held me in high regard, as the only son of my beloved mother, it was Aunt June who had the courage to give me back what I had lost. The knowledge had come in the form of heartbreaking news, but it had come. The mystery of who I was gave me a sense of belonging. What I felt so much a part of, no longer existed, but it had existed in a faraway place in a wonderful time, and its re-gained memories made me feel like a whole person. I understood my attraction to the Catholic Church. I understood my feelings of being different. I understood the importance of belonging, and the pain of being alone. I understood all the lessons I learned as a child from an old Indian man named Tony Two

Hats, and yes, I understood the warnings I had been given by a wonderful old black lady we simply knew as Old Bea. Thinking back to the many times she sat with me, drying my tears, I wanted to try and find her. It saddened me to know that I never even knew her name; simply Old Bea. In later years, I came to believe in angels. They were as real as persons who walked the journey along side of us each day. Tony and Old Bea had been angels. They were real, but nevertheless, angels who watched over and guide me still today.

My aunt and uncle drove me to Duncan, Oklahoma in August of 1961. From Duncan, my Uncle Paul would drive me the remainder of the way to Denton, Texas. They had already been advised that I knew everything, and was doing well with the knowledge. Being big football fans, everyone was excited that I was going off to college to play ball, even if it was not for the University of Oklahoma. It was sort of a joke that I would cross the state line into Texas where all the rival schools were located. We all laughed about it. It was a good reunion, and I was treated well and given hugs and encouragement as we prepared to leave.

Walking to the front door, my Uncle Paul said,

"Larry, I've got something to give you that I found in an old box of your things that have been stored in the garage."

I had no idea what it could be, but was happy at the thought of getting a going away present. Uncle Paul walked into his bedroom and soon returned. He was carrying something concealed behind his back that I couldn't see. Approaching me, he took a deep breath, and handed me the gift. It was an old deerskin bag with a beautifully beaded Thunderbird adorning the front flap, and while it was showing some age, and wear, I recognized it immediately. It was my bag. Unable to take my eyes from the small, worn bag, I could only nod, "Yes," in an attempt to thank my uncle for the gift.

"And just in case those Texans get squirrelly down there, there's something else that came quite a while after you had left. They said it had been lost in a move, but thought it belonged to you."

Grinning from ear to ear, my cousin Don took something he was concealing and handed it to me. It was a small bow and two arrows. Laughing, he said,

"You'll probably need this in Texas!"

Again, I was speechless. It had been a long, long time since I had made a trip with my bag and my bow. Unable to speak, I held the precious items to my chest. I could feel my heart pounding, and knew beyond a shadow of a doubt that I was in the company of one of my angels. In some magical way, I could hear this barely audible voice talking. Very faintly, but clearly, I could hear,

"Somebody die?? Dis look more like a funeral than a homecoming. Let's go boy, we gotta long ways to ride!"

Before long, I again crossed the big steel bridge that separated Oklahoma from Texas. "Welcome to Texas," the big sign read, as we crossed over and continued to Denton which lay a short 30 miles farther south. In the deep recesses of my mind, I recalled a trip to Texas. It had been years ago, and very different. It was a different time, yes, a totally different time, and even in a different life it seemed. I was a little boy on that first trip. I was returning a young man; a young man on an adventure that would take me into an exciting world I was eager to explore. I remembered the people in my last year of high school cheering for me, and how our little team had come from a losing history to the Oklahoma state finals. The memories were good, and now I had the opportunity to make more good memories. I wanted to be a champion, and a new opportunity had been given me to show I was no loser.

"Oh Dear God," my Aunt Blanch said quietly to herself as we pulled into the drive in front of the athletic dorm at North Texas State University. Her comment resulted from seeing what were obviously other team members either sprawled out on the beautiful lawn in front of the large dormitory building, or throwing a football around as they laughed and played together.

All kinds of things were racing through my mind, as

several turned to look at me exiting the big, white Oldsmobile. Jokingly, this huge black guy with arms about the size of my legs, pointed at me and yelled,

"Hey, white boy, you mus be de managuh!!" We don't play no ball wif no miggets!!!"

All the players laughed, and joked and I did sort of stand out as I was a white boy, and it seemed about half their size.

"You got any money, smart ass?" I yelled at the guy that had made the comment. Behind me, I heard Aunt Blanch gasping for air.

"Whatchu mean, white boy, does I have any money?"

By this time, Aunt Blanch, a granddaughter of General Braxton Bragg of Civil War fame was back in the Oldsmobile begging Uncle Paul to grab me and leave.

"Get your money, if you've got any, and get your ass over here!" I yelled the challenge to him. By now, I had the undivided attention of the twenty or so black giants that were all joining in on the fun.

"Dis white boy's crazy!" he spouted as he strutted the few paces to where I was standing.

I pointed to a sign at the far end of the block which had directed us to the Athletic Dorm. Pointing at the sign, I told him,

"See that sign, gorilla! I've got ten bucks that says I can run to that sign and be back here before you get to the sign!" His mouth dropped open, and suddenly all the other black guys were laughing at him, and telling him,

"Go on big mouth!! Run yo big black ass roun that sign and sho us how hot you is. Dis white boy gonna make you look like sum big ass chimp!"

One of the black guys winked at me, and I recognized him from the previous year. He and I had run at a track meet in Fort Worth, Texas, and he remembered that I could fly. I had run a 9.6 hundred, and just managed to edge him out. We had met after the race, and I liked him a lot. He was an amazing athlete, and we had both ended up here at North

Texas State. Walking to the front of the crowd of boys, he pulled out his wallet and said,

"Nuthin' ginst you brutha, but I gots fifty says this honky gonna smoke yo black ass!"

It was quiet for a second, and I thought I could hear Aunt Blanch crying in the car. The silence was broken when Uncle Paul, stepping into the middle of the intimidating crowd, raised his wallet and said,

"Any of you high rollers cover a hundred?"

All of a sudden everyone was reaching into their pockets and pulling out money they had made over the past summer. They were loud, boisterous, challenging, name calling, laughing, and shoving. Out of the crowd, this enormous guy approached me, and pulling me completely off the ground by the collar of my shirt, put his face directly in my face. In a frightening manner, he asked,

"Just "how" fast are you mother _____?"

"Fast," I responded, knowing that if something went wrong, this black monster would cut my throat and leave me for the buzzards.

Finally, all the bets were collected for the race. My friend James looked at me again and almost laughed out loud. He KNEW his money was safe betting on me, and I was about to earn my place amongst my new team mates. My opponent's name was Carl. I would later learn that he had made All-American the previous year, but had the bad habit of thinking he was as fast as a running back. He was fast for 6'4" and 255#. He just wasn't fast enough.

Carl, as I predicted was just circling the pole when I ran full speed into the group of laughing and yelling team mates. They grabbed me, and pulling me to a stop, one of the big kids said,

"White boy, you run like a goddamned nigguh!"

By this time, the boys who had bet on me winning had picked me up like a sack of potatoes and were parading me around while yelling insults at Carl.

One of the bigger kids walked over to me and rubbed my cheek.

"Yea, dis mother_____'s white! Sho don't run like it!"

Waving goodbye to Uncle Paul and Aunt Blanch, who sat leaning against the door of the car looking unconscious, the guys helped me carry my bags into the dorm.

"Whas dis mother_____ bow fo, white boy? Aint' no mother_____ Indins roun hea! You one strange mother_____!"

We were greeted at the front door by one of the assistant coaches. He commented to the boys who had me circled to "leave me alone and not tease me!"

"Whatchu mean, Coach Thomas! We LUV dis white boy! He gonna make us sum signifcant revnues racin de bruthas what don't know bout him yet! We LUV dis white boy!"

Looking very puzzled, Coach Thomas walked me into the dorm office, and a nice lady named Ms. McCreedy told me I would be rooming with my friend, James. I was excited at my good luck to be assigned to a boy I already knew and liked. As we walked en masse towards my new room at the end of the hall, I began to see a few other white boys, mostly laying around on their beds, or playing cards. One of them yelled,

"Hey, you criminals don't be corrupting this poor little white boy! We need all the white boys we can get around here!"

Everyone laughed and joked until my things had been put away in my room. Turning to look at my new friends and team mates, I felt very good. I wanted to play ball with these guys. I wanted them to like and accept me. They obviously did, even though I was a relatively small, white boy in a world of very large young men.

"It's good to see you, James, I said, offering my hand."

"Good to see you again too, Larry," he said with a big grin.

I stretched out on my small dorm bed, and took in all my new surroundings.

Around 5:00, James guided me to the athletic cafeteria where a feast was waiting. Sitting around the big tables, I immediately recognized the faces of several boys I had competed against in the yearly Oil Bowl Game; a contest between the All-State players from Texas and Oklahoma.

"Hey cacahuate!" I heard coming from across the cafeteria. The yell was coming from a guy I recognized as Rufino Mesa. Rufino was this giant lineman who had knocked me unconscious in the last quarter of the Oil Bowl Game.

"I thought I killed your scrawny ass. Whatchu doin heer?

Laughing, I made an obscene gesture at the giant Rufino who was the largest of the high school players at 6'4" and 250#. He had dominated the Oil Bowl Game for the Texas team and put several of my Oklahoma team mates out of the game with injuries. He was brutal. He remembered me vividly from a comment I had made to him in Spanish during the game. I was desperate to distract him in any way I could as he was literally killing us. I thought the comments I made about his mother in Spanish might do the trick, but it just seemed to bring out more violence. "Thank God, I thought, that this Mexican mass murderer was on MY team. I would hate to ever meet him again as an opponent. As Rufino half jogged his massive body towards me, we shared insults in Spanish to the amazement of all our new team mates. When he approached, he shoved his meaty paws up under my armpits and "threw" me into air like I was a toy. Surviving his greeting, I was appreciative that we were now friends. Thank God, Rufino Mesa and I were friends.

Laughing together and walking towards the food line, one of my new black friends grabbed me by the arm, and overcome by curiosity asked,

"What kine of Mescan talkin, nigguh runnin fool is you? You is one peculiar mother_____, if I eva saw one!!!"

Everyone was laughing and joking with each other as I picked up my tray and stood before the largest feast I had ever seen. I liked this place.

We ate until no one could eat any more. After about an hour, we all headed back to the dorm. The guys were still laughing and joking when we walked through the big doors of the athletic dorm. Passing the first open door, I noticed a nice electric guitar and amplifier sitting in the corner of one of my team mate's room.

"Do you play?" I inquired.

"Like shit," his room mate responded.

"How about you?"

Picking up the guitar and turning on the amp, I broke into one of my Chuck Berry favorites. Suddenly, every kid on the team was crowding into the room and going wild at the sound of my playing and singing.

"I'm takin this honky home to meet my sistuh," this enormous black guy named Marcus said. Another giant black guy from across the room yelled back,

"Yeah, that would sho be an improvement over yo mutha!!!"

Everybody in the room was laughing, dancing, and singing along with the songs. We were having a great time, when Ms. McCreedy flashed the lights on and off to the dorm room.

"Good Lord, boys…..settle down a little bit! You'll wake up the whole town!"

We kept laughing and playing.

Later that evening I crawled into my new bed. James was reading a book, but stopped to ask me,

"You think you'll like it here?"

"I love it here, James! I love this place!"

Before drifting off to sleep, I recalled all the funny things that had happened since arriving earlier in the day. I had met so many new guys, and their joking, easy manner made me laugh. The crude humor they exchanged was different from anything I had ever heard, but it was funny, and I guess; harmless. Having a hard time keeping my eyes open, I thought one last time, "I'm sure glad these guys like me. Otherwise they would have been scary beyond belief!"

As I drifted off I wondered what Kip was doing. I wondered how quickly she would forget she ever met me. I might write her a letter some day.

For the next two weeks we lived football. We were up at 5:30, ran and exercised until 6:00. Breakfast was served at 6:30, and at 7:15 we began team meetings where we discussed everything from practice schedules, to dedication to the team. At 8:00 we were suited up and on the practice field and stayed there until 11:00. Lunch was served at 12:00, and at 1:00 we returned to team meetings. Afternoon practices lasted from 3:00 to 6:00 PM, and was followed by a two hour meeting where we studied offense, defense, special teams strategy, and philosophy of winning football. At these late meetings, we also watched endless films of previous players who had "paid the price to be winners!" I enjoyed the films and remember thinking that someday, the coaches would be showing "my" films. I was willing to pay the price, and would stop at nothing to excel. I had tasted success, and was starving for more.

By the end of the second week of practice, our team was really taking shape. We had size, speed, and a large number of guys who shared a winning attitude. We were tough; physically and mentally tough! What I liked about so many of our players is that we were not rich, city kids who had been given all the opportunities afforded many college bound students. We were from all over the United States, and came from little towns like Abilene, Texas; Apache Junction, Arizona; Lafayette, Louisiana; Erie, Pennsylvania and Tupelo, Mississippi. I had never heard of most of these towns, but through aggressive recruiting, a staff of dedicated coaches had pulled together a talented group of young men who had one goal in common, and that was winning.

Practices were very hard. I had managed to gain up to a weight of 168 pounds over the summer which I had hoped would stay with me. At this weight, I was a minimum of 25 pounds smaller that even the lightest wide receivers that played. The average weight of our running backs and receivers was about 205 pounds. The line averaged around 230. At 168, I did, for a fact look like a "scrawny white boy!" The second week of two a day practices took me down to 160 which is what I weighed the day we gathered information to put in the first Game Program. We were playing Texas Tech at Lubbock, Texas, and I was one of four freshmen who made it into the roster. "If" I got the opportunity to play at all as a freshman, it would be on special teams, running back punts and kickoffs. I wanted to play all the time, but it just wasn't realistic to hope for that. I had been practicing very well, and had even been called in one day after practice for a "coach's session." It started with a very surprising question.

"Young man, do you want to play ball here at North Texas?"

"Yes sir, you KNOW I do! Have I done something wrong?"

Somewhere along my journey, I had come to believe that eventually, everything I did would lead to a mistake. No matter how I tried, I would eventually always fail. Hearing this question from Coach Montgomery, I assumed I had failed again.

"Kid, do you know anything about "Physics?""

"No sir," I replied, "I'm not a very good student."

"Let me put it to you this way, kid. If one very large object traveling at high speed, collides with a very small object traveling at even higher speed; what have you got?"

"Well, sir, like I said, I'm not a very good student."

"Whatcha got here kid, is a fuckin' nightmare!"

"I guess the smaller object would get pretty messed up, huh Coach?"

"I think you're getting' it boy, I think you're getting' it."

"So what's that got to do with me, Coach? Have I done something wrong?"

"Kid, did you ever see King Kong?"

"Yes sir I did…good movie!"

"Well kid, you're not King Kong! You're more like that goddamned monkey that hangs out with Tarzan." You've got King Kong's heart but it's trapped in that monkey's ass! You're playin' a game that's determined by size, strength, speed, agility, and toughness. God knows you're a tough little bastard, but these guys are murdering you. I see you limping around out there. These guys would kill someone for you. They love you, and God knows they try not to run over you when they can avoid it. What the hell is going to happen when we run up against those jack-offs from OU, or the University of Texas, or Baylor, or LSU? Do you think that they give one iota about a pea brained kid from nowhere New Mexico? They'll break your fuckin' neck!"

"I'll be OK, Coach, just give me a chance. Please don't cut me from the team. I can make it!"

"Hell, how could I cut you from the team? Half the black kids in Texas would be cuttin' my fuckin' tires. I'm stuck with your scrawny ass. Do me one favor kid?"

"Anything you say, Coach!"

"Just chill a little out there. You're one hell of an athlete, but remember the goddamned Physics lesson, you are NOT King Kong! Now get your ass to bed. See you at 6:00AM."

I could hear him chuckling a little to one of the assistants who had been sitting and listening in a nearby office. Faintly, I could hear him comment to the other coach,

"I hope we don't have to bury the little bastard!"

I was not affected by the coaches' warning. I played the way I played. My smaller size had never been a matter of concern even though it was brought up to me almost daily. A couple of days earlier, I had tried to take down a senior running back we called RL. He had already earned All Southwest Conference, and All American Honors. RL was large for a college running back at 6"3, 235#. What made him really outstanding was his speed. I was faster than RL, but my 160# versus 235# was a mismatch. I think our collision was where Coach Montgomery got the Physics lesson. Regardless, I had been knocked unconscious on the field and woke up at the school clinic where a physician was examining me.

"You took quite a lick, boy," the team doctor commented. "I don't like the look of your eyes. Can you see me?" Do you know who I am?"

"Yes sir, you're Dr. Clark!"

"Boy, I was taking a look at you when you first came in, and you're pretty beaten up. I think I'm going to suggest to the coach that you take a week or so off before going back to practice."

"Please sir, don't do that; please! If I miss even a day of practice, I won't make the trip to Lubbock to play Tech. Please sir, don't do that to me."

I returned to practice the next day. My head was pounding, and I felt a little sick even before the long practice started. It didn't help that it gets pretty hot in Texas in late August. The thermometer at the clinic had read 101.

It was Thursday, and we were leaving Friday afternoon for the six hour trip to Lubbock. I don't recall ever feeling as excited for an event in my life. I wasn't optimistic that I would get into the game, but just being there, suited up as a freshman was enough to make my head feel a little better. The big reclining seats of the Greyhound Bus were very comfortable and gave me an opportunity to rest my shoulders and neck which had both been pretty sore from the previous weeks of hard practice. Looking at the big gray bus, I recalled seeing ones like it on my first trip to Texas. It was called a SceniCruiser, and had a top section you could ride in for a better view. Again, I thought Tony might have enjoyed riding in a bus like this.

My first thought was to climb the short stairs into the viewing area, but was still feeling a little sick to my stomach. I claimed the first available seat, and joked to Carl Smith who was passing by, that I think "his kind" have to ride in the back. Everyone was laughing at my comment as Carl made a make believe left jab at my head. Carl was popular, and it was a good thing he had a sense of humor. His, was the only time I had ever seen a new Riddell football helmet broken in half.

The boy he hit, sort of a wise guy type from California, never returned to practice. Carl was a frightening human being.

By the time the game started on Saturday afternoon, I was so excited I couldn't breathe. I remember as a kid, having trouble breathing from time to time, but this time it was because I was so happy. I wasn't going to play, but at least I made the traveling team as a freshman, and was there to enjoy it.

We were on fire by the time kickoff came. Even though there was a lot more red and black in the home stadium in Lubbock, there was a large section of green, with loyal fans from Denton waving banners. There were TV cameras, and people running all up and down the sideline dragging cables and carrying equipment. It was a madhouse, and I loved every minute of it.

At the half, we led Tech 44-14. We had played a flawless game and were relishing in our imminent victory over the Red Raiders. By fourth quarter, we had increased the lead, and it appeared a blowout was in the offing. With four minutes left on the clock, I noticed our special teams coach whispering to the head coach. As was normal for me, any time there is a private conference going on, my paranoia makes me instantly think "it's about me!" To my amazement, IT WAS!

"Come here kid, Coach Murphy shouted to me. You wanna get in on this?"

"YES SIR!" I shouted back.

Our defense had played so well that Tech had been forced to punt to us a lot during the game. Our punt return specialist were pretty beaten up as Tech, even though we were beating them was a VERY physical team and had no quit in them.

"Looks like they're going to have to punt to us again pretty quick. I want you to go in and return the punt!"

"YES SIR!"

The referee signaled it was fourth and long, and the Tech kicking team ran onto the field. Coach Murphy yelled,

"Get your scrawny ass out there, kid, and don't hurt anybody," he added jokingly.

I was so excited, I almost fell running onto the field. All my team mates were yelling for me, and I just knew that I'd drop the ball or do something stupid because I was so pumped! The kick was a very high, long spiral and it came straight to me. With my hands shaking, I fielded the punt, and took off down the right sideline. I made the first two tacklers miss and temporarily broke into the clear at about the forty yard line. For a brief second, I could see an opening all the way to the goal line. Crossing the forty and right in front of our bench, I could hear team mates yelling,

"Run, white boy, run!"

Crossing the fifty, I could see the two last defenders coming at me full speed. In desperation, I lowered my head and plunged up the sideline in an effort to get every last yard I could get.

"Bang!"

It was one hell of a crash, and the blow carried me off the field and into the bench cemented firmly into the visiting team sideline. That's all I remember.

The emergency room at Lubbock Memorial was pretty crowded, but I could hear the voices of the guys rolling me through them directing everyone out of the way. Everything was pretty fuzzy but I knew where I was, and that I had taken a pretty hard hit. After an hour or so of poking, probing, and taking x-rays, I was happy to see the faces of the coaches peering into the room.

"H,mmm," I remember Coach Murphy saying as the hospital doctor waved them into my room.

"Looks like the little bastard is still alive."

I tried to smile, but felt like I had been run over by a train. When the coaches were all inside the room, the doctor said,

"Gentlemen, I'd like to show you something."

Pointing to an x-ray of my head, he began,

"See this, gentlemen. This is today's concussion. It's significant and we're going to have to keep a close eye out for swelling."

Pointing to a second and third cloudy spot inside my head, he inquired,

"When did "these two" concussions occur?"

Looking surprised, the coaches looked at each other and shrugged their shoulders.

"No idea," they responded in unison.

"Take a look at this x-ray, if you will. This is a full frontal of this boy's shoulders. That right clavicle is broken, but the injury appears to be a week or so old. The left clavicle is floating; doesn't appear to be attached to anything."

Pointing to another x-ray, I could recognize a neck and spine; "my" neck and spine,

"There is remarkable damage to the first and third vertebrae. Again, looks to have happened before today."

I just lay there, halfway dazed and wishing he would stop with the x-rays. He finally did.

"Gentlemen," he began again, showing them a report of some kind. "This kid has enough blood in his urine to infuse an elephant! We found the same thing in his GI tract."

Turning to me, the doctor asked,

"Son, do you have a history of stomach ulcers?"

"What's that?"

Looking frustrated, Coach Montgomery asked,

"Doc, what the hell does all this mean?"

Looking pessimistic, the doctor responded,

"This boy is totally and unequivocally beaten to a pulp!"

"How soon can he play?" one of the coaches asked, looking a little shocked by the doctor's evaluation.

"My concern is keeping him ALIVE!"

The response hit me harder than the two guys that kept me from scoring a touchdown.

Two weeks later, I arrived back at school in a large, white ambulance. The guys all came out to greet me, cheering and yelling things like,

"He's back, he's back. They didn't kill our little white boy no ways!"

Everyone was laughing and hugging me as I hobbled my way up the stairs into the athletic dorm.

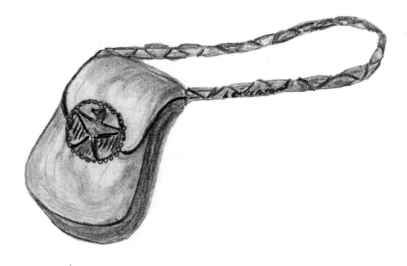

Chapter 35
Going Home?

I spent the rest of the day laughing and visiting with my friends in the athletic dorm. Dinner at the athletic cafeteria was a real treat after two weeks of hospital food. Stopping by the table where I sat eating and joking with my friends, Coach Montgomery walked over, patted me on the back, and said,

"Come see me first thing in the morning, boy. Glad you're back."

I didn't sleep at all that night, partially due to the pain, but mostly due to my fear that once again, I had done something wrong.

At seven, the next morning I walked into the coaching office. To my surprise, all the coaches were there. They smiled as I entered, and one pointed to a chair. I sat down rather stiffly, and asked,

"What's up Coach?"

After a pause, Coach Montgomery began,

"Son, you are one hell of a football player!"

"Thanks, Coach, I try my best."

"You do at that. I wish everyone had your desire to play."

He continued with,

"Boy, you know that football at this level of the game is a business. We have a business to run here. I wish there was room for everybody to stay whether they were playing on the field, or just hanging around to be part of the team. We have a limited number of scholarships, and have to use them sparingly for the benefit of the whole team. It hurts me to tell you that you won't be playing any more for us this year. There's just no way you would ever heal in time to get back on the field."

At some level, I already knew that I was done for the year. I just didn't want to hear it.

"So what do I DO, Coach?"

"We need your scholarship money to spread around to some of the other boys who could use it. We've already been talking about it. We've talked most of the night, and just can't justify paying your way to school this fall."

"So what do I DO, Coach?"

"Son, why don't you take the year off, and come back to us in the fall?"

"So what do I do, Coach?"

"Hell boy, just go home and relax. Hopefully, you'll be a little bigger by next fall, and we'll just pick up where we left off."

"Coach," I began almost apologetically, "I don't have a home to go home to.

There was little more to be said. I was at a loss for words, and by the looks of the men in the room, they would rather be anywhere than stuck in that office doing what had to be done. Walking out, every single one of these big men gave me a warm hug. I liked them all, and didn't blame them for this very bad situation.

To my surprise, my Uncle Paul drove up in front of the athletic dorm the very next morning. The other boys had been avoiding me, and it was very obvious that they knew what had happened, and didn't want to tell me goodbye. Not a single boy was left in the dorm as Uncle Paul and I carried my bags to his car.

We spoke very little on the drive back to Duncan, Oklahoma. About half way there, my uncle told me that he had some pretty good news for me. Ready for anything good, I listened intently,

"Your dad," he began, "has really wanted to mend things between the two of you."

This "good news" came as a shock, as there had been essentially no contact between he and I for a long time. Uncle Paul went on to say that I would be staying with my dad until I got well and could go on from there.

"What do think about that, boy?" he asked.

"Sure, why not," I responded, knowing there were minimal options.

The old house on Pine Street looked pretty much the same as we approached the driveway. Turning in, I saw my dad in the front yard mowing. He turned, and offering a smile, seemed pleased to see me.

"Hi Dad," I offered.

"Hi Son," he responded, offering me his hand.

"That college ball is pretty rough, huh?"

"Yes sir, it's pretty rough."

"You boys have a good evening," my Uncle Paul said, as he got into his car to drive away.

My dad suggested a while later that we go to the Parkview Café and have dinner.

"Sure, Dad," I agreed.

We didn't talk a lot for the next several weeks, but at least we didn't fight either. I told him that as soon as I was able, I wanted to go back to school. He agreed that would be a good idea.

It must have been about my fifth week back in Oklahoma when I got an official looking letter in the mail. The envelope was addressed to me, and the return address was the US Government, Selective Service Department. Having no idea whatsoever of its contents, I opened it and read:

"GREETINGS: You have been selected for induction into the Armed Forces of the United States of America."

"GULP!"

When my dad returned from work that day, I showed him the letter and asked what it meant.

"This means you don't have to look for a job, son. You've got a job waiting for you."

As he explained its significance, I almost died! Thinking this was a mistake of some type, I walked the ten blocks or so to the US Post Office the very next morning. I knew from being in the post office that the Army guys had an office in there too. Walking into the recruiting office at 8:00 the next morning, I presented my letter to the sergeant sitting behind the desk.

"Congratulations, boy, you're gonna be one of US!"

"CONGRATULATIONS MY ASS!" I spouted back at him. "I'm no soldier, I'm a football player!"

"Ah, good to see a boy with some spunk!" he responded.

"This is BULLSHIT!" I yelled at him.

"Mercy me, son, you'll have to get your attitude right before some drill sergeant who lacks my good nature sticks his boot up your butt."

"Holy Shit!" I thought as I walked at a fast pace to my Uncle Paul's house hoping he could tell me how to get out of this unexpected mess.

"Well," he started, "Looks like you'll be carrying a gun instead of a football for a while."

He went on to say that my injuries would probably keep me out of the service, but until the Army docs rejected me, I was headed for the service. Up until this time, I had refused to accept that I had anything at all wrong with me. Now, I was hoping and praying for a physical relapse that would render me a hopeless cripple, or at least keep me out of the friggin' Army!

The big green bus I stepped into on October 21, 1961 was nothing at all like the Greyhound SceniCruiser we had taken to Lubbock. We were headed for Oklahoma City where following our physicals; we would fly on to Fort Carson,

Colorado for Basic Training. Assuming that I would flunk my physical, I was not overly concerned. I even thought I might call Kip after I got rejected by the Army. The idea of going to Colorado sounded pretty good, but not as a soldier. I might be coming up that way to play a game in a year or so, but I definitely had no interest in seeing the Rocky Mountains from the ass end of an Army truck. The Physical Examination line at the Induction Center was long. To my amazement, every single guy in line, just like me, was a hopeless cripple. They limped, coughed, blinked uncontrollably, jerked, and visibly demonstrated every affliction known to man. As each cripple told his sad story to the Army doctor, he was poked, probed, violated, and all to the same conclusion;

"You'll do!"

Telling the doctor about my terrible injuries was like telling an Eskimo it was cold outside. It fell on deaf ears.

"You'll do!"

The flight to Fort Carson, Colorado was miserable. I've never heard that many men cussing and crying at the same time. We arrived at 1:00 in the morning, and were herded off like cattle to be examined AGAIN, and told to get in this line, and that line, and pick up this, and stand there, and bend over, and "ouch" the friggin' shots were nightmarish!

I was in a state of shock when we lined up at sunrise in our newly misfitted, baggy green crap. I looked like an idiot. I felt like an idiot. At least, I wasn't alone; there was an abundance of idiots standing in front of us, marching up and down the lines of the unfortunate prisoners yelling obscenities at the top of their lungs. It was an ugly scene.

Finally, the idiots yelling at us marched us off to breakfast. I sat down beside a black guy who looked just as depressed as I was.

"Ain't dis sum fuckin' white man bullshit!" he mumbled as I sat down.

"Without a fucking doubt!!!, I responded.

Part IX
Reflections in the Mill Pond

Chapter 36
Saving the World from Communism

After three hard weeks, I still wasn't making a very good soldier. I tried to improve my attitude and do my duty, but when I saw a sign hanging in the Fort Carson gymnasium requesting "interested candidates" to try out for the newly organized Fort Carson All Stars Football Team, I was first in line. Getting permission to try out for the team, I showed up at the gym with renewed hope that I would somehow adapt to the military. I was still feeling the beating I had taken while attempting to play major college ball, but if there was any chance that I could make this team, I would stop at nothing.

Checking in with a 2nd Lieutenant who managed the gym, I knew I had made an ally. From the looks of his uniform, he was bona fide ROTC, and not fitting in much better than I was. Immediately spotting me for a college boy down on his luck, he winked at me and said,

"Beats the shit out of marching, huh dude?"

I agreed wholeheartedly as he checked out my equipment, telling me that the first tryouts would be at "1600 hours" today. When I asked him,

"What time is that?" he responded,

"Beats the hell out of me, man. It's sometime this afternoon."

"Just stick around the gym. Some asshole will surely show up and tell us when we're supposed to start."

"Cool," I responded. I liked this guy.

The other hopeful players began showing up at the gym around 3:00. They were an interesting lot, ranging from second team high school heroes, to some really scary looking giants I imagined had flunked out of college ball. We all shared one thing in common; we preferred football to marching.

I breezed through the tryouts and it was immediately apparent that I could play well at this level. Returning to my barracks with a letter from my coach indicating that I would be playing on the base team, I could not pack my Army stuff fast enough. I moved into the gym with the other guys who had made the team, and we celebrated by going to the base PX and getting roaring drunk. The next morning was a total bitch as we were awakened at 7:00AM for the first practice session. At least I wasn't dragged out at 5:00 to march around like a friggin' idiot.

Our team took shape pretty quick. To my surprise, there were a lot of guys who had been drafted right out of college like me. Everyone was talking about the "Cuban Crisis," but my biggest concern was staying in good standing as a member of the Fort Carson All Stars. Somebody else could worry about the Cubans.

At the end of the tenth week of service to my country, my entire unit was ordered to Fort Sill, Oklahoma of all places. Fort Sill was only 28 miles from Duncan, and I found myself going right back to where I started. Football season had ended at Fort Carson, and I found myself wondering what in the world would happen to me now. Arriving at Fort Sill, a personnel officer looked at my records, and laughingly commented,

"Hell, you haven't even had BASIC soldier!" Where the hell have you been for the last ten weeks?"

"Playing football, sir."

"Your ass is headed back to Carson for basic, Private!"

"Dear God, Lieutenant, PLEASE don't do that to me. It's friggin' winter up there, and I'll die within 24 hours!"

Fortunately, I had run into another ROTC Lieutenant who was just putting in his time. The guy looked at me and asked,

"Are you a basketball player by any chance?"

"Was on a contract to the Celtics when I was drafted, sir," I lied.

"No shit?" he commented.

"No shit, sir," I responded.

Walking into the Fort Sill base gymnasium reminded me of my first day at North Texas State. The only other white face I saw was that of a rather scruffy looking 2nd Lieutenant; obviously another ROTC hero whose only possible Army success would be coaching a basketball team.

"What's up private?" he asked as I approached him.

"Here to play basketball, sir!"

I could hear the laughing from a dozen or so huge black guys who were standing on the basketball court looking on curiously.

"No shit?" the coach responded.

"No shit, sir," I responded.

The guys on the court were laughing and pointing as I obviously looked like a duck in a flock of swans.

"Can you play, private?" he probed.

"I'll do my best, sir," knowing that I didn't have a prayer of making this team. Silently sharing my unspoken thoughts, the lieutenant said,

"Hey dude, we don't have a manager yet. You got any problems washing jocks and socks for a bunch of aborigines?"

"Sir, it would be my pleasure!"

I spent the next ten weeks in the gym with Lieutenant Jones, and an all black basketball team. These guys were awesome, and we beat the crap out of every base team in North America. I became the best manager a team ever had, and gave thanks every night on my knees that I was living in the gym instead of learning to be a Forward Observer for a friggin' artillery unit.

I had time on my hands during basketball season, and when I wasn't hanging out with the team, I was writing letters. I wrote several letters to Kip who was in her junior year of high school. To my amazement, she wrote back. I read each of her letters over and over, dreaming that somehow she could stoop so low as to actually like me someday when I was done serving my country. In a couple of my letters to her, I alluded to being trained as a Forward Observer which is a desperately dangerous assignment. I confided to her that I probably wouldn't survive the Army should a conflict break out. It was total bullshit, but sounded so much more impressive than telling her I was washing socks and jock straps for an all black basketball team.

The situation in Cuba was getting worse according to soldiers we visited with, and at the end of my tenth week with the team, my entire unit was sent to Germany to be assigned to units guarding the border between East and West Germany.

Arriving in Bremerhaven, Germany in March, I experienced the second "deja vous" experience in my life. A personnel officer inspecting my records, asked,

"Where the hell have you been, soldier?"

"Well, sir, it's a little confusing."

"How the hell did you land in Germany when you've had absolutely zero training?"

"Well, sir, it's sort of a long story."

"Get you ass out of line, private. I don't have a clue what to do with you!" he said angrily. "You're not a baseball player by any chance are you, soldier?"

"Was on contract to the Yankees when I got drafted, sir," I lied.

I had landed in Germany on March 1st of 1962. My

assignment to the 7th Army was part of a massive buildup in preparation for what was looking like war against the Soviet Union. President Kennedy was taking a hard stance in Cuba, and if a war started there, defense of Europe would be a priority.

It just so happens that military buildup is closely followed by concern for troop morale, and an all out effort to provide entertainment for the troops. Part of the all out effort was the organization of division level sports whose games were the source of entertainment for the many soldiers who supported the teams enthusiastically.

While thousands of concerned soldiers were being sent out en masse to various combat units, I and three other potential baseball team members sat and joked in the back of a truck headed for Frankfurt. Arriving there about 8:00 in the evening, we were greeted by not one, but two ROTC looking Lieutenants who obviously had been throwing back a few German beers, and greeted us like long lost fraternity brothers. They were apparently celebrating the same good fortune we had met.

Baseball practice began the very next day, and it was immediately obvious that I could play on this team. There were some terrific ball players, and roughly half of them had spent time with a number of professional teams, playing at various levels from the big leagues down to "Double A" ball. We had an amazing group of baseball players, and I knew this would be a great way to spend my first spring and summer in Germany. I quickly secured the Short Stop position, and my room mate and starting 3rd baseman was a kid who had been drafted right out of the big leagues. His name was Tito Torres. Everyone called him "Taco" and we became friends immediately. I couldn't believe I was playing right next to a player of his caliber. It was fun, and I felt pretty proud. This Army thing was not as bad as I had anticipated. Best of all, we were living in a converted German hotel right in the middle of Frankfurt. We practiced and played home games in a beautifully manicured stadium about a block away from the hotel. In the evenings, we frequented the many bars of Frankfurt, and traveled the country if games were not scheduled.

In my second week of living in the hotel and playing baseball for the 7th Army, I met a kid named Alan Matsuzaki. "Matt," as we called him was assigned to Special Services like the rest of us in the hotel, but his sport was Karate. Matt traveled all over Europe putting on karate demonstrations for the troops. For a kid of Japanese decent, Matt was very large at 6'3" and 200#, and like so many of us was a college student who got nailed by the draft. He had completed three years at Cal Poly, but couldn't obtain the deferment needed to avoid being drafted. One evening Matt and I were sitting in a bar when another soldier spotted us. We knew him as a kid assigned to the hotel cafeteria where we lived in comparable luxury. The soldier had been drinking, and wanted to borrow money. When I handed him a ten, Matt asked,

"How much interest are you charging him?"

"None," I responded. I told Matt that I have given him a few dollars a week before and he paid me back quickly. Matt continued talking about how so many of the soldiers either drink up their money, or gamble it away. He suggested that we let it be known that "we" were available for loans, and the loans are due in full the next payday along with 50% interest! I thought that was a little opportunistic, but trusted Matt completely. What made it even better is that the thought of failing to re-pay Matt was patently unthinkable; quite possibly suicidal.

The first month we loaned out $200.00 to party goers, crap shooters, and poker players whose money management was as poor as their gambling skills. Matt and I split the $100.00 profit and loaned out $600.00 the following month. Within three months, my soldier pay was considerably smaller than my banking proceeds. Fortunately, Matt and I stayed together our entire 18 month tour. In our final months in Germany, we were loaning out thousands of dollars, and collecting large profits which became very problematic the day I was released from the service. It's hard to explain how in 18 months, you manage to save $15,000.00 on a monthly salary of $118.00. A lot of strange things happen in the Army.

Between baseball season and the beginning of football season, I had a lot of time to spend essentially free from the military. It was a wonderful way to spend almost two years. I traveled, ate good food, and was thankful for my good luck. Matt, who enjoyed the same good fortune and freedom, shared the cost of a used Volkswagen convertible, and paying for it in cash, I had the freedom and pride of owning my first car.

One of my favorite trips was driving the short distance to the Bavarian Alps which lay to the south of Frankfurt a couple of hours. I must have made the trip a dozen times or so, and each time felt that somehow, I was going home to a place that I remembered from long ago. Having the time to think and remember, I was determined more and more to go back there and re-visit all those places I recalled from my childhood. Being completely on my own, I now enjoyed the freedom to attend the Catholic Church again, and made a practice of doing so. The many old cathedrals of Europe intrigued me, and twice while on game trips to Paris, I visited the Notre Dame. The memories of my youth and the painful recollection of learning that Father Bill had been killed in the same accident that took my grandfather and Aunt Ruth were particularly vivid when I visited these holy places. With every thought and memory of Father Bill, I thought of Bernie and wondered where she was now. I had not seen or heard from her in almost eight years. It was like those people never really existed, but were just fragments from childhood stories I had somewhere, somehow collected. I wanted the stories to be true. I wanted to know that I had lived there in that time, in that special place, and that those people I recalled so were real. I knew that someday, I had to go back there to search for evidence to validate my childhood. I wanted to re-visit the trails I had ridden with Tony Two Hats. I wanted to smell the aroma of piñon smoke burning in the kiva fireplaces. Most of all, I wanted to stand at the mill pond and magically recall all the faces of those who had left the reflections I remembered so dearly.

During my stay in Germany, I continued to write Kip. Surprisingly, she always wrote back. I sent pictures and shared my many experiences with her. Even though I was traveling a lot; playing games, or sightseeing Europe, I was always eager to get back to the hotel to see if I had received a letter. Many times I did. During my time in Europe, my father had begun to write. I received a letter almost weekly and always responded. While I always felt estranged from him, I enjoyed the letters and in turn, shared my experiences with him. I wasn't sure how it would be once I returned, but it didn't really matter as I would most likely return to New Mexico, and hopefully re-establish some kind of home there. Even though I anticipated the possibility that everything had changed, I still had a strong commitment to the pledge I had made to Father Bill and Bernie. I had met a lot of interesting people in my travels. I had seen a lot of the world that I had only read about in earlier years in school. I had learned from my friend, Alan Matsuzaki, that I had a pretty good sense for business, but aside from all that, the feeling I immediately enjoyed upon entering a small Catholic church told me that this was my home. This was where I was supposed to be. Unfortunately, every time I had this thought of spending my adult life serving in a small Catholic parish somewhere in New Mexico, another, much less pleasant thought would come steamrolling it's way into my head. This thought, while dormant much of the time would come visiting; telling me that I was not only different from the other kids in my family, but that in spite of successes I had enjoyed in sports, I was still a loser in life. I was certain that if I shared my ambitions of becoming a Franciscan, I would suffer the same condemnation that fell to me upon disclosing that I was attending the small neighborhood parish church in Oklahoma City. That incident had reassured me once again, that not only was I different, but I perhaps didn't fit in at all in my mother's family. I loved them, and I especially loved my cousins. I was just different. Old Bea had known this from the very beginning, and tried to warn me. With my paternal side of the family now essentially non-existent, I was left to fit in with my mother's family, or have no family at all. It was a dilemma I struggled with constantly. On one hand, I fantasized about returning to Oklahoma, marrying Kip, and becoming hugely successful in business, just like my mother's brothers had done. On the other, I just wanted to disappear into a small parish in the Sangre de Cristos and spend my life exactly like my hero, and mentor, Father Bill had done. It was a constant struggle between a need to prove myself to my family, or following my heart in the footsteps of Father Bill.

Whatever my path would be, I was running out of time to make a decision. The two years I spent in the Army had flown by, and the need for choosing a direction was at hand. Whatever the direction, I was rested, healing, and ready for civilian life. During my two years of serving my country, I had become a little larger, and had more experience as a football player at a level beyond high school.

My Army coaches had assisted with applications to various colleges. One was a state school in Oklahoma which had just won a national championship and had a reputation for taking poor students. That appealed to me. I had learned to play tennis and golf from fellow Special Service colleagues who had previously played the games professionally. At tennis, few could beat me. In golf, I played to a two handicap. In a desperate attempt to locate players, the 7th Army Polo Team had given me a tryout and I made the team and played with them two seasons. I played two seasons of baseball, and thanks to my friend "Taco" Torres, who was anticipating going back into the New York Yankee organization following discharge, he contacted a recruiter who invited me for a tryout the spring following my release from the Army. Last but certainly not least, if all else failed, I was an experienced basketball team manager, and could wash socks and jockey straps to perfection. Then there was always banking.

It had been a busy two years serving my country, but I had a lot to show for it above the occasional saddle sore, tennis elbow, being hit by a errant golf ball, athlete's foot, and the always present; jock itch. I had almost $20,000.00 in savings in the American Express Bank, and was going home.

Chapter 37
Home?

I was detained for two days at the debarkation station in New Jersey, while personnel officers attempted to find the source of my $20,000.00 on deposit with the American Express Bank. I continued to tell them that I was an exceptional gambler, and had done pretty well while stationed in Europe. I think they would have been a little easier on me had my service record not been stamped, Special Services; Sports and Entertainment, 7th US ARMY, Europe. Perusing my record, it was obvious that I had enjoyed my service a lot more than a personnel officer sitting at a desk in New Jersey. Their jealousy showed, but unable to prove any illegality, they finally released me AND my money.

It was October of 1963 when I found myself at La Guardia Airport in New York City. I had two years of nice memories, a pocket full of money, and no place in the world to go. By the time I had completed my service, my sister Judy and her husband had returned to Duncan, Oklahoma. We had written several times during my absence, and I knew she would welcome me in their home. Unfortunately, I had mostly bad memories from Duncan, and didn't want to return there. I had various aunts and uncles scattered around Oklahoma, and while I was probably welcome to stay for a while with them, it was only temporary. I wanted to return to New Mexico, but had absolutely no one left there to live with until I could get on my feet. Everyone was gone. Sitting in the big airport feeling pretty perplexed, I remembered that one of the coaches I had communicated with had given me a phone number to call when I returned from the Army. I had the number in my billfold, and decided to make a call just on the chance that he could help me out. It was around lunchtime when I made the call from a phone booth at the airport. To my surprise, a pleasant girl's voice answered saying,

"Athletic Department, University of Central Oklahoma."

Surprised at my luck, I inquired,

"May I speak with Coach Murdock?"

"You certainly may," she responded, "He's in his office right now."

Transferring me to the coach, I remember my knees shaking in anticipation of his having no clue who I was, or telling me he was unable to help me with my situation. I was really shaking when I heard him pick up the call from the secretary.

"Larry, my boy, where the heck are you?"

The young girl working in the athletic office had told the coach it was me making the call, and he did remember me. Feeling immediately relieved and a little excited, I told him,

"I'm at the airport in New York, coach, and I'm looking for a place to go."

"Well get your butt down here boy, and let's see what we can cook up!"

Coach Murdock was a man I had met almost three years earlier while I was still playing high school ball. I had liked him during those first visits, but was determined that I wanted to play major college football, and playing for a smaller state school in Oklahoma just didn't carry the prestige that my frail ego was needing. I remember him telling me at the time that

I was too small, and the guys in the Southwest Conference would eat me for lunch. Looking back, I realized that he knew exactly what he was talking about. I was a little larger now, and had the benefit of playing two years of Army ball. Unfortunately, I was likewise suffering from two more years of abuse to broken shoulders and damaged vertebrae, which were never given the opportunity to heal. Nevertheless, football was my ticket to college, and the $20,000.00 I had on deposit could be saved for a rainy day.

"Are you talking to any other schools, son?" Coach Murdock asked as our conversation continued.

"Not really, Coach. Mainly, I'm just looking for a place where I can come now, and start school in the spring."

While the University of Central Oklahoma had a reputation for winning, it also had a reputation for taking athletes who had for any number of reasons bombed out of major universities. There were grade issues, discipline issues, attitude issues, and on occasion, legal issues. While the team's reputation was not blemish free, there were a couple of redeeming qualities that were indisputable. UCO had won frequent national championships in Division II football, and secondly, UCO placed a large number of players into the National Football League where grades, and to a lesser degree discipline, were not serious issues. Winning was the issue. My history was anything but blemish free, so coming to UCO was an apparent fit.

In addition to fitting in at the University of Central Oklahoma, there was a second factor that drew me to the school. UCO was located a short drive north of Oklahoma City, Oklahoma. Though Kip had chosen to attend Sophie Newcomb College in Louisiana, she would be home for summers and holidays, and her home was less than thirty minutes from UCO. Assuming I could never be anything other than a friend's cousin, I still thought about her a lot, and had written during my time in the service. Surprisingly, Kip had always written back. In a month, she would be home for Christmas holiday, and I was hoping that maybe I could see her.

"You need money for a plane, kid?" the coach inquired as his question interrupted my daydreaming about returning to Oklahoma and the possibility of seeing Kip again.

"No sir, I'm in pretty good shape."

"Well, get a plane into Will Rogers Airport in OKC, and call me back with an arrival time. I'll pick you up at the airport."

I was feeling very good about the conversation with the coach and suddenly all of my anxiety about having a place to go disappeared. I was going back to Oklahoma to school, and I could pick up where I left off two years before. I was bubbling over with excitement as I thanked the coach and told him I would call back in a few minutes with an arrival time.

Before boarding the plane to Oklahoma City, I made two more calls. The first was informing Coach Murdock of my arrival time at Will Rogers Airport. The second call was to Sophie Newcomb College in Baton Rouge, Louisiana. After a dozen or so transfers and inquiries, I finally located her in the game room of the freshmen girl's dormitory.

"Hi!" was all I could get out.

"Who is this?" I heard a friendly voice respond.

"It's Larry, Larry Wood," I told her.

"LARRY! Where are you?"

Suddenly, all my anxiety disappeared, and I told her where I was, and that I was on my way to Oklahoma.

"When will you be there?" she asked excitedly.

"I'm leaving this afternoon!"

After what seemed like a hundred questions, she told me she would be home on the 18th of December, and that we could get together her first day back.

There had been times in my life when I had felt excitement. I had known some good moments, mostly coming from athletic events. Thinking back, however, most of my recollections had been of difficult times that I had preferred to forget. Hanging up the phone after talking to Kip and hearing her voice telling me she wanted to see me and at the same time knowing that I might have a place to go upon my return filled me with an excitement I had not known to that point in my life. After all the difficult times, the anger, the disappointment, the loss of my loved ones, my life was finally beginning to turn in a direction that felt good. I STILL had that longing to go into the church and be like my mentor and hero, Father Bill, but this opportunity was knocking, and it was just too good to pass up. With a big smile on my face, I picked up my heavy bags and headed straight towards the loading gate for my flight to Oklahoma City.

Part X
Reflections in the Mill Pond

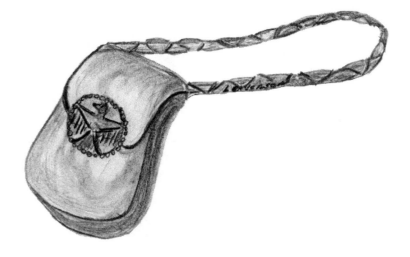

Chapter 38
To Those Who Wait

Due to my inexperience as an airline passenger, I had chosen a counter with a pretty lady selling tickets instead of finding a ticket with some airline offering a direct flight to Oklahoma City. By the time I realized my error, I had already made the call to Coach Murdock to pick me up at the airport. I was a little curious why the flight would not get me into Oklahoma City until 10:00AM the following morning, but after two years in the US Army, I questioned nothing. I was determined to enjoy the flight and after all, I had never visited the airports in Albany, New York, Trenton, New Jersey, Canton, Ohio, St. Louis, Missouri, or even Tulsa, Oklahoma; my last change before flying the final twenty minutes into Oklahoma City. It was an experience.

The one benefit of turning a three hour flight into an overnight, 17 hour adventure is that you have a lot of time to think. I thought a lot. In two months I would be twenty years old. Sitting in the comfortable airline seat, I drifted back through all those years, trying to understand why I had the misfortune that had visited me with regularity and frequency. My journey had begun so wonderfully, surrounded not only by persons I loved and admired, but nestled so securely in my beloved Sangre de Cristo Mountains of northern New Mexico. I reflected that if a kid, any kid had an opportunity to select a childhood; it would be mine they would select. It was like a chapter from a wonderfully written book, detailing all the things that make childhood wonderful. Exactly why I had chosen to leave that idyllic setting remains somewhat of a mystery still today. The recollections of conversations with Father Bill, who so badly regretted that he never knew his family, played a big part in my decision to leave. Father Bill wanted me to have something he had lost and never found. I think he was right in wanting that for me. One thing I've come to believe over the years is that we are all part of a plan. We all share a journey we are compelled to travel throughout our lives. We have the freedom to make certain choices along the way, but eventually those choices lead us right back to our journey. My choice to go live in Dallas, Texas had led to disaster. I had added loved ones into my life, but in doing so had lost almost everyone along the way. In my early Catholic learning, I accepted that when we make bad choices, we suffer the consequences. I was suspect that my choice to go live in the big house in Dallas with all the things that money afforded had cost me my loved ones. I made a bad choice; I paid the consequences. Standing in the large doorway of the mission church in Taos with Bernie and Father Bill, I had been given a direction. I chose to leave the path that revealed itself so clearly that day. I erred, I paid.

Again, as I looked past that harvest of broken dreams, I saw myself being given a second chance for success and eventual happiness. While the old cameos of Taos, New Mexico, and spending my life working with children, maintained a special place in my vault of memories, they had become merely memories. I was a young man now, and it was time to move on. With these thoughts I briefly remembered a reading I had heard long ago in some church that I've now forgotten. The passage went something like, "When I was a child, I spoke as a child, but now I am older, and etc., etc."

Anyway, whatever the passage, I was no longer a child, and it was time to find myself in a different time, a different place. The biggest difference this time is that I was a young man who had seen a large part of the world, and had a pocket full of money. I had a place to go to where I was confident I would be accepted and successful. In a month's time, Kip would return from school, and I would have the opportunity to meet her again, not as her friend's cousin, but as a young man attending college and playing football. Closing my eyes for a few minutes on one of the many legs of my flight, I could see a dark face peering at me though a mist. The face was smiling, and I could hear a voice speaking to me in an unmistakable dialect.

"Mistuh Larry, yous jus keep walkin dat path an one of dese days yu gonna fine dat rainbow. You jus be patient, and dat pot o' gold be waitin' right dere fo you."

I could see it. It was right there in front of me; there for the taking. Feeling the tears well up in my eyes thinking about how much I had loved Old Bea, and how I would have loved to give her a big hug and thank her, I took a deep breath and sank back into the seat of the plane. I had known some hard times for a kid of twenty. I had essentially seen everything I cared about flicker, fade, and then vanish into nothing but memories. They were just that; just memories, and the bad choices I had made along the way had been paid for.

It was almost 10:00AM the following morning when the pilot announced we were approaching Will Rogers Airport in Oklahoma City, Oklahoma. There was a slight rain falling, and looking out the window of the big jet, I thought I could make out a rainbow. Approaching the runway it was obvious that a storm had just passed, and as I took a deep breath and viewed the familiar Oklahoma landscape, I touched the small silver St. Francis medal I had worn for the last two years, and gave thanks that my storm, like the one cleansing the red clay earth of Oklahoma, had finally, finally passed.

Chapter 39
How Good Does It Get?

Coach Murdock was there at the gate to meet me. To my surprise, he was accompanied by three young men I immediately recognized as guys I had played with, and against during the Texas-Oklahoma All State Game. It was a wonderful reunion as they laughed and joked about how two years of growing had essentially done nothing for me, and I was still a runt. I remembered all three of these guys very well, and knew what exceptional athletes they had been in high school. Unlike me, they had gotten even bigger, and it was North Texas State all over again. This time, however, I had learned my physics lesson well enough to know that "If a very large object moving at high speed runs headlong into a much smaller object moving at even higher speed, the end result is me lying in a Texas hospital bed with a brain concussion and a broken body." I was a little older now, and I prayed to God, a little smarter!

We laughed all the way back to Edmond, Oklahoma, and pulling up in front of the Athletic Dormitory, I enjoyed another familiar scene. On the beautifully manicured lawn of the big building were about twenty huge black guys. Looking at me, a kid I recognized as having played for the Texas team in the All State game, pointed at me laughing and yelled out,

"Look hea! Dats dat Wootz boy! I member his white ass! Dat motha_____ run like a goddammed nigguh!"

We were all laughing, and I was amazed and pleased at how many of these guys I recognized and liked. We had an amazing bunch of football players, and I felt like a million dollars that I was a part of it.

"How much better could it get?" I thought, as an old acquaintance helped me carry my things to my new room. On top of having a place to live and an abundance of friends, the second semester didn't begin until after Christmas holidays. I was free as a breeze.

In less than ten minutes I had found the phone in the dorm hallway and called Kip. In two weeks, she would be home, and by that time I would have my own car, my own money, and the world by the tail.

After dinner, that first evening, I went to the campus chapel and gave thanks on my knees; that after all the hardships, I had finally been blessed with good fortune. My only regret was that so many people whom I wanted to please were no longer alive to tell me how proud they were of me. I've regretted that my whole life.

Contrary to NCAA rules, I lived in the athletic dorm for the next several weeks, although not attending classes. It was a good time for me to re-adjust from two years away. My second day back at school, a friend drove me to a car dealer, and I paid cash for a fire engine red '57 Chevy 2 door hardtop. It had red leather seats and spoke wheels. We were an awesome pair I thought, me with my All-State letter jacket, a ton of money in a local bank, and driving around in the '57 Chevy! I wasted no time in locating and purchasing a brand new, candy apple red, Gretsch Chet Atkins guitar, and the best Fender amp on the market. While my fellow athletes were struggling with final exams, I was entertaining them nightly.

It was a good time, and I counted the days until Kip would be home from Sophie Newcomb.

It was around 7:00 in the evening on the 16th of December when one of the guys walked into my room and announced that I had a call on the dorm phone. Thanking him, I walked down the hallway wondering who might be calling.

"Hello, Larry! How are you doing?"

I would have known her voice anywhere, but was surprised as she hadn't called me at school. Now she was on the phone, and my heart was about to jump out of my chest.

"Hey, Kip!!! Where are you?"

"I'm still in Baton Rouge, but I'm flying out of here at noon tomorrow. I thought I might call around and see if I can find some football star with a flashy car to pick me up at the airport!" she said jokingly.

I had told her already about my red Chevy, and now the thought of picking her up at the airport the next day was almost more than I could deal with.

"You found one!!!" I shouted back, "This must be your lucky day!"

Without a doubt, I felt like it was my lucky day. I don't recall ever being so excited about anything ever. We talked for a short while and I promised her I would be there when she walked off the plane. Hanging up the phone, I yelled out loud!!! A couple of the guys stuck their heads out of their rooms and inquired about my excitement. I couldn't even answer. I just kept yelling at the top of my lungs. Walking into the room, Don my best friend and room mate, looked up from a copy of Ebony Magazine and said,

"Settle yo white ass down boy! You jus inherit sum money o sumthin"?

"No, my man, but I'm feeling pretty rich right now!"

I WAS feeling rich!! I couldn't imagine anything in the world that I wanted or needed more at that point in my life than to feel like someone I really cared about might care a little about me too. All those times when I felt sad or even angry that I didn't fit in were just fading away. I was OK. I was OK enough that the most beautiful girl I had ever met was obviously thinking I was OK. The feeling was indescribable, absolutely indescribable. I don't think I slept a minute that night. Before going to bed, however, I made the short walk a second time over to the campus chapel, and gave thanks for my good fortune.

Walking back to the Athletic Dorm that early winter evening, I could hear people singing Christmas Carols and celebrating the holiday season. The air was crisp, and I could smell the aroma of firewood burning in the chimneys around town. It wasn't the smell of piñon or cedar that I loved so much back home, but it was still the smell of home, hearth, and happiness. Happiness had finally come my way and never again, I thought, would I feel the pangs of loneliness, loss, and even despair that had been my constant companion for so many years of my youth. Old Bea was right; I had found the end of the rainbow, and having found it, I would guard and keep it. Everyone, I contemplated has their ups and downs. My downs had just been disproportionately distributed into the very early years of my life. Now that those days were just memories, I was more than ready for the ups!

The ups began at noon the following day. I had bought flowers for Kip on the way to the airport. This was a lesson I had learned many years earlier from my grandfather, who told me many times,

"You get to make a first impression one time. Make it a good one!"

I planned on doing just that, and by the look on her face as she exited the loading ramp, it had worked well. She grabbed me, flowers and all, and gave me a huge hug. I don't recall what I even said in response, but I'm sure it was something pretty stupid as I stood there in the airport feeling like the luckiest, and most inept, person in the world. The icing was pouring out all over the cake!!

It was one of those times in your life when you want to do

the right thing, say the right thing, and present yourself as a thousand things you'd like to be. Unfortunately, I was so awestruck, I could just only look at her and grin. It seemed like every time I tried to say something impressive, I sounded a little more stupid. Oh well, such is youth, and at least I still had the '57 Chevy waiting in the airport parking lot.

"It's gorgeous!!, she said as I pointed to it proudly.

"Yeah, pretty cool!" I admitted.

Putting her bags in the trunk of the flashy red car, I got in and she slid in right beside me. I was REALLY shocked at this as we had never really even had a date the summer that I have lived with my cousin in Oklahoma City. Whatever it was that possessed her to be this friendly, I didn't care. I was in heaven, and it was just getting better all the time.

Before heading to her house, we cruised a popular kid hangout that was called the Split T. There were always kids hanging out there, and as we drove through with her waving at the countless number of kids that she knew, I felt like royalty! I had come a very long way from the little kid riding his pony through the dusty streets of Taos, New Mexico. Somewhere in the resources of my mind that kid still existed I imagined. I just didn't know where.

Chapter 40
Meeting the Family

Driving across the north end of Oklahoma City, I became a little nervous about meeting Kip's parents. My concern was based on the fact that I was pretty much of an unknown kid who had just returned from the Army, while Kip, on the other hand, was a well known debutante, presently attending one of the most prestigious colleges in the country. We weren't exactly what you would call a match. Had my cousin Cindy and she not been best friends, it is doubtful that I would have ever met Kip, as we obviously traveled in different circles. We had met however, and liked each other from the beginning. While coming from a fairly wealthy, social background, Kip lacked all the snobbishness that sometimes accompanies the social circumstances. My being more or less a hard luck kid with a sketchy background didn't seem to bother her in the least. Regardless, we were driving to her house, and I would meet her parents for the first time. I wanted them to like me, and most of all; I wanted them to accept me.

Kip's house was a short distance from where I had lived two years previously with my cousin. Pulling in the drive, I was impressed to see not one, but two very large and new Lincoln

Continentals. The house was beautiful, and as we walked to the front door, I could hear what sounded like boys playing in a backyard swimming pool. Kip's mom met us at the door with a huge smile and big hug. She hugged me too, and I was immediately relieved by her reception. Kip's mom was also named Kip! They identified themselves as "Big Kip" and "Little Kip!" Looking at Big Kip for the first time, I immediately saw where Little Kip got her good looks! Big Kip, whom I guessed to be in her early forties, was drop dead gorgeous. She wore shorts and a tank top, and looked more like an older sister than a mother. She was beautiful, and better yet made me feel immediately that I was welcome in their home. It was just getting better all the time. Pulling us into the house, she informed us that Kip's two older brothers, Chad and Charles were in the pool and I needed to come meet them. I liked her brothers immediately. Both were students at Oklahoma State University, and likewise made me feel welcome in their home.

At nineteen, I had experienced a few good things in my life. I had some talent of which I was constantly reminded. I had traveled a lot, done a lot, seen a lot, for a kid my age. I had memories of a wonderful childhood, and had been surrounded by loving caretakers. Unlike many, I had been given a direction when I was a very young kid, and that direction was most likely a result of the environment in which I was living at the time. Now, standing here essentially in a different world, the notions of living my life in a Catholic orphanage, and being a spiritual leader for a bunch of homeless children not only seemed impossible, it seemed ridiculous. Those had been childhood notions based on my adoration of Father Bill and Bernie. They were gone, and along with them any foolish notions that I could have ever entertained thoughts of such a life. I was standing in the backyard of an expensive home, surrounded by intelligent, ambitious, and beautiful people. If I was ever to erase those old nagging suggestions that I was a loser, I would do it not by being a priest in some obscure orphanage, but by dedicating myself to being a financial success in the environment I now found myself. One of these days, I thought, those Lincolns in the driveway would be mine.

Snapping back into the scene at the pool, one of Kip's brothers yelled,

"Get a suit, and come in!!"

"I don't have a bathing suit with me," I yelled back.

"Hell, we've got several, help yourself!"

The pool did look like fun, and turning to Kip, I asked,

"You wanna?"

"Sure!"

Within five minutes, we were all in the pool, splashing and playing. Big Kip brought us drinks, and we played until we were all exhausted. Sitting by the pool, the boys commented that they had heard, obviously from Kip that I was a football player. Both brothers had been very good athletes and seemed impressed by that. I thought they were amazing. They were. It flashed through my mind that I would love to have a couple of brothers like them. I really liked them. I liked them all. From the very first day, I wanted to be a part of this family. Kip's dad was working that first day, but I was sure that from the warm reception I had received in their home, he would be just as nice. He was. The boys and I made a golf date for the following Saturday, and the four of us had a great time. It would be the first of many.

Driving back to school following that first meeting at Kip's house, I had no doubt about what I wanted to do with my life. I wanted to marry Kip, make a fortune, have a houseful of kids, and live happily ever after. It was as simple as that.

Five years later, I was married to Kip, making a lot of money, and anxiously awaiting the birth of our daughter, Brittany Jane Wood.

Part XI
Reflections in the Mill Pond

Chapter 41
The Ups

After a wonderful Christmas Holiday, Kip returned to school in Louisiana. I would have rather drunk poison than see her walk down the ramp leading to her plane. We had spent most of the holiday together, mostly at her house with her family who made my holiday, for the first time in many years, wonderful. The thing I wanted most in my life seemed to be happening right in front of my eyes. With Kip came a mom, a dad, brothers, grandmothers, grandfathers, cousins, beautiful homes, cars, friends; the whole enchilada. Best of all, Kip liked me. I worshiped her, and watching her walk up that loading ramp, I promised myself that I would do anything, and everything humanly possible to spend my life with her.

Driving the thirty miles that separated Will Rogers International Airport, and the University of Central Oklahoma, I made a vow to myself. I promised myself that whatever misfortune had befallen me in the past; would stay in the past. Whether deserving or not, I had been given a second chance at a good life and I would not let anything deter me from capitalizing on that opportunity.

Driving around the loop that circled Oklahoma City, I noticed a road sign indicating that US Highway 66 West eventually led to Amarillo, Texas and on to Santa Fe, New Mexico. A part of me still wanted to take that road west and go in search of the life I had left behind years ago in Taos. I knew it was gone forever, but those things, those people, who had been so dear to me during my childhood still occupied a place in my heart that no amount of time, nor circumstance could eradicate Driving past the exit sign leading westward, I recalled a line from a poem I had written. I was obviously thinking at the time about my life journey and still wishing I could return to my youth. The line I was recalling went something like,

"Yesterday, just memories,
 we can't turn back the clock;
Life's journey, a path through many doors;
and on each door, a lock."

It struck me as I remembered lines from this poem that I had spent the majority of my short life wanting to go backwards to a better time in my life. Now, for the first time, I was having thoughts of tomorrows, and the thoughts were filled with excitement and great expectations of things to come. No, I couldn't take the long road west and return to my childhood. Those days were gone. I would go forward. It was time to make a life for myself in the world that I had been forced to remain in, and the prospects of finding happiness in this place was looking better every day.

As my drive brought me closer to Edmond, Oklahoma and school, I felt the excitement of being part of a team again. We had an extraordinary group of young athletes, and I would do whatever it took to make a place for myself on this team. In doing so, I would establish myself as a person of value, and feed the badly damaged ego that had been my constant companion for so long. I was not the loser that I had been labeled, and I made a pledge to myself that I would stop at nothing to prove myself a winner in the eyes of anyone who had ever doubted me. The focus of my achievement would be proving myself to my mother's family. I had given them good reason to doubt me over the past few years, and while they had been good to me in every way, I felt like I was always under the microscope, and it was just a matter of time before I embarrassed them with my erratic behavior. I had done it before, and given time, I would do it again. At least that's the perception I had.

Walking into the dorm, I found that several of my team mates had returned from the Christmas break, and in no time what had been a quiet college dormitory was reverberating with shouts and greetings. Though early January, the weather was pretty nice so I put on my sweats and joggers and headed for the gymnasium to prepare myself for the task at hand. Some of the other players were kidding me as I headed out for an unscheduled workout. It didn't matter at all to me. I was on a mission, and willing to work longer and harder than anyone to accomplish what I needed to accomplish.

After dinner that first evening back at school, I made a call to Baton Rouge. Just hearing her voice reassured me that what I was doing was right. Closing our conversation, Kip had said that she wished she attended school closer to home so that we could spend more time together. I shared those feelings, but had a busy schedule ahead of me and knew with her close, I would be very easily distracted.

Classes began the following Monday and along with classes came preparation for spring football. Every day we met in the training facility, and on pretty days moved onto the practice field. It was a good time. I was doing pretty well in my classes. While it was tempting to ditch on occasion, I disciplined myself into a routine, and insisted constantly that this was all part of my proving myself, and becoming a worthy catch. My old football injuries continued to plague me, but it was 1964 and pain pills and steroids were as common in a training room as vitamins. I helped myself to both having no idea whatsoever of the potential hazards to my health. I loved playing football, and if medication made that easier for me, I wouldn't hesitate. I didn't hesitate.

By the time spring training came around I was in great shape, both in the classroom and on the field. Starting the first of April, we would have three weeks of intense afternoon practice, culminating in a yearly ritual called the Blue and Gold game which was a preview of the coming year's team. I was in the best condition of my life, and with the aid of medication I would again, prove the old adage that, "It's not the size of the dog in the fight; it's the size of the fight in the dog!" I demonstrated this on the very first day of practice. While many players, regardless of how aggressively they play the game, don't look forward to full contact scrimmage during practice, it was my opportunity to prove that I could play the game with much larger players. While I didn't relish the idea of attacking my fellow team mates and friends, it was my opportunity; the only opportunity I had to establish myself. So to the occasional "oohs" and "aahs" from coaches and spectators, I played the game with a vengeance. As a defensive Free Safety, I had the flexibility to attack anyone, anywhere within my range, which thanks to my speed, was all over the field. When I had the opportunity to unload on some unfortunate running back, I felt like something inside me was released, and I exploded on any ball carrier I could get at. To me, football was a gift. It afforded me the chance to not only prove myself as a winner, it gave me an outlet for frustration and anger that loomed dangerously just below the surface. I couldn't have been more suited for the game.

Within the first week of spring football, it was obvious that I would be on the field when fall season rolled around. It was just a matter of staying on the straight and narrow until that opportunity availed itself. I would be patient.

For the remainder of the spring school semester, I was a model student athlete. I attended classes, studied my coursework, and called Kip twice a week. Within days, she would be home for the summer and the thought of spending more time with her and her family brought an almost uncontrollable excitement. Summer jobs had been arranged by the athletic department at sites not far from school so that training could continue through the summer months. We were likewise provided with apartments not far from school where players would live together and train while not working our summer jobs. I liked the comfort and security of having my summer pretty much planned out for me. I would have plenty of free time to play, but still enjoyed the regimen we had been provided for being college athletes.

Spring semester ended on a Friday. I and my fellow team mates moved into our apartment on Saturday. On Sunday morning, I was back at the airport waiting to pick up Kip. I could barely contain my excitement and the anticipation of a wonderful summer. As she walked down the unloading ramp smiling from ear to ear, I thought my life just couldn't get any better than this. In my naivety, I had no idea of just how good life can be. I had no idea that I was standing on the threshold of what would become magical years that brought with them everything and anything a person could want. Old Bea had been so right. Her advice had been the secret to my newly acquired success. I had been patient. I had stayed on the path regardless of obstacles, temptations, disappointments. Finally the pot of gold she had so accurately predicted lay before me and nothing would deter me from harvesting my treasure.

That first evening of our summer together, Kip and I went to the movie and saw Audrey Hepburn in "Breakfast at Tiffany's". I spent half the time watching the movie, and the other half admiring the beautiful girl beside me. To this day, I can't hear the song "Moon River" without being taken back to those first magical times that we spent together. The song became our song, and the lyrics promise of "Crossing you in style someday," foretold of unimaginable treasures we would share and enjoy in the coming years. In my mind I could picture the two of us standing knee deep in a large gold filled chest. I wasn't sure just why I had suddenly been blessed beyond my wildest imagination, but it was happening right before my eyes. I was totally and completely in love with Kip, and amazingly enough, she liked me, too.

After dropping her off at her home that first evening, I drove to the parish church I had first attended when I lived with my cousin Cindy. It was almost midnight but I knew the chapel would be open. I remember so well that as I entered the small chapel, I could distinctly feel a presence. The smell of burnt candles permeated the small, dimly lit sanctuary and reminded me of the aroma of piñon fires. The small pictures that hung from the walls and Santos depicting the Stations of the Cross all took me back to an earlier time and place. They were so familiar, so comfortable, so inviting. Folding down a prayer bench, I lowered myself to my knees and began reflecting on the journey that had brought me to this particular time and place in my life. I recalled from somewhere that just before a person dies, their entire life passes before them. I was experiencing something similar, but instead of it happening at the end of my life, it was happening at the beginning. I actually felt that my life had just begun, and all the events that led me to this place, were just hazy recollections that existed within the amber recesses of my mind. I knew that what I recalled from my past was factual. Rosa Montoya was real, as was Tony, Father Bill, Bernie, and Roma. All those people were real people, and Taos, New Mexico was a real place. What was also real is that I had for some reason been transported from that life into this one, and in spite of the tragic circumstances that had defined much of the previous six years, I had been rewarded beyond my wildest dreams, and for that I was grateful. I remained with my thoughts and prayers of gratitude for a number of hours. In between prayers and lighting candles for loved ones who were gone, I just sat there in the chapel knowing beyond a shadow of a doubt that I was in the presence of loved ones. They were all there, and every one, even little Rosa was smiling and telling me they were proud of me. In the dim light of the small chapel,

I spotted a very familiar form. As I recognized him, I couldn't help but laugh out loud as a familiar voice asked,

"Somebody die here? Looks more like a funeral than a homecoming!"

As those words quietly drifted through the little chapel, I knew beyond a shadow of a doubt that I heard the muffled laughter of loved ones. As my tears mixed with laughter, I clearly heard a voice inquire,

"Anything to eat around here, I'm starving!"

Again, the muffled laughter, and I knew at that moment that I was armed and ready to begin the second leg of my journey. I excited the chapel to the first hints of sunrise peeking over the Oklahoma horizon.

Chapter 42
The Magic Wand

I arrived at the apartment parking lot just as my room mates were leaving for work. Four of us had been given jobs at a moving company for the summer, and I held the guys up just long enough for me to change clothes and join them. The guys knew that I had been with Kip at least some portion of the previous night and chided me relentlessly about spending the entire night out. Most of the guys already knew Kip, either from personal visits or the picture I kept on my desk. As we got into one of the guy's cars, one of them said,

"You know, Wootz, we've been wondering about what this hot chic sees in your scrawny white ass, and I think we've got it."

He paused, waiting for me to take the bait which I did.

"OK, you assholes, what do you great minds think she sees in me?"

"Not a goddammed thing," they responded as they all got a big laugh at what they thought was the world's funniest joke.

I didn't mind at all as teasing and taunting was normal communication among guys. Anyway, I had wondered the very same question myself many times before. Regardless, we all laughed, and after sharing a huge breakfast at a pancake house, drove on to our first day of work. I didn't relish the idea of moving furniture all day after having missed an entire night's sleep. On the other hand, I could care less. I'd probably do the very same thing every night if I had the opportunity.

In spite of the very hard work at the moving company, the summer passed very quickly. I had developed a routine of getting up, going to work, coming home to a brisk workout with my friends, then going to Kip's for the evening. On weekends, I usually played golf with her dad and brothers and later, Kip and I would see a movie or lounge around her pool. It was a lifestyle I adapted to with ease and a great deal of pleasure. In spite of my very different childhood, I found I had a lot of potential as part of the country club set, and I was developing that potential rapidly.

How far away, how very far away I had traveled from my little room in the old adobe house at the fish hatchery. Not many evenings passed, as I lay in my bed in the athletic dorm at school that I didn't stare at the ceiling and wonder at what those people in Taos would think of me now. I spent sleepless hours wondering what they would think of the big college I attended. I wondered how they would relate to all my new friends. I wondered what they would think of my flashy '57 Chevy, and most of all, Kip. I spent a lot of time wondering how I could possibly explain to those people I had known and loved what the daily routine of my life was now. While I knew they would be interested in my new life, I doubted seriously that they could in any way relate. What troubled me even worse was the converse of these very thoughts. How could I ever explain with any degree of success what my life had been like prior to moving from New Mexico. While many of the young people in Kip's circle had similar "Old Beas," no one had experienced a Tony, and my attempting to explain his significant relationship to my life was hopeless. The fact was, I had lived another life, one which had very few similarities to this new one. I don't doubt that most people's lives change from youth to adulthood. That's common. What I struggled with was that while so many of my new social friends, mostly kids I had met through Kip and my cousin Cindy had very similar backgrounds. Many had moved from one neighborhood to another, and some even from one town to another. The common thread that bound them I would eventually learn was that these kids were products of middle class America. What was even more analogous was that they were mostly middle class kids from Middle America. Some had traveled a little. Most were bright kids from educated families. All were white; very, very white. While these kids were learning golf and tennis at the local country club, I had been begging nickels from tourists. The irony was now that I could beat them all in golf and tennis, and any other game they might want to play. I just didn't have the proper background and that haunted me as I envisioned myself adapting into the country club life. It was like I had a secret I needed to conceal. The problem with keeping that secret was that I was enormously proud of my background, and the thought of hiding any of those people from my new friends disgusted me.

One night while reminiscing, I imagined that Tony had decided that he might like to give golf a try. I imagined Tony and I riding down the fairway in our electric golf cart, driving from shot to shot. I imagined that Tony was saying very little but thinking a lot. I imagined that we played a whole round of golf and had not spoken a word, something that was not too uncommon for Tony. Anyway, as we completed the round and put our clubs away, Tony turned to face me and meeting eye to eye, we both broke out laughing uncontrollably. No explanation was stated, but the realization that we had just spent an entire afternoon banging a small white ball all over this beautifully manicured landscape to hopefully and eventually putt the ball into a cup just struck us both as horrifically funny. We just kept laughing. No one in the world would have understood our amusement. I understood, and I also understood just how ridiculous it would have appeared to Tony Two Hats. How could I ever explain golf shoes to Tony, or could he ever fully grasp the need for a wedge to get out of a sand trap? In a way, I was almost glad that I would never have to try. I imagine that he would have thought that I had lost my mind. Maybe I had lost my mind. If not that, I was certainly living in a dreamland that only a few years before, I had absolutely no knowledge of. For some reason, my entire life had been transformed. What had appeared to be bad decisions leading to catastrophic consequences, suddenly presented me with a new and exciting life with promise of things yet to come that in my wildest imagination, I could have never dreamt of. It was as if my bow had been transformed into a wand, a magic wand, and everything that I wanted or dreamed of just appeared before me. Before going to sleep that night, I said another prayer of thanks that all the bad things in my life had passed and from this time on, only good things would come to me. I had a magic wand, and everything I wanted in life was mine for the taking.

Chapter 43
Roses without Thorns

Summer flew by. By the time August rolled around, Kip and I had decided that Louisiana was too far away and we wanted to be closer together. Leaving a prestigious school like Sophie Newcomb would have made most parents hysterical. Kip's parents on the other hand, took it in stride and happily accepted her desire to attend the University of Oklahoma in Norman, Oklahoma. I would have loved to have her attend school with me in Edmond, Oklahoma, but leaving Sophie Newcomb for OU was a big enough step. Leaving Sophie Newcomb for UCO was like shopping one day at Nieman's then the Salvation Army Store the next. UCO was a good school and fairly large, it just didn't carry the prestige that Kip was accustomed to. Regardless, we were very excited that she would be within an hour's drive and we could spend a lot of time together.

In late August, Kip went off to rush where she would naturally be grabbed up by the top sorority on campus, PI PHI, and I would move back into the athletic dorm to begin two a day practices. It was an exciting time for both of us, and when she wasn't busy at school and I wasn't playing an away game, we would meet at her parents for the weekend. Things couldn't have been much better.

I began the fall semester with a lot of enthusiasm. My love of animals had given me an interest in studying Veterinary Medicine. I enrolled in a couple of biology classes, but quickly found that I was pretty deficient in math. So much for the Veterinary Medicine. By the end of the first week of school, I had changed all my science and math courses to history and anthropology courses as I had watched a movie with the guys one night in the dorm about Egypt and decided that Archeology was my new thing. I liked Archeology and Paleontology. One of the courses I had enrolled in was called Archeology of the American Southwest. I was surprised and happy to find out how much I had learned as a kid from Tony. Thanks Tony! Shortly into our study, I was likewise shocked to realize that Tony probably knew more than Dr. Thompson did! H,mmmm, Dr. Two Hats. Sort of had a ring to it. I also had enrolled in two different Spanish classes but learned I could test out of them if I felt I had the necessary skills. I did so the second week of school. I tested out with "A's!" I replaced the Spanish classes with European History and German, and could have passed them both without attending a lecture. While the professor was exposing the large classes to the nuances of those "faraway places with the strange sounding names," I sat smugly by the aisle, yawning conceitedly, and thinking....been there, done that!!!! Even my being drafted into the Army had turned out to be a blessing in disguise.

While I was taking a fairly serious beating on the practice field, I had earned my position of starting free safety. I also ran back punts and kickoffs and was assigned "head hunter" for the kickoff team. That was my favorite assignment as I was free as we kicked off to an opponent, to run the length of the field and attack anyone unfortunate enough to be within my range. It was the one time during a game that my smaller size didn't matter. I could use my speed, agility and totally reckless abandonment to assault a ball carrier. Being the "headhunter" was an assignment that I was born to do. When playing this position, I was free, and there seemed to be something inside of me that still needed to strike. I didn't feel consciously aware of it, but it was called to my attention frequently by coaches and team mates that constantly reminded me that "football is a game, and the object is to score more points, not kill the other guys!" I didn't consider myself an angry person. On the contrary, I was feeling great about all the good things that were happening in my life. I didn't know where the rage was coming from and that's exactly what I told the doctors after being transported from the field late in the fourth quarter of the first game of the season. Again, I had regained consciousness in a hospital after being knocked out while tackling an opponent. I learned later that we both had been ambulanced from the stadium. He didn't survive our collision much better than I had.

On Friday of the following week, I was headed for the plane with the rest of the team and would, in spite of new injuries, be playing. In the mid sixties, pain pills were as plentiful as steroids, tranquilizers, uppers, downers and whatever might help to bring you to a level of maximum performance. I routinely took downers to sleep, uppers to play, steroids to grow, and lots and lots of pain killers to keep me going. Football was my ticket to an education. Football meant my name in the papers. Football meant success, and most importantly my success at football meant popularity and Kip.

Part XII
Reflections in the Mill Pond

Chapter 44
All Good Things....

It was the fall of 1964, and time was flying past. With the season progressing well, I had slipped into a routine which I found workable. Each morning I was up early, breakfast at the training table, off to classes, practice in the afternoon, recovery in the training room, and dinner at the training table, team meetings with scouting films, evenings in the dorm studying or playing music. At precisely 9:00PM, each night, I made a call to the Pi Phi House at the University of Oklahoma. At 10:00PM each night, I went to bed and gave thanks for my good fortune.

During the season it was difficult to see Kip as much as I would have liked. In addition to playing Saturday games which sometimes were a long distance away, we typically had Sunday afternoon sessions where we would discuss the previous game, and hear a scouting report for the next. After the meeting, all injuries were assessed by the trainers and team doctor. I usually stopped in just long enough to tell them I was doing fine, and to load up on enough uppers, downers, and pain killers to get me through the week. The uppers helped me study; the downers allowed me to get some sleep and to rest on long road trips, the steroids helped me maintain weight, the pain killers allowed me to hold on to, even if loosely, the brass ring.

The season ended with a Thanksgiving Day game. It had been a good year for me and my father attended the game. Meeting me outside the locker room at the end, he congratulated me, and we had dinner together before he returned home. It was pleasant enough but a little melancholy I recall, as I actually did want to have a good relationship with my dad, but neither of us had a clue about how you go about doing that. At least, I felt like my dad was trying, and I appreciated that. There had been so much bad blood between us that building a bridge that was open, comfortable, and rewarding to either of us, just remained beyond our grasp. After all that had happened between us, however, my father was trying, and that's the way I choose to remember him.

After my dad left for home, I drove to Kip's for a late Thanksgiving gathering. She and her brothers had attended the game, but left quickly to prepare for the big event. Driving to her house and reflecting on the visit with my father, something very disturbing hit me. My father had been enormously successful in business and was a well respected, brilliant man, yet I had no desire to prove myself to him. My mission was to prove myself worthy to my mother's family. Whether or not, I succeeded or failed in the eyes of my father, I did not care. I think I felt like my efforts would have been pointless. Too much damage had been done between us to make me want to do well just to please him. I had somehow given up that notion long before. The haunting desire to be successful in the eyes of my mother's family had an entirely different effect. Like my father, they had all acquired wealth. They lived in beautiful homes, drove expensive cars and belonged to the country club. Their kids, my cousins whom I loved, all seemed to do the right thing all the time. I had not always done the right thing. My past had been checkered to say the very least. For the last year I had done everything well and I felt like I had overcome the difficult years of high school. What struck me now, was that the very people for whom I wanted to succeed the most, the people I needed to impress the most, the people whose respect and acceptance I needed the most: my mother's family, didn't seem to care in the least.

It was funny, that it had taken my father's coming to a football game to open my eyes to something I needed very badly. I needed the respect of my aunts and uncles. They attended football games every Saturday of the fall, but they had never attended one of mine. They had chosen to bypass my games to watch the University of Oklahoma games where they knew not a single player. The reality of this hurt me deeply. The one exception to this was my cousin Mike, with whom I had lived for a while in high school. Mike was always there yelling for me, and to this day I have loved him for that. Not another member of my family ever saw me play college football.

As this painful realization ate at me while I drove into Oklahoma City, I vowed that someday I would do something to make them proud. I would be hugely successful or die trying.

We ended our season at 9-2 and I spent the entire Thanksgiving Holiday with Kip and her family. It was wonderful and they made me feel very special. When I was in their home, I felt like a person of value who was given the respect I had worked so hard for. When I spent time in my own family's homes, I always felt like I was not quite up to standard, and regardless of what I was accomplishing, it could never live up to the accomplishments of my cousins. I loved them all, but could not help feeling jealous of the unconditional, immeasurable love they received from their parents. I had known that twice in my young life; once from my grandfather, and later from my mother. I resented that both had been taken from me. I loved and respected my mother's family. I just needed more from them than they were able to give me, and the more I realized it, the more determined I was to make them notice me. There was still an enormous driving force within me as I envisioned myself standing at a crossroads. In one direction was the love of my life, her wonderful family, money, acceptance, respect. When I looked at the other fork, I saw a long, dusty road leading far off into the distance. There were no big homes, expensive cars, fancy clothes or country clubs. There was no Kip. There was only the dusty road leading far away into the Sangre de Cristo Mountains of New Mexico, and a feeling that there, and only there, could I actually and honestly be at peace.

Feeling that I was once and for all closing the book on all those things I held so dear in my memory, I turned away from that dusty road.

Adios, recuerdos de me juventud!!

I buried those memories with my grandfather, with Mom, with Father Bill, with Old Bea, with Rosa, with Aunt Ruth, and with my dear friend, Tony.

Before we could recover from the Thanksgiving holiday, Christmas came and with it more times with Kip's family in Oklahoma City. The more time I spent with all of them, the more I felt welcome and I was appreciative that I had been taken in as a family member. I was working hard and doing well in school. When I wasn't in school, I was in Oklahoma City with Kip's family whether she was home or not. Her mom, dad, and brothers accepted me in a way that I wish I felt with my own family. I spent time with them occasionally, but never felt that I was quite up to their standards. Whether real or imagined, it was a feeling I had developed, and even though I hated it, it was alive and well within me. I still loved all my cousins, but unfortunately, I envied them as much as I loved them. I wanted my family to be just like their family but it just wasn't to be. It wasn't their fault, it just wasn't to be. Had my mother lived, perhaps it would have been different. Unfortunately, she didn't. So I spent more and more of my free time with my adopted family. With them, there was no scrutiny, no waiting for the next disappointment, and no criticism of my past, only acceptance of me and what I was doing in my life today. It was everything a person could want in a family and I had been lucky enough to find it.

By the end of the Christmas Holidays, 1964, Kip and I were seriously involved. To my constant amazement, she had become to feel about me, the way I had always felt about her. We had even discussed the logistics of how we might marry and finish school together. We were both very young, but with each day apart, and the growing love we shared, the idea of being apart for several more years was difficult. The spring semester came and went and with it, the routine of evenings on the phone from our separate campuses, and weekends at her parents home in Oklahoma City. The only deviation was spring football practice where I was involved seven days a week in preparing for the next year's season. Again, I played with a vengeance, as I saw this as my ticket to an education and the status I needed to maintain the relationship with my beautiful debutante. My grades were good, my thoughts were good, and my future was good and looking better each day.

With summer vacation, I was back in the apartment with team mates. It was fun going into our summer routine again in spite of the constant harassment when I raced home each day from work to get to Kip's house. If the truth were known, they were envious of me. Who wouldn't be? It appeared I had found the reward at the end of the rainbow, exactly like Old Bea had predicted. The thing I didn't know was this was only a small taste of what was to come. I had found the pot, but had no idea of the riches it contained. By some quirk of fate, I had been given the magic wand and for the next ten years of my life, our lives, everything I touched would turn to gold.

When football began in the late summer, a new coach had taken over the head job at UCO. Within a week of practice he had let us all know that "things were changing" in the football program and he had no intention of letting UCO continue as a "cesspool" as he called it, for football misfits. I clearly recall

sitting in the team meeting room with my fellow team mates
and looking around the walls at the numerous Conference
and National Championship pictures that adorned the walls
of the room. Several players were sharing looks of amazement
and resentment that he viewed our team as misfits. It was true
that many of us had been in other schools prior to UCO,
and it was also true that several players were here because of
relaxed academic standards. What was even more true was
that regardless of why we were on this particular team, we
had come together as a team, and as a team of college athletes
been given a chance to perform in the classroom and on the
field. To a man, we had taken that opportunity and done well
with it. Now to be referred to as misfits in a football cesspool
was not winning any points for the new Coach Hall. Before
we even had the opportunity to begin practices, two of our
top players left the team. When Coach Hall announced their
leaving with a flippant, "Good riddance," another key player
made a comment about the new coach's mother, and he was
dismissed from the team on the spot. The rest of us shared
our fellow player's views about the coach and his mother, but
we needed to play to stay in school. It was as simple as that.

We lost our first two ballgames to teams that rarely had
beaten us. By mid season, we were 3-3. Morale was very low
and the number of injuries very high. The new coach reached
an all time low when he announced in a team meeting that
all players who were too injured to participate in full contact
practice, would wear "pink" practice uniforms and watch from
the sidelines as the other members practiced. Reaching into
a sack, he arrogantly extracted a newly dyed pink practice
uniform which he held high for the team members to see. Two
more key players mumbled something under their breath,
and walked out of the meeting room. We were shocked at
the emotional brutality of this supposedly educated mentor,
but found ourselves in a situation that compelled us to stay
and endure his mistreatment of us if we wanted to continue
school and play football. I hated this man, but I had no choice

but to stay and accept whatever abuse he doled out to us. To me, it wasn't just football. Staying and playing meant a whole different life with all the rewards that an education and social recognition would afford me. I had come too far to fail now. In spite of the abuse, I was staying. To leave, I would have felt like a loser and no one would ever call me a loser again.

It was late in the third quarter of our 7th game that I attempted to intercept a pass thrown to an opponent's wide receiver. Neither of us came down with the ball, but the opposing player fell to the ground on top of me with his knee and the full weight of his body landing on my left shoulder. In spite of the pain pills which I took prior to each practice and game, there was an excruciating pain that shot through my shoulder and into the left side of my chest. Reaching through the neck of my dark blue game jersey, I felt blood on my shoulder. It wasn't too bad I thought so I wiped it on the turf and finished the game. Following the ballgame, I removed my jersey and pads to find dried blood covering a small hole not much larger than a pea in the front of my shoulder. Anticipating a problem if detected, I quickly showered, put on a large sweat shirt and left the locker room. I covered the hole with a Band Aid.

Among other things, UCO was noted as having one of the larger Schools of Mortuary Science in the country. Several thousand students from all over the world came there just to study to be morticians. We called them "Diggers," and they enjoyed their roles and several drove old outdated hearses for their personal cars. They constantly amused us by placing body parts around the girl's dorms and sorority houses. One of the jocks had heard that a "buyer" would be on campus in a couple of days to purchase bodies for later use in medical schools and mortuary science colleges. The price for your body was $100.00 which would be paid on the spot. Your body would hopefully be delivered at a much later date. I still had money from my Army days, but the lure of an easy $100.00

was too much to pass up. I likewise didn't really care what happened to my body after I was finished using it.

All that was required for the sale of your body was a quick x-ray, and proof that you were of adult age. No problem. The full body x-rays were being done in the school clinic by none other than Dr. Clark who also served as our team doctor and laughed at us as we entered the clinic with our birth certificates. The doc was a likeable man and good team supporter who was sharing the disappointment of the current season with the new coach. When my time came to be x-rayed, he grimaced a little as I had trouble getting up onto the large, flat table.

"What's this?" he immediately asked noticing the small, now badly infected hole in the front of my left shoulder.

Not wanting to make an issue of the new injury, I jokingly answered back,

"Oh that, that's where they inflate me before the games! Makes me look a lot bigger you know," I said with a laugh.

"That's a goddamned hole in your body, son!" he said angrily.

"It's OK, doc. Really it is!"

Probing the small hole with a metal instrument that looked a little like tweezers, the doc extracted a small piece of bloody bone.

"Oh, shit!" he said.

"Oh, shit." I said.

The doc didn't do the full body x-ray. He did from my waist up and told me to go wait in his office until he had finished with the other boys. I did. In less than an hour he came in with my x-rays.

"Doc, do I still get my $100.00?"

"You stupid little bastard, I NEVER should have let you play last year, much less this year. You're done!"

His words hurt a lot more than the hole in my shoulder. The broken shoulder hurt. Both shoulders hurt. I couldn't turn my neck to either side. There was normally blood when I went to the bathroom, but all things considered…I was doing OK.

"Do you want to tell 'em, or do I tell 'em?" the doctor asked, inferring that one of us would tell the coaching staff that I would not be playing football any more. Knowing that I couldn't let this happen, I told the doc that I would tell them. I felt like if I could maybe take a week off from full contact, I would heal again and be OK. In a desperate attempt to manipulate the situation, I told the doc that if he would just write me a note stating that I could not practice the following week, it would give me a few days to heal a little. Unbelievably, the doctor bought my lie and wrote a note stating I was not to participate in practice the following week. It made no mention that I was finished with football.

That afternoon before practice, I presented my temporary excuse to the coach. As I sat on the bench in front of my locker, I noticed him approach. As I turned to face him, he handed me a pink practice uniform. I didn't take the dyed jersey and pants and he just sort of tossed them onto the bench beside me. Observing this unfolding scene, and fully aware of my sometimes explosive nature, I heard a couple of my friends and team mates quietly mumble,

"Oh shit!"

For the first time in my sports career, I walked slowly onto the practice field. I was proud of what I had accomplished as a student. I was proud of what I had accomplished as a student athlete. I was proud that my hard work had rendered me worthy of a wonderful girlfriend and the respect of everyone that knew me. At this particular moment, what I was the proudest of was walking onto the practice field suited up in the dark blue colors of my team. The dyed pink practice uniform lay in the garbage can in the locker room.

"Come here, Woods!" he shouted as soon as he saw me.

He was pointing his finger at a spot on the turf immediately in front of him indicating that I was supposed to report to him and stand at attention while he did whatever he was going to do to me for disobeying his orders. I walked some twenty yards to where he was standing, glaring at me. Helmet in hand, I walked up and faced him, looking him squarely in the eyes and remembering too well how he had referred to us as misfits, and the cesspool of college football. I was not happy. He began by reminding me that I was not one of the players that he had personally recruited, and that I was just exactly the type of player that he was going to weed out of his program. He told me that he had clearly observed my attitude getting worse over the season and now, on top of it all, I was trying to fake my way out of a few practices.

"Quiet, quiet"...the voice in my head kept telling me as I stood listening to his ranting. I could put up with anything as long as I stayed on the team and in school.

"Quiet, quiet," I kept telling myself, but I could still hear his demanding voice telling me that NO ONE disobeys him, and he doesn't tolerate losers like me. At that moment something strange happened. I recalled all the hundreds of times that my friends and team mates had made jokes about each others mothers. It was a game they played called "deuces" which I never quite understood, but meant that you could say horrible things about someone's mother, and even use the most derogatory terms about each other in the process. The word, "nigger" was commonly used between my friends and most amazing of all the term "mother_____" was used as if it had no meaning at all. The difference was I had come to learn, was that there was a mutual respect in a bizarre sort of way, between the boys using the terms. God forbid, some stranger, or worse yet, an enemy take that liberty. The result would be very violent and justly so.

I was trying to drown out the ranting and raving coming from this imbecilic person as I just stood there refusing to return to the locker room to put on the pink uniform. I was just praying for the attack to end when I heard him use the term,

"You cowardly mother _____!"

I've often wished I hadn't been holding the gold Riddell football helmet with the Bronco and my number 41 painted on it. I'm sure I would have exploded, but the result would not have been so severe. Coach Hall made a habit of wearing dark metal framed sun glasses that made him look like an abusive cop from some small town in Alabama. He used that look to intimidate us. As the glass shattered from the first blow from my helmet, I saw parts of the dark lenses embedded in his forehead where the blood was gushing out. My second and possibly third hit splattered the mouth that had abused us so routinely. The final blow knocked him completely off his feet and gave him a severe brain concussion. I wiped the blood from my gold helmet onto his shirt as he lay there gasping for air.

Chapter 45
Landing On Your Feet

I vaguely remembered being in jail before. It had been a long time, but not much had changed. I think if they had done a year book and had categories like Best Dressed, Most Likely to Succeed, and definitely Most Popular, I might have won. I had tons of visitors. Unlike so many of the prisoners, my visitors wore Polo shirts, Weejuns, college sweaters, letter jackets and Levi 501's. They were a pretty classy lot compared to most of the visitors.

Thanks to Kip's folks and an expensive attorney, my stay was less than six months. People had lined up in the courtroom to attest to the brutality demonstrated by the recently retired coach Hall. Even the assistant coaches, including my good friend, Coach Murdock had testified that it was just a matter of time until someone retaliated. Fortunately, my previous assault history was acquired as a minor so it didn't come into evidence. I was given a suspended sentence, a long probation, and counseling which curiously enough led me into a new career direction.

In the late fall of 1964, I was not yet 21 years old. I had lived what felt like a multitude of lives in a variety of places.

My history was somewhat normal excluding the fact that I had been rejected at birth, raised by a grandfather and four Flamenco dancing grandmothers, didn't speak English very well until I was 9, pulled my mother from her coffin at 14, institutionalized at 15, drafted at 18, played college football at 21, and faced my second attempted murder charge at 22. At times, I still saw myself as a fairly conservative altar boy, with aspirations of becoming a Franciscan priest in a New Mexico orphanage some day. What I found even more interesting was while I was awaiting trial for the attempted murder of my football coach, I began to get a considerable amount of publicity. What was even more interesting was that the publicity I was receiving was not horrible accounts of an enraged student athlete who had attempted to kill his coach. It was more along the nature of "Abused student athlete strikes back at oppressive system." In a twisted sort of way, I found myself in the roll of a folk hero who had taken a stand against the evils that existed in college sports at the time. In the numerous eloquently written articles there was reference to the slightly undersized athlete who under the influence of loosely administered drugs sacrificed his health and well being to afford a college education. It was good stuff. I couldn't have written it better myself, and the effect it was having on the reading public was extraordinary. Within my first month of incarceration, while waiting trial, I received more than enough contributions to pay the next two years of college. Regrettably, by the time my trial came up, second semester was well underway and I had missed it. I didn't mind taking a short break from school, as it still wasn't my favorite thing. An education was a means to an end and I fully intended to use it as such.

During my stay as a guest of Oklahoma County, I had so many visitors that they were forced to start scheduling visits. The only exceptions were Kip and her mom who visited me daily. After my blow up which was plea bargained down to Aggravated Assault, I quickly assumed that any future I had with Kip had gone the way of my playing career. I was shocked to learn that the first morning of my incarceration that I had visitors and it was none other than Little Kip and Big Kip. They brought gourmet coffee and brownies which I had enjoyed many times before while visiting their home. I was shocked at seeing them and delighted that I had not been condemned as a mad man. On the contrary, they treated me as always and promised that I would soon be free to resume my life. I couldn't believe it as I had spent several previous years feeling that anything and everything I did was subject to constant scrutiny and probable condemnation. It was too good to be true.

Once again I found myself, even though sitting in a jail cell, looking at my future with optimism. It kept crossing my mind that if these people I had learned to love would still have me after what I had done; then I would not let them down. With renewed determination, I planned for my hopeful release and the steps I would take to make myself someone they would always be proud of.

An interesting thing happened just prior to my trial and release. Friends from school brought my mail daily, and I would read the various cards and letters usually encouraging me to keep a positive attitude and I would be free soon. Interesting enough, one day Coach Murdock and Dr. Clark showed up with my mail and to say, "Hi." I was always happy to see them. Glancing through the small stack of letters, I noticed one particularly impressive envelope which bore the logo of the Minnesota Vikings Football Organization. Seeing the logo, I was immediately excited and showed Coach Murdock and Dr. Clark. Opening the letter I found a player questionnaire which is commonly sent out to college players who are perceived as having the potential to play at the professional level!

"Holy Shit!!" I exclaimed showing the questionnaire to my visitors.

Before my brain could even engage, I saw visions of myself playing ball for the Minnesota Vikings. I was running up and down the field, dodging tackles and being interviewed on the TV by some hot sports caster. Kip would love me forever once I became a professional sports star! Suddenly, I noticed my visitors looking at each other with looks of disbelief.

"Son, you couldn't pass the physical to get into Four Seasons Nursing Home!"

I knew Dr. Clark was right. I didn't want to believe it, but I knew he was right. Even reaching out to shake hands with a friend had become a painful experience. I couldn't raise either arm above my shoulders. When I was arrested at school, I couldn't put my arms behind my back. A few days later, I couldn't raise my right hand to be sworn in to testify on my own behalf. Worst of all, it hurt to hold Kip. She had just recently begun to tell me that she loved me, and oftentimes a tear would accompany her profession. I could barely wipe away the tears. As much as I wanted to attempt professional football, my playing days were over. It was time to move on to another dream.

I pled guilty to the charges, and walked out of the courtroom with no further jail time. Just before sentencing, I was asked by the judge if I had learned my lesson. I responded,

"I think we both did."

When the magistrate inquired who the "we" was I referred to, I timidly responded,

"Me and Coach Hall."

This was obviously not the answer the judge was soliciting and seeing his concern for my rehabilitation, the courtroom got very, very quiet while everyone waited to see if I had once again screwed myself.

"Young man, I hope counseling assists you in getting a better handle on your anger."

Well, it didn't exactly help with the anger, but it did help me get a better handle on my class schedule for the next year. I filled in two gaping holes in my schedule with Psychology classes.

Part XIII
Reflections in the Mill Pond

Chapter 46
Assume Nothing

The trial ended on March 27, 1965. It was Good Friday and also the day of my mother's birth and death. I walked out of that grim place with the determination to make her and all those who had supported me during this time very proud of me.

Returning to the dorm to pick up my belongings, it came as no surprise that I had received a letter from the NCAA telling me I was banned from participation in all future NCAA college activities. The insinuation was painful, but I knew I was finished anyway. It was just another disappointment I would learn to deal with.

With the new setbacks I once again found myself in a position of not having a home where I might take refuge and regroup. Being a "folk hero" had its upside but didn't carry much weight when you have no place to sleep. I had done well investing my Army proceeds and decided to rent a small apartment until I could decide what to do. I rented a nice place very close to Kip's parents' home and began pondering my future once again. Momentarily it crossed my mind to finally go home to New Mexico. The people I cared about were mostly gone, I was sure, but the mountains would always be there. The St. Francis Mission would always be there, and the memories of a wonderful childhood were indelibly etched on my mind. With every thought of those magical days a smile came to my face.

My telephone was installed in my apartment the same day I moved in. I called the Pi Phi house at OU to give Kip my number. She was in class but I left the number with Kip's room mate and best friend, a very cute young girl named Julie Levinstein. Julie sounded happy to hear me and said that Kip had something to talk to me about, and would make sure she got the phone number as soon as she returned from class. Without hesitation, the old tapes in my head began to play, and I knew beyond a shadow of a doubt that Kip had come to her senses, deciding that I just wasn't what she was looking for in a boyfriend. It was over and I might as well get used to it. It was too good to be true anyway. Things like Kip and her family just don't happen to a loser.

There was a liquor store in the same block as my apartment. I walked there, bought a fifth of tequila, and was nearly half way through it a couple of hours later when my phone rang for the first time.

"Howdy!"

"Larry, is that you?"

"Yup!"

"Are you OK? You sound funny!"

"Yup."

"Larry, are you drunk?"

"Yup."

"Do you know it's only 2:00 in the afternoon?"

"Nope."

"Larry, I've got something very important to talk to you about and it can't wait! Don't drive; I'll come to the apartment!"

"No need. Just say it now and get it over with."

"Larry!! What are you talking about?"

"Julie already told me!"

"Julie didn't tell you anything, you idiot. She's sitting right here beside me!"

"Larry, you moron! Stay right there and I'll be at the apartment in half an hour! Don't you dare leave!"

"Well crap," I thought as I bit into another lime to lessen the bite of the Jose Cuervo.

They didn't knock on the door, or if they did, I didn't hear it. I was nearing the end of my relationship with my friend, Jose when I squinted my eyes and saw Kip and Julie staring at me in disbelief. All I could offer was,

"Howdy!"

I could hear them talking about getting me into Kip's Corvette and throwing me into Kip's pool. I also remember sort of sitting in Julie's lap in the two seater sports car, with the wind hitting me in the face just enough to keep me conscious. With the help of Big Kip, the three of them carried me from the car and dumped me into the pool clothes and all, then jumped in with me to keep me from drowning. My mind was spinning, and I recall thinking that I would prefer the drowning over what I assumed I was about to be told. As if things weren't bad enough, I was still sloppy drunk but sober enough to notice that Kip's beautiful mom was not wearing a bra under her pink Polo shirt. Fool that I am, I grinned at her and commented,

"Nice tits!"

It might have been an hour or so when I began to regain a little of my senses. I was sprawled out on an overstuffed chaise lounge beside the pool with a large cup of coffee being poured down me. In addition to Julie, Kip and her mom, Big Kip, we had been joined by her brother Chad and her dad. It was like they had come to the wake of some newly departed that they didn't really care was dead anyway. I was wishing I was dead. Why in hell did they save me?

"Larry, I've got something important to talk to you about!"

"Oh shit," I thought, now she's going to tell me in front of everybody. I wanted to jump back into the pool for another shot at ending my misery.

"Julie's dad has a job for you in Indianapolis! Isn't that great?"

"Yea, that's great alright," I thought, knowing they had managed to find me a job about a thousand miles away from them."

"Gee thanks," I mumbled, still wishing I had drowned in the pool.

"Hurry and sober up, we've got a lot of planning to do!"

"What's to plan, I'll just get my stuff and leave."

"Oh no, you won't you idiot, we're getting married first!"

Several seconds passed as I struggled to comprehend what Kip had just said. I was trying to process what was happening when an enormous urge to regurgitate overcame me. Half falling and half climbing out of the chaise lounge, I lunged for the side of the pool as the Jose Cuervo and half a dozen partially digested limes hit the cool blue water. They were accompanied by a Chili Burger I had eaten at the Split T earlier in the day. It made a pretty awful sight floating around in that beautiful pool. As I hung there on all fours, Kip knelt at my side and said,

"I love you, Larry," to which I politely responded,

"You're out of your friggin' mind!"

"Hey, let's celebrate!" somebody yelled from behind me.

"Get the champagne!"

Hearing this, I lowered myself back to the edge of the pool and unloaded the very last of the Chili Burger. Kip had asked me to marry her, and there was almost a whole slice of pickle floating in front of me on a partially chewed piece of hamburger meat.

Chapter 47
The Six Tiered Cake

It was about 2:00 in the morning when I pulled myself out of bed to get water. I felt horrible. The house was quiet and everyone was sound asleep. Stumbling back from the kitchen, I decided to begin my apologies early instead of waiting until morning, so I very quietly entered Kip's room and knelt beside the bed to begin the first of my appeals for forgiveness. A beautiful hand was all I could see sticking out from underneath the satin sheets, so in an attempt to maximize the apology, I kissed the hand and sincerely asked,

"Sugar, will you ever forgive me?"

"Holy Shit!!" Julie yelled as she woke from a dead sleep to someone kissing her hand in the middle of the night.

"Oh crap, Jules, what are you doing here?" I apologized.

By that time, Kip, and everyone else in the house was awake, and her head popped out from under the sheets beside Julie.

"Oh God, Jules, I'm sorry! I thought you were Kip!"

No more had I said it when the lights came on in the room and there at the door was Kip's dad holding a shotgun in anticipation of shooting an intruder.

"Oh God, just shoot me Mr. Siegel! Let's just get it over with!"

"Damn, son, I thought you were a prowler!"

"No Sir," I responded meekly, "just your basic village idiot."

"Will you guys ever forgive me?" I pleaded, feeling a little nauseated again.

"That's doubtful," Kip mumbled as she pulled the sheets back over her head.

I could hear the two of them giggling as I left her bedroom in hopes of getting a few more hours sleep and feeling a little better in the morning.

"Hey, let's tee 'em up?" was the first thing I heard the next morning. It was Kip's brother, Chad, insisting that we play golf.

"I'll call for a tee time! Off your ass, let's go!"

By that time Big Kip was in the kitchen cooking breakfast. I could smell bacon frying and amazingly enough, it smelled good. I vaguely remembered that I had only eaten once the previous day, and the thought of that was like recalling the worst scene from a Frankenstein movie. Now, the guys wanted to play golf and I was just barely able to walk again. Aha, then it hit me. The three of them, Kip's dad and two brothers were planning to get me on the golf course and beat me to death with their golf clubs. I could only hope it would be a quick and merciful death.

"Son of a bitch, you were REALLY wasted!" Charles commented as I tried to wash the previous day off my face.

"Actually, it was just the flu," I answered, half laughing, in an attempt to regain my old twisted personality.

"Yeah, right," he laughed, slapping me on the back and almost causing me to start throwing up again.

"We're playin' $20.00 skins today, so you'd better come back to life pretty quick!"

"Oh crap," I thought. Our golf was always a very competitive event as all four of us loved to gamble, and taking each others money was particularly enjoyable. I usually came out on top even though Chad and Charles both played very well. Today was their big chance to pick me like a chicken and they did; all three of them. The long, miserable episode cost me about $600.00 and as the four of us sat in the bar at the club afterwards; them enjoying their drinks and me, attempting to hold down milk, they jokingly suggested we return home for a nice swim.

"Ah shit," I thought, I'll be the rest of my life apologizing for the pool episode. It had been a day to remember, and we would all laugh about it in later times. My soon to be new family had seen me at my very worst and was able to laugh about it. I had been truly blessed, and that evening at the dinner table, as I attempted a very small sip of champagne, I toasted my new family, and genuinely thanked them for making me very, very happy.

As a child I had known unconditional love and acceptance. Dramatic circumstances had taken that security away and made me doubt myself as a person of value. On numerous occasions over the previous years, I had sunken to the point of questioning my desire to continue my journey. At desperate times, I had acted upon my thoughts of bringing my journey to an end. During those dark moments I had recalled something that had been said at my mother's funeral. The pastor was reading from the Bible and read the words, "I shall look onto the hills from whence cometh my strength." Hearing these words, and on desperate occasions, recalling those words, I pictured my home in the Sangre de Cristo Mountains. I recalled my grandfather's hand on my shoulder as I looked through the frosted window at Tony and Scout for the very first time. I recalled the faces of the grandmothers when I placed flowers on the table. I could hear Bernie and Father Bill yelling congratulations to me when I first rode Bernie's yellow bicycle around the courtyard of the mission church. And like a beautifully painted picture, I could see each and every one of the people I had loved staring back at me from the still surface of the mill pond. Regardless of how far I had traveled and how different my life had become, they were still there, indelibly etched in my memory and ready to support me through difficult times. Now, it appeared the difficult times were past and my new family, though knowing little of my youth, opened their doors and their hearts to me. I vowed they would never regret having done so as I made a toast to them all.

After a wonderful dinner, we remained at the table talking for hours. There was obviously a lot to discuss, not the least being that Kip wanted to marry me, and move to Indianapolis, Indiana, a place neither of us knew anything about, much less visited. When I inquired about school, both parents agreed that Kip was paying more attention to me than school anyway, so we might as well be together and continue our educations together in whatever manner worked out. Again, I was amazed at the resolution her parents showed in not only allowing their debutante daughter to entertain notions of marrying me, but their willingness to allow us to work out college in whatever manner worked for us. It was just too good to be true.

Julie's dad was an executive for a large jewelry store chain. I had met her parents many times and liked them both. Her dad had told me more than once that he would gladly employ me after I had finished school. Now, I found myself temporarily out of school and getting married. The offer still stood and it would give me a way to support us. Now, we just had to figure out where Indianapolis was.

The conversation at dinner was happy and very animated. I more or less just sat there listening to my life being planned out in front of me. It all sounded great but I still couldn't believe that Kip's parents were allowing her, allowing us, to do this seemingly outrageous thing. They couldn't have seemed happier. At one point in the planning, I asked,

"Mr. and Mrs. Siegel, are you folks absolutely positive that you want your daughter to marry me?"

After a brief pause, Kip answered back with,

"Well, there is ONE condition."

I braced myself for the worst, and reluctantly asked, "And what would that be, Kip?"

"I want a six tiered wedding cake!"

Everyone laughed and I felt very relieved by her request.

The following morning I returned to the apartment. I had been in the same clothes for two days, and only taken them off to dry after the pool disaster, and to allow Big Kip to launder them for me. I kept the red Polo shirt as my lucky shirt even though it had not prevented the $600.00 loss at the country club. I kept that lucky shirt for years until it was just a worn out rag. After changing clothes, I got in my '57 Chevy, stopped by the Mayfair Bank, and went straight to Zales Jewelers. I nervously told the salesman I was there to buy an engagement ring. It was my plan to get this on Kip's finger before she had an opportunity to come to her senses. Spotting me for a college kid with limited funds, the man pulled out a tray of rings. Taking a quick glance at them, I told the guy I was looking for something with a little more dazzle. I saw a ring that wasn't in a tray with other rings. It sat by itself and I suspected that it was placed where it was in order not to make the other rings look unimpressive.

"Wow, that's pretty!" I told the guy, pointing at the solitaire that looked about the size of a lima bean.

"Yes," he replied, almost acting like I was annoying him and perhaps wasting his time. He reached for another tray of rings.

"Can you guys gift wrap?" I asked him.

"Certainly, we gift wrap. First let's find a ring."

"Well, I think I want THAT one!" I said, pointing again to the big solitaire which he still had not pulled from under the glass case.

"Sir," he responded, "That ring is a little in excess of 3 carats. It's quite expensive."

"No shit! I hope I brought enough. Does the gift wrap cost extra?"

"Sir, the price of THAT ring is $9,000.00!"

"Oh Baby!" I said, "This has got to be my lucky day!!! That's exactly what I brought with me! Do you promise you'll wrap it for free?"

All the store employees were watching as I counted off the ninety, $100.00 bills. When the salesman turned to an attractive lady wearing a Store Manager tag, and inquired about the taxes on the purchase, the pretty lady smiled and said,

"We'll just include the sales tax in the sales price."

I told her, "Thank you," and she took the big diamond ring personally to a table covered with gift wrapping paper. In a very few minutes, she returned with a beautifully wrapped box and commented,

"This is going to make some lucky girl very, very happy."

"Well, Ma'am," I responded, "I'm the lucky one!" I don't think I had ever made a more truthful comment in my life. I was indeed, the luckiest guy in the world.

After stopping by the bank for more money, I darted into a flower shop and bought red roses for Kip. My grandfather would have been proud. This was probably the happiest day of my life.

Later that evening at the dinner table with her entire family, I pulled out the ring. When she opened it, the first thought that came to my mind was a picture I had seen on a Christmas card. The picture showed a choir of children singing Christmas Carols, and each singer's mouth was wide open almost revealing their tonsils. The picture at the dinner table was very, very similar.

"Holy Shit!" I heard Chad comment, looking at the size of the big solitaire.

Kip stared at me as if dumfounded. It was the first time that I had noticed that the back of her throat was as pretty as the rest of her. It crossed my mind that my ring selection had achieved the desired result. Amazingly enough, it fit her perfectly without any need for sizing. I had certainly bought the right ring.

Kip spent the rest of the dinner and evening staring at the almost gaudy diamond on her finger. I had never known her to be so quiet. She just kept looking at the ring, then looking at me, she'd look at the ring, she'd look at me, she'd look at the ring, she'd look at me. Finally, she asked the question that I knew would eventually come,

"How in the world could you afford this, Larry?"

"No biggee," I answered. I saved up some money while I was in the Army and when I got home I invested quite a bit of it in a computer company. My friend Alan Matsuzaki was right; I did have a head for business. I also had almost $60,000.00 in my savings account at Mayfair Bank which wasn't bad for a guy who hadn't had a real job yet. Just before going to jail for assault on my coach, I had bought another sizable block of stock for a dollar a share. It was another computer company called Hewlett-Packard. My broker had called me while I was still in jail to inform me that "if the court didn't find me innocent, I might be able to buy the jail and let myself out!" I had made some very good investments.

Part XIV
Reflections in the Mill Pond

Chapter 48
The Crystal Ball

"LOCAL DEBUTANTE TO WED CONTROVERSIAL SPORTS FIGURE."

This was one of the articles that appeared in The Daily Oklahoman the following week. There was a gorgeous picture of Kip accompanying the article. It was a picture which had been used at the University of Oklahoma when she had been named Sophomore Queen, or one of the many other honors she had won during her first year at OU. The most recent picture taken of me was done by Oklahoma County, and it had a rather unattractive line of numbers beneath it. I was glad it was not included in the article.

Kip remained in school to complete the spring semester and I decided that I would make the trip to Indianapolis to find an apartment. The date set for our wedding was June 11. It was going to be a very busy couple of months, but as I knew very little about planning a wedding, it was just as well that I ventured out to find a home. The very thought of "finding a home," sent good thoughts from my head down to my toes. Just the thought of it kept me smiling. Leaving Kip in Oklahoma was difficult, and I couldn't get it out of my head that if I left, she would surely change her mind and that would be the end of the fairytale. Kip assured me that she was committed and that come hell or high water, we would be married in the First Methodist Church in Oklahoma City on June 11, 1965.

The day before I left for Indianapolis, I was driving down May Avenue en route to Kip's. I passed a Ford dealership, and sitting on top of this big car display stand was the prettiest car I had ever seen. I pulled into the dealership and inquired about the car as I had never seen one like it. The salesman told me that it had just come in that morning and it was sure to be the hottest thing Ford had ever produced. He called it the "Mustang," and was talking a hundred miles an hour about all the features.

"OK, I'll take it," I interrupted just to shut him up. "How fast can you get it down off that platform?"

"Well, don't you want to see it up close?"

"Nope, just get it down and put some gas in it. I'll be back in about half an hour to pay you. Can you give me something for the Chevy?"

"Sure," he said.

I left to go to the bank and when I returned the new red Mustang was still up on the stand. Walking into the showroom, I found the salesman I had talked to sitting at a desk smoking a cigarette.

"I'm sort of in a hurry," I told him as he looked at me like he was surprised to see me back.

"What's the problem?" I heard, as I turned and saw a face I recognized from the country club as one of Kip's dad's good friends. He asked again what the problem was and I told him I was trying to buy the red Mustang, but the salesman didn't seem to believe me.

"You got five minutes, kid?" the owner of the Ford dealership asked.

"Sure, Mr. Richardson!"

Turning to the salesman who was still sitting at the desk smoking his cigarette, the dealer turned to him and said very emphatically,

"Get off your ass and get this boy his car!"

Mr. Richardson, the owner, walked me over to the cashier and politely said,

"Pay the lady."

I smiled, and said,

"You bet!" as I pulled a roll of hundreds out of my pocket. In less than five minutes, I had paid for the car, signed registration papers, and was driving out of the dealership in the very first Ford Mustang sold in Oklahoma City. It was fire engine red with tan leather seats. I was beyond cool.

I left for Indianapolis on a Sunday afternoon. Kip was returning to school in Norman, and I was leaving for Indiana. It was a little frightening thinking that we would be apart for a while, but I kept telling myself that it was just my old paranoia making me doubt all the things that were happening. It was frustrating, I told myself, that I could not relax and enjoy how my life had changed so much from those first difficult years after leaving my home in Taos. The bad times had been very bad, but they were offset by the quality of what I was experiencing now. Still, I worried as I drove the Tulsa Turnpike, heading off in a direction I had never been in my life. Everything was new and strange, and the solitude of being in the Mustang alone had given me a chance to really sit back and think about the long, sometimes bumpy road behind me, and of the possibilities of the journey ahead. In my wildest dreams, I had never seriously considered that someone like Kip would want to spend her life with me. In my own mind, I thought of myself as a good person. I was kind, very trustworthy, and was always the first to stand up for a good friend or just cause. Yet I was plagued by old demons that haunted me with warnings that the road I had taken was not the road intended for me. One day many years ago, I had been given a clear and simple message about the direction of my life. There was no mistaking the message I thought, but still I chose to take my life down a different path. In my Catholic way of thinking, the tragedies that had befallen loved ones was probably due to my refusal to follow the clear and simple direction I had once been given. In my own twisted way, I felt like the deaths of my mother, my grandfather, Aunt Ruth and Father Bill were resultant of my refusal to keep my vow to God. When I had mentioned this feeling of guilt with priest friends, they had assured me that God was certainly not punishing me. I was trying to make sense of those tragic losses and since it was obviously not God's fault, it must be mine. Regardless, I held my breath as I contemplated all the good fortune that had been dumped into my lap. I knew I was not worthy, and that thinking, along with the persistent feeling of not having the love and admiration of my mother's family, kept me from sleeping at night. It also kept me in a constant search for medication that would ease the pain of my ulcerated stomach. Tequila, I had found was definitely not the magic elixir. Unblended Scotch and Half & Half on the other hand allowed me to continue drinking a little without irritating the ulcer too much.

I spent the first night of my trip in St. Louis, Missouri. I called Kip from my hotel room just to say "Hi" and tell her I loved her. She assured me that she loved me too, and that she trusted me with finding a beautiful place to call our first home. I gave her that assurance, as in recent years I had definitely developed an eye and taste for fine things. I would locate and lease the most beautiful apartment in Indianapolis. It was a promise I kept.

Before attempting sleep that first night away, I lay on a big king sized bed staring at the ceiling of my room. In my imagination, I saw myself and wonderful things hovering above me. The illusion was clearly presented as a very large, brilliant crystal ball. In every direction radiated light and color. Every facet of the crystal ball contained its own spectrum, or rainbow, as Old Bea would say. It was a beautiful sight as it slowly turned, showing the myriad of rainbows which now were mine to enjoy. Looking into the crystal ball, I saw the faces of everyone dear to me. I saw riches, mansions,

limousines, country clubs, exotic travel, and the faces of little
children sitting lovingly with Kip and me. It was all there, and
it was all mine. The more I saw however, the more concerned
I became about keeping all those wonderful things. As I
studied this magnificent picture, I saw that the crystal ball
wasn't floating in the air at all. The large ball was perched
very precariously on a very, very small golf tee of all things.
The enormity of the ball made the golf tee look even smaller.
The closer I examined the tee, the more precarious the perch.
Trying hard to put this uncomfortable scene out of my mind,
I could not, and spent the rest of the night worrying about
the perceived delicacy of my situation. Instead of enjoying the
things that had come to me, I was terrified at the thought of
losing them all.

By 7:00AM, I was on the road again. I felt exhausted from
the previous night, but tried to think good thoughts as I
continued on to Indianapolis. I arrived there in late afternoon
and called Kip as soon as I entered my hotel room. Everything
was great she assured me, and I felt a little better.

To the disgust of my waiter, I had a couple of scotches
and cream with my dinner, and slept much better the second
night away from Oklahoma.

I found the number of an apartment locator in the yellow
pages and called right after breakfast. I arranged to meet with
a lady later in the morning and together, we would find a nice
place to live. Indianapolis was a beautiful city; dense with
large trees and parks, and I knew there would be something
special here for us. There was. After telling the apartment
locator lady exactly what I was looking for, she drove me to
a beautifully secluded area with awesome Spanish looking
buildings. Interestingly enough, the complex was called,
"Old Santa Fe." Trees and fountains were everywhere. When
I saw the stucco exterior, large pines, tiled floors, and kiva
fireplaces, I knew I had found it. The nice lady showed me
a wonderful apartment with a balcony overlooking the pool.
The model apartment was decorated with expensive looking

leather furniture which made the place look like something out of a magazine.

"I'd like this one, just exactly like it is; furniture and all."

The lady looked surprised and turning to the apartment manager who had joined us, she sort of raised her hands in a questioning manner.

"Well," the manager said, "The furniture was placed here just for show purposes, but I guess we could sell it. I need to tell you; however, it's pretty expensive."

"Yeah, it looks expensive! Just put it on the bill and I'll pay you for the first six months for everything."

"God, this place was beautiful!" I thought. Kip is going to love it!"

Chapter 49
Here Comes the Bride!

After spending a few days in Indianapolis meeting my fellow employees, I made the trip back to Oklahoma City. With my third speeding ticket of the return drive, I decided it would all be there waiting for me, and maybe I could slow down a little.

Seeing the "Welcome to Oklahoma" sign sent my thoughts racing, and knowing I would see Kip later in the day was just too exciting. The feelings I had for her was something I had never known before, or since. It was an overpowering desire just to see her, be with her, and hear her voice. I was wildly and uncontrollably overwhelmed with my feelings for her. Being with Kip, I was able to put every painful event of my youth behind me. She was my Alpha, my Omega and I would give her everything in the world she wanted or die trying. It was that simple.

I arrived at the Siegel house late in the evening. It was good to be back in familiar surroundings, and the usual reception awaiting made me feel good. It was a Friday evening and Big Kip told me she was expecting Kip at any time as she would be home for the weekend. My apartment in Oklahoma City was paid for another two months, but I preferred being with the Siegels and anxiously awaited the arrival of my fiancée. Kip would be in school for the next four weeks, but we would have weekends together planning the big event scheduled for June 11. Hearing her Corvette entering the driveway was exhilarating, and I met her at the front door. It was really happening, and seeing her smile as I greeted her was just beyond description. That evening, we sat on the couch watching old movies and eating popcorn. It was a scene I imagined would be repeated over and over again for the rest of our lives together. I couldn't have been much happier.

We spent the entire weekend talking about the apartment I had rented in Indiana and planning what was to be an enormous wedding. My head was spinning as I listened to Kip and her mom telling me all about it. It would be a colossal event, and all I could do was nod "Yes" to each and every suggestion for the huge ceremony. My only interest was making sure it was really going to happen, and that I would be there to enjoy it. Late that evening, I drove the short distance to my apartment and lay in my bed for a while still disbelieving it all.

The next morning I returned to the Siegels just in time for breakfast and the demands that we go straight to the club where the Siegel boys would take more of my money. With my head spinning from all the excitement and the considerable loss of sleep from the previous night, they did just that. At least it was fun playing with these guys who were very soon to be my family, and we would do it over and over again in the years to come.

After the golf beating, we returned home for steaks and drinks by the pool. The rest of the day was spent looking at thousands of pictures of wedding dresses, sterling silver samples, and the fine china which would be picked out for wedding gifts. Again, I could only nod, "Yes," and respond with,

"Yes, dear, that's lovely."

I was swimming in uncharted waters, and all I could do was trust the impeccable taste of my lovely bride-to-be and her charming mother. They DID have good taste, and it crossed my mind that I was very fortunate in having an uncanny ability for making money. I would need it!

Before returning to school Sunday afternoon, Kip told me that I needed to start thinking about "groomsmen." My only experience with "groomsmen" had been the enlisted men who painstakingly cared for the polo horses we rode in Germany. It had never crossed my mind who these guys would be that would join me at the altar. Kip had decided on eight bridesmaids, and without a doubt they would all be gorgeous debutantes like her. I was picturing my friends from college that I had played ball with. The visual I was getting as I matched up these mostly black giants with the eight snow white debutantes was a little disconcerting. Of course there would be Rufino, who would lend a bit of Latin flavour to the occasion. Then it crossed my mind that these guys would all need to rent the tuxedos which had been selected to compliment the dresses the girls would wear. The likelihood of the tuxedo rental place having the gray, pinstriped tuxes to fit eight guys ranging from 6'3 and 230pounds to 6'6 and 275pounds was very small. As an added touch of pizzazz, it crossed my mind to have the guys wear their flashy blue and gold game uniforms. While a little different, it was not much more outrageous than the thought of Kip marrying me. Anyway, I quickly dismissed that thought and drove straight to UCO to gather the guys who would be my groomsmen. We had about five weeks for the rental store to perform a miracle. Still pondering how it was going to look with my guys matched up with these gorgeous white chicks, I was somewhat consoled in thinking that if any kind of trouble were to break out at the wedding; my guys could beat the shit out of anyone wanting to spoil the big event.

Kip was home again the following Friday afternoon, and I assured her that the boys and I would be ready. It was not until the pool party the following night at her house, with her girls and all my guys invited, that I realized for the first time that Kip must indeed love me.

Kip knew my friends. She had met and liked all of them. The girls were already sitting around the pool when my groomsmen showed up. It looked like a picture from a Hugh Hefner Playbunny Party. When the first of my buds stripped naked and jumped in the pool with a loud "Geronimo," I thought we had lost the girls. After what seemed like a very long silence everyone started laughing uncontrollably and we partied all night long. We were half way through the second case of champagne when the sun peaked over the eastern Oklahoma horizon. I had witnessed some pretty crazy stuff during my twenty years, but nothing had ever come close to that party. It was plain to see, and was no longer questionable, that Kip did, for a fact love me unconditionally.

When June 11 rolled around we were ready! It was the largest crowd I had seen at a church since my mother's funeral. There were lines of limousines, hundreds of Cadillacs, Lincolns, Benz's and even reporters from the Daily Oklahoman. The entire Pi Phi House from OU was present along with what looked like half the student body. A huge contingent of rowdies from UCO was making a lot of commotion in front of the church and I had to ask Rufino to instruct them to keep their beer out of sight until after the ceremony. It had all the colour and flare of a Roman Circus with dashes of a Papal Coronation and WWF Championship title match thrown in for good measure. Above the hum of a rather rambunctious and irreverent crowd, I finally heard the minister proclaim,

"I now pronounce you man and wife," as the humming in the large auditorium turned into an uncontrolled roar.

It was done! The little white boy from nowhere New Mexico had married the princess. I had won the Super Bowl of marriages!!!

Thank God, Big Kip had the foresight to anticipate the massive gathering and changed the six tiered cake to a ten tiered cake. I later learned that the bar tab at the reception was around $7,000.00. Great God almighty!! The insanity of the occasion was only crowned when one of my guys left the reception with one of Kip's debutante bridesmaids and didn't reappear for three days.

Two days later, we left in the Mustang for the trip to Indianapolis. We said very little; just sort of sat dumfounded as the road unfolded before us. It was Dorothy and Toto all over again and Kansas was nowhere in sight!

Chapter 50
Young, Dumb, and Married

I hated the job at the jewelry store! I had spent all twenty years of my life feeling different from everyone else, and now I'm the only Catholic kid amongst 300 Jewish employees. I was constantly teased, harassed, and on occasion even abused I thought, as my fellow colleagues chronically left work for the myriad of holidays I had never heard of. Worst of all, I worked six 10 hour days a week, and on occasion had to come in on Sundays to inventory. I didn't even have the excuse that I had to take time off to attend Mass. St Joseph's Cathedral sat directly across the street from the downtown store where I worked. When I inquired about attending church, visiting with a priest, or even going to confession, which I had never done in my life, my boss would simply point out the large glass store window to the cathedral some fifty feet away.

In spite of the terrible hours and my complaints of abuse, the other employees seemed to like me. It probably didn't hurt that I accounted for almost a quarter of all sales generated in the big store. That doesn't sound like a lot until you consider there were over a dozen other employees. We shared a common "commission" pool so my hard work kept everyone in Hickey Freeman suits and Ferragamo shoes. To reward my hard work and large contribution to the store, I was given the title of Assistant Manager. There was no raise attached to the new assignment, only more hours and responsibility.

I imagine I would have died there on the job from exhaustion had we not all gone to B'Nai Brith Hospital to donate our blood to some Jewish organization I had never heard of. After taking a blood sample from my arm, a nurse returned rather quickly and informed me that I had a very bad case of Mononucleosis, and that I could not leave the hospital in that condition for at least a week.

"Oh Thank God!" I said, making the sign of the cross on my monogrammed Yves St. Laurent shirt. "Thank you, God!" I repeated.

My fellow employees were very concerned that I would not be at work for several days. They weren't nearly as concerned about my dying as they were for sales volume dropping. I was absolutely beat!

I called Kip from the hospital and told her the wonderful news that we could spend more time together even if it was in the hospital. She was excited too, and brought me a bar-b-que pork sandwich and some fries from our favorite rib joint. The staff at B'Nai Brith looked on with disgust as I gobbled the pork sandwich with gusto. I was dreaming of a Bud Light to go along with it, but that was just asking too much.

As I sat enjoying my lunch, a thought suddenly struck me, and without any hesitation, I blurted out,

"Kip, let's go home and go to school!"

Kip looked at me in disbelief, then with tears streaming asked,

"You mean, home, home?"

"Absolutely!" I responded.

While I was still bound and determined to make our fortune, I had decided long before the hospitalization that the jewelry business was not my thing. It had been a good experience, and I had developed an enduring taste for delicatessen food, but I was ready to turn in my keys to the big store.

Kip was overjoyed. I knew she was missing home and all her friends, but never for a moment had she complained. She had given up her education, her posh life, and all her family to be my wife and sit countless hours alone in the apartment. She deserved better and would soon get it.

We called from the hospital room, and when Big Kip answered the phone, Kip yelled,

"Mom, I've got some great news! I'm in the hospital with Larry and he's almost dead!"

With this initial information, I could hear Big Kip's voice loudly yelling,

"WHAT?"

"Larry came to the hospital to give blood but instead he's getting several quarts and we're coming home to go to school!"

Kip was so excited; I knew she was making little sense to her mom, who kept answering with,

"WHAT?"

Taking the phone from Kip, I said rather cheerfully,

"Hi Mom! We're coming home!"

"WHAT?"

"MOM, WE ARE COMING HOME!!"

Kip kept grabbing at the phone to talk with her mom, but I held the receiver long enough to tell her what we had decided. Naturally, Big Kip was excited too, and began offering hundreds of ideas about how we could find a little house, and work for them part time in one of their numerous businesses. It was exciting stuff, and I finally gave in and returned the phone to Kip. A nurse stuck her head in the room, and putting her finger to her lips, offered,

"Shhhhh!"

Later that evening, Kip returned to my room with a corned beef sandwich; one of my favorite meals, and some chips. This time she managed to slip the Bud Light past the nurse's desk.

She had been thinking she said, about how we could afford to go to school and support ourselves. I reassured her that we could work while we attended school and it would be fine. I also had GI benefits that would help us financially. Then there were my investments. I mentioned that my sandwich was not as good as the ones at Saul Rosenthal's, a diner next to the jewelry store, and a while back Saul was looking for capital to open a second deli. I supplied the capital for a percentage of the business and options on any further expansion. While the jewelry business didn't really do it for me, seeing those Saul's Delis pop up over the next several years was really fun. I likewise wondered many times over the next few years if that massive infusion of Jewish blood I had received at B'Nai Brith Hospital had anything to do with my business successes.

Part XV
Reflections in the Mill Pond

Chapter 51
School Days

It didn't take long for Kip and me to pack up our things, call the movers, and set sail for Oklahoma. The first trip we had made coming to Indiana was fun, but the excitement of going home to friends, family, and fun really had us flying.

"Good afternoon Officer!" I offered as a familiar looking face walked up to the window of the red Mustang.

"Well, I'll be. Aren't you the same kid I stopped a few months back in about the same spot?"

"Yes, sir, I believe that might have been me."

"Son, do you have any idea how fast you were going when I clocked you?"

"No idea, sir."

Looking into the red Mustang, he looked at Kip and shook his head.

"Son, that's an awfully sweet looking lady whose life you are endangering," he suggested very politely.

"Yes sir, she's pretty awesome," I agreed.

"Son, where are you going in such a big hurry?"

"We're moving home, sir."

"Didn't like Indiana, kids?"

"Loved it, sir, but we just want to go home."

Smiling and shaking his head, he said,

"Well, I don't want to leave you kids with a bad taste about our state. In five miles, you'll be out of Indiana. Any chance you can keep it down for five miles?"

"Yes sir, you have my word on that!"

I thanked the State Officer and cautiously pulled back onto the highway.

"Jesus, Kip, how fast were we going?" I asked as we crept the next five miles.

"Sort of looked like 125 to me, sweetheart."

"Damn!"

We had just passed the "Welcome to Missouri" sign when I heard the siren. He must have been hiding behind the welcome sign and nabbed us red handed. Damn, I couldn't believe it. Well, about all I can say is that the cops in Missouri were not nearly as friendly as the ones in Indiana. It was an expensive drive home, but regardless of the cost, we were going home and we laughed non-stop for two days.

Within thirty minutes of arriving at the Siegel home, we were both relaxing in the pool with steaks on the grill. Coming home was everything we had hoped for, and once again, I found myself the happy recipient of many blessings. At every turn it was just getting better and better.

We had been spoiled by the beautiful apartment in Indianapolis and had trouble finding something in Oklahoma City that suited us. After a couple of disappointing days of looking, we decided to take her parents up on an offer to temporarily live in a little house that sat beside one of the family businesses. It was a funny little house with creaky floors and a leaking roof. What it DID have was a small corral out behind the house. It had been several years since I left Scout behind, and the idea of finally having another horse excited me. Again, Kip was willing to sacrifice anything, even her creature comforts to make sure I was happy. That was just Kip.

We moved our expensive furniture into the little house the same week, and in spite of the leaky roof and creaking floors, we couldn't have been happier. No house is a home without a pet we decided so the day after moving into our little hovel, we went to the pound and adopted two rather scroungy dogs. One was almost a Beagle and the other some type of coon hunting hound. We named them Tuffy and Troubles. Within a week, we had become a family. They immediately endeared themselves by keeping most of the field mice out of the house, and therefore were allowed the run of the place. Like me, Tuffy and Troubles had come a long way, I thought, as I watched them sleeping comfortably on the $4,000.00 Italian leather couch.

Kip and I both took summer courses and enrolled in a full time schedule for the fall. We had decided for a number of reasons to attend UCO, my old school. First of all, it was affordable and secondly, a short commute from our little house in Oklahoma City. We were up at the crack of dawn each day and off to school. Like everything else I did with Kip, it was fun. Just being with her made anything fun.

I met a cowboy-looking kid my first day back in school, and we struck up a conversation. He was married too, and worked part time for his dad who was a calf roper and ran a construction crew. I met his dad after school and he hired me on the spot. He also had a nice little sorrel mare for sale, and after roping a couple of calves on the little mare, I bought her. Her name was Susie and we added her to our ever-growing family the same day. Now, I attended school with Kip during the mornings, worked for Danny's dad in the afternoons and began attending rodeos on the weekends. Again, Kip was always in agreement with anything I wanted to do, and encouraged me when I came up with the idea of buying horses at the monthly horse sale in Ft. Smith, Arkansas, and re-selling them to a growing market of families moving to the suburbs around Oklahoma City. It was like finding money. Danny and I used his dad's large truck and trailer, and my money to buy the horses. On an average trip, we would buy fifteen to twenty head of horses, bring them home, clean them up, and sell them to the ever growing list of buyers. We typically paid around $150.00 apiece for the animals. Our resale price ranged from $500.00 to $1,000.00. We sold them faster than we could bring them home and clean them up. It was a veritable gold mine, and we did this all through college. The income was good and coupled with money we earned working for Kip's parents, my GI benefits, some really good investments, an occasional check from Danny's dad, we had more than enough funding to pay for the two of us to attend school full time. While other married students were going in debt to pay for college, Kip and I were driving new cars and taking nice vacations. With Kip's help and constant encouragement, I was even able to maintain decent grades. Kip made all "A's." Kip was not only beautiful, she was extremely intelligent. She excelled at everything. I had less talent than Kip, and was subject to occasional questionable behavior. I did have two undeniable assets which no one could dispute. I had the world's greatest young wife, and I could turn dirt into money.

We had just begun our senior year at UCO, and it didn't seem possible that we had come so far so fast. Kip had focused on Special Education, and would get her undergraduate degree in that field. Education was definitely not my thing as it had been a struggle for me since day one when I first mistook the ABC's for a departed grandmother. I wasn't dumb, I had been told a thousand times. I just wasn't "focused." Admittedly there had been a couple of deviations in my studies as I vacillated from Veterinary Medicine, to Archeology, to Business, to Psychology, then lastly to the study of Foreign Languages. This came about following a conversation I had with an FBI recruiter who had visited the campus looking for candidates with unique backgrounds. Since prior to my military career, the United States had been knee deep in maintaining intelligence in Cuba and Central America. The need for bi-lingual and bi-cultural agents had skyrocketed, and the supply was minimal. The thought of being an FBI Agent, I thought was pretty impressive and the money was very good. The FBI Agent who was recruiting was extremely impressive, and even when I mentioned that there might be a couple of issues on my record, he didn't seem overly concerned. He explained that had I been involved in activities like fraud, theft, conspiracy, that could be problematic. Having banged up a couple of people actually seemed to excite the agent, and he encouraged me to begin the very lengthy application process. I did.

"Hey Kip, I've got some big news," I said meeting her at the parking lot after talking with the FBI recruiter.

"I've got some big news too, Larry!"

"You go first," I insisted.

"I think our family is getting bigger!"

I didn't realize my mouth was gaping open until one of the ever present Oklahoma flies landed on my tongue. I was speechless. I knew I had heard Kip, and more so, I knew exactly what she meant. I just couldn't react. After what seemed like forever, the tears came streaming down both our cheeks. I never dreamed I could love Kip more than I already did, but at that moment, I did. The thoughts that this lady, who had given me more happiness than I could ever imagine was now giving me even more was beyond my wildest dreams.

"Paco!"

"Paco??"

"Absolutely!! Let's name him "Paco!"

"Sure, why not?" she said grinning from ear to ear.

By this time, we were both laughing uncontrollably and raced from the car to call Big Kip and tell her our family was growing again.

"Mom, we're going to have a "Paco!"

"Oh God, Larry, not another dog??"

"No Mom, a HUMAN being!"

"Dear God," was all she could say.

Chapter 52
Just Not to Be

Paco didn't make it. In spite of all our efforts and prayers to let it happen, Paco didn't survive. We lost him at four months into the pregnancy, and in spite of our optimism, it appeared that future additions would be difficult. The set back was devastating to all of us, but when the news came a few months later that Paco #2 was on the way, we re-gained our hopes. While we couldn't understand why the initial tragedy had happened, we begrudgingly accepted it, and prepared for the second blessed event fully aware that Kip might have problems.

In spite of all our efforts and the best medical care money could buy, Paco #2 never took his first breath. He was nearing full term when we lost him. He was fully formed and was in fact a Paco. He just wasn't ready to join us and we gave up our second little angel.

For several weeks following the second loss, I frequently visited a small parish not too far from our little house in Oklahoma City. While her heart was breaking, Kip remained strong and courageous through the terrible ordeal of losing both attempts at a family. She had proven herself much stronger than I, and in my sadness I turned back to the God I once had been very close to for answers. I was angry with God, and didn't want to hear things like, "It's all part of God's plan and everything happens for a reason!" I didn't care about plans or reasons, I just wanted to have a family with Kip, and make her the happiest mom in the world. I hated God and God obviously hated me. Every time the priest made mention of his "loving God," I got a little more upset. In spite of my anger, I continued stopping by the parish when no one was there. I cursed God, and challenged him to take out his seemingly heartless wrath on me instead of my wife and children. I had done bad things. I was totally aware of that. I was likewise totally aware that many years before I had made a pledge to God to serve him, and follow in the steps of my beloved mentor, whom God had also seen fit to take away, along with the others I had loved. In my rage, I had decided that maybe there was no God at all, and that anyone who believed in one was simply foolish and naïve. I had been foolish and naïve I thought, but just then, the old memory tapes began to play and I saw myself as the loser I had been taught to believe I was. There was a God, alright, and he was punishing me again for breaking my vow to serve him. I had turned my back on God, and I would spend the rest of my life feeling his wrath. My God was not a loving God. He was an omnipotent Master over those who didn't keep their vows, and a vengeful executioner of innocents to teach a lesson to the unfaithful. I knew God. I had seen His work and I hated Him.

Part XVI
Reflections in the Mill Pond

Chapter 53
Going On

Kip and I began school again the following semester. We had spent a couple of days re-arranging the room we had prepared for Paco. Many tears were shared as the funny little clothes, toys, cowboy boots, and various baby things were placed in boxes and stored in a closet. In spite of the terrible ordeal that had marred our happiness, we had each other, and for that we were grateful. It also seemed that every time we would reach a low point either Tuffy or Troubles would run through the little house playing chase, or doing something funny that made us laugh again. It was interesting that every time we thought we could not handle the pain of what had happened to us, something silly would turn our tears into laughter. Some friend had said to us,

"God never gives you more than you can handle."

Well, I had my doubts about God having a hand in drying the tears, but somehow we dealt with it and with the support of family, we went on.

Kip had missed an entire semester and doing so, allowed me to catch up with her. In the fall we began our senior years, and that in itself seemed like a miracle. Without Kip, I would have never returned to college following the debacle I had made of my previous attempt. Without Kip, God only knows where I would have been. I certainly would not have been graduating from college.

I had continued my application with the Federal Bureau of Investigation, and as always, Kip supported me. I think if I had developed an interest in playing my guitar professionally in a Mexican whorehouse, Kip would have supported me. That was Kip.

Time flew by during our senior year. We had decided early on that the little house beside the auction business suited us just fine. As long as we had each other, we didn't need much else. We were best friends, we had Tuffy and Troubles, and we had Susie to ride in spite of a harrowing experience one day when we returned from school and saw that she was not in the back yard where I placed her early in the morning to "mow" the grass. Susie had obviously smelled something through the flimsy screen door that led to the back yard and had helped herself into the house. We had joked many times about the creaky floor in our humble hovel but it was not nearly as amusing when we entered the front door and saw Susie standing quietly on the ground beneath the floor which failed to support her. Like the gentle mare she was, she just stood there quietly still holding a half eaten loaf of bread she had found in the kitchen before venturing into the living room where she crashed through the rickety floor. A lot of people would have been upset finding a horse had fallen through their living room floor. We laughed. Kip and I had experienced worse. We laughed together again a few weeks later.

We had covered the massive hole in the floor with a large piece of plywood and it looked so good, we invited friends over for dinner.

Kip and I had worked hard to prepare a big ham we were serving with sweet potatoes covered with marshmallows; one of my personal favorites. The table which sat in an adjoining room was adorned with the fruits of our labour, and did look quite nice even if we admitted it ourselves. We were seated in the living room enjoying a glass of Ripple with our guests when Jimmy's wife Linda suddenly went pale and her mouth dropped open. Following her eyes to the door leading to the dining room, we saw our mutt Troubles proudly holding in his mouth what remained of the large ham. He had most of it consumed right down to the bone. Beside him sat his ever present partner in crime, Tuffy with so much gummy sweet potato on his face that he was wheezing to breathe. He was licking his Beagle chops laboriously to clear his olfactory senses. Perched on top of the villains nose was the remains of the very last marshmallow.

"Jesus Christ!" I exclaimed, vacillating between killing the mongrels and laughing my butt off.

We laughed. We all laughed for half an hour, then went down the street for a hamburger. We were still laughing as we ate our greasy hamburgers at the less than stylish diner. Again, we had seen worse. Kip was laughing again, and that's all I needed to make me happy.

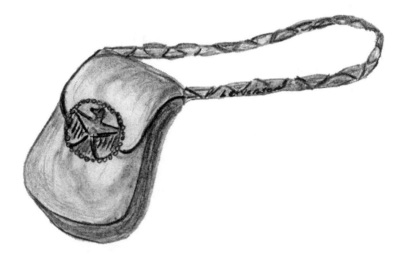

Chapter 54
College Graduates!

Kip and I had been married for over two years, and the two heartbreaking experiences coupled with the further doubt that we would ever have a child, was filed away in our memories. In a very short while, we would graduate together from college and another improbable milestone in my life would be reached.

It was understood that I would travel somewhat working with the Bureau but again, Kip was always willing and ready to take on the next adventure. The adventure exploded prematurely two weeks before graduation when I was called by the Oklahoma City Bureau Chief and informed that the FBI had just announced a "hiring freeze" resulting from some investigation of the head of the Bureau, J. Edgar Hoover.

"Holy cow!" I responded, asking how long the freeze might be and what I was going to do between now and then.

"No idea; maybe as much as a year."

I had come to know this agent very well over the past months as the application for employment with the Federal Bureau of Investigation was long and arduous. He had encouraged me all along and now sounded very disappointed and concerned as he knew I was married and had no other plans other than to enter the Bureau. I was devastated, and shared the bad news with my old friend Coach Murdock while waiting for Kip to finish a class.

"Hey kid, you wanna coach football and teach high school?"

"Hell no, coach, I'd rather keep selling horses than do that!"

"Well you think about it Sport, and if you change your mind, give me a call. There's a school just outside of Tulsa; a big 4A school that is looking for a head football coach who can teach Spanish. The chances of finding that combo are slim and none."

"Coach, I barely dodged a prison sentence the last time I had anything to do with football. Even the Tulsa people read the Daily Oklahoman, and I can just see their faces when I show up grinning and telling them about attitudes and behavior. They would run me out of town! Are you kidding me, Coach?"

"Well, my boy, you ARE a little rough around the edges, but let me tell you something; this school up there has some issues of its own and you just might be the ticket!"

"Aw crap, Coach! What kinda "issues?"

"I'm sure all the stories are just exaggerated about this old hard ass superintendent who can be a little....archaic???"

"What the hell is archaic, Coach?"

"Aw, it really nothing. Just something silly about their game schedules. Nothing you can't handle, my boy. Nothing you can't handle."

"Are they competitive, Coach? Do they have a winning tradition?"

"Welllll, kid, I'm not sure about the exact statistics," he lied through his gold teeth!

On the drive home, I broke the bad news about the FBI to Kip. As always, she took the announcement in stride. She was unshakable. In an effort to assure her that my education had not gone for naught, I told her about the coaching job in Tulsa.

"Larry, that's wonderful!!!"

Only Kip would have responded like that.

"That's absolutely perfect!! Everybody is hiring Special Ed teachers and if we're lucky, we can both be at your school! What's the name of it?" she continued as excited as if I was taking over the reins at Texaco Oil.

"I think it's called, Berryhill; Tulsa Berryhill."

"Oh, I love that name!" she went on. "I bet it's wonderful!"

Chapter 55
Moving to Tulsa

Two weeks later, Kip and I graduated from college. Her family was proud. My family was shocked. Once again I must say that without Kip, I would have never made it. I had accepted the job over the phone at Tulsa Berryhill. They didn't even ask me to interview which should have been a warning. I had told them that Kip was a Special Ed teacher and they hired her likewise over the phone. Our first employment as college graduates was less than financially rewarding. Adding our two teaching and coaching salaries together, we made roughly half what I made in two weeks of buying and selling horses. My annual bonus check from Saul's Deli was larger than my teaching contract. Oh well, I thought...the prestige of being a head coach in a 4A school will make up the difference.

Thank God, I had also saved quite a bit of the money over the past three years of horse trading. The little house by the auction company had cost us nothing thanks to my wonderful in-laws who helped us out at every opportunity. We were in good shape financially compared to other new graduates. To celebrate our graduations, I surprised Kip with a brand new Buick Riviera, and traded in the Mustang for a Datsun pickup truck for myself. The plan was for Tuffy and Troubles to ride in the back of my truck to Tulsa but Tuffy growled when I attempted to pull him from the back seat of the new Riviera so I didn't make an issue of it. I just waved goodbye to the three of them as they pulled out in front of me for the drive to our new home.

Leaving Oklahoma City for the second time was not a joyous occasion but we were just going an hour up the Tulsa Turnpike so it was nothing like moving to Indiana. We had been looking in the Tulsa Tribune for the past two weeks and had a few possibilities already lined up for our new home. We didn't get past the first. It was beautiful. Our first real home was a red brick Victorian in an older part of the city. The large lawn was covered with big oak and pecan trees which shaded the lovely older home during the warm hours of the day. In the back yard was a beautiful fountain with large goldfish. Tucked away in a corner of the yard and almost obscured by Ivy vines and other lovely flora, was a very comfortable sized dog pen with a heated dog house. Tuffy and Troubles refused to enter the relatively luxurious dog pen and instead waited impatiently at the back door of the house, ready to go in, and looking somewhat disturbed that we might suggest the dog facility. The interior was charming. The main room sprawled out before a large red brick fireplace with a double opening; one into the living room and the other into a den. Picture windows looked out to both the well landscaped front and back yards. The moment we saw it we both knew it was home, and within 20 minutes had signed and paid for a twelve month lease. Before I could catch my breath from the paperwork, Kip said,

"This place needs Early American furniture and we passed an Ethan Allen store on the way here!"

"Race you to the car???"

We essentially bought the store. Kip was right about the décor and the massive dark pine pieces made our new home look like something out of a magazine. My wife certainly had taste, and she could be a good little manager too, as she instructed the store people to have all the furniture at the house first thing the next morning. They did!

I just sort of stayed out of the way as the entourage of moving guys hauled in load after load of beautiful furniture. Kip was busy telling them to,

"Put that here, and put that over there, and don't scratch that, and leave THAT room empty!"

In less than an hour, it looked like we had lived there for a year. It was beautiful I thought as I sat down on the overstuffed couch and propped my feet up on a very comfy matching ottoman.

"Holy smokes, Kip, it wore me out just watching you work those poor guys! You know, Kip, its beautiful! Oh, and by the way, I noticed you kept that back bedroom empty. Were you maybe thinking a private room just for the dogs?"

"Oh yes, I must have forgotten to tell you. We'll need some "different" furniture for THAT room."

"Good Lord, Kip, we bought the whole damn store!"

"Yeah, we did OK, but they didn't have what we will need for that room."

"So what the hell do we need for THAT room, Kip?"

"We'll be needing baby furniture!"

It seemed like hours passed before either of us spoke again. We looked at each other in perfect silence as if either of us made a sound; the magic of the moment would be broken. I had known that feeling maybe once before in my life as I stood at a frosted window with an old man's loving hand resting on my shoulder. When his voice said,

"He's Scout," my childhood prayers had been answered.

Now for the second time in my life, hearing the person I loved most in the world tell me,

"We'll be needing baby furniture," my heart almost burst with joy. Speech or even movement was almost impossible. I did manage to reach out for Kip, and hold her for a very long time. I just held her for a very, very long time.

Chapter 56
Making the Sports Page (again)

There were very good reasons why Berryhill School was looking for coaches and teachers. The old Superintendent whom my friend and coach had described as "archaic," was an asshole!!! I had looked up archaic in the dictionary and it did little to prepare me for this jerk. His name was Carmine Ogeldorph and that pretty much said it all. He had been the Superintendent of Schools at Berryhill for thirty three years when Kip and I had the misfortune to land there. The old fool himself had attended Berryhill back in the first half of the century when all the small communities around Tulsa were just starting sports programs and pretty much all had the same number of students and playing talent. The "other" communities had grown with the times and become schools which were not just a good place to get an education, but a great place to participate in interscholastic sports.

All the neighboring schools, consistently sent teams to the state playoffs. Not so Berryhill. All the neighboring schools consistently sent students and student athletes off to colleges around the country. Not so Berryhill. The neighboring schools took pride in keeping up with the times and preparing their kids for an ever-changing world. Not so Berryhill. In fact, I learned from a fellow teacher the first day on the job that Berryhill had the distinction of putting more kids in correctional institutes than in schools of higher education. It was an academic and athletic purgatory. At the helm was the omnipotent superintendent Carmine Ogeldorf. Carmine's philosophy was,

"We beat 'em back in '38, we can still beat 'em!"

His "it worked back in '38," attitude carried right into the classroom, and I was shocked to hear him comment that "these damn computers are just another fad. They will come and go and we don't need to waste money on the fool things!" So we didn't.

As far as Coach Murdock's inability to recall statistics pertaining to our win-loss record, I was suddenly suspect at my old friends' mental acuity. Berryhill had not won a game in 5 years. How hard is THAT to remember? When I mentioned this amazing statistic to my new team of mostly scrawny, raggedy, and totally unconcerned looking miscreants, one unusually small and anemic looking youngster looked up at me almost excitedly and offered,

"But Coach, we almost scored twice in that game with Bixby last year!"

"Holy cow!" I thought. "What in the world have I gotten myself into?"

I had read some books, seen some movies, heard some motivational talks about how the right coach can pull together a group of marginal athletes and they end up being a great team. Well, that crap makes really good movies. Unfortunately, that wasn't the case in Berryhill. In the first game of the year, I personally witnessed something I had never seen happen in a football game.

With the help of my assistant coaches whom had never personally played the game; possibly not attended one, I had the guys honed, hot, and fired up to play an old time rival, Jenks. It wasn't even fair to say it was a "David and Goliath."

David had a sling shot. We had zippo. Our kid's lack of athletic ability was only equaled by their small size, ignorance of the game, and general desire to be spending their Friday nights elsewhere. It happened so quickly, I couldn't exactly recall the events myself until I read it over a couple of times in the next morning's Tulsa Tribune. It went something like this;

"Berryhill loses the toss and kicks off to Jenks. Jenks runs the short kickoff into the end zone for a TD. Extra Point attempt; good. Jenks kicks off to Berryhill who fumbles the ball into the hands of a Jenks player who runs it in for a touchdown. Extra point attempt; good. Jenks kicks off to Berryhill and Berryhill player falls on ball to take possession. First play from scrimmage, Berryhill throws pass into the hands of Jenks player who runs interception into end zone for touch down. Extra point; good. Jenks kicks off to Berryhill. Player fumbles ball before he can get out of own end zone. Jenks recovers for touchdown. Extra point; good.

Amazingly enough this account went on and on like that for what seemed like a hundred years. I think it notable to stop at this point and mention that at this particular time in the game, the score was Jenks 32- Berryhill 0. That really would not have been so significant except for the fact that only 15 seconds had elapsed from the clock. This first game pretty much summed up our season. On a brighter note, not a single opponent scored a hundred points in a game that first year. Almost all of them came close, but no one made it. Shockingly enough our ticket sales soared as perverted football aficionados came out to see if the opponents would reach 100 points on the scoreboard.

"Assholes!"

While things digressed miserably at school, home was a happy place. Kip was doing remarkably well with the third pregnancy. We began to add small pieces into the empty room, and counted each day, sometimes each hour, with guarded anticipation. We had sadly learned not to count your chickens, or Pacos before they hatch. In the evenings we walked through the lovely neighborhood where we lived and recounted the laughable circumstances of our workday.

Berryhill, true to tradition had not won a game that first year. We did manage to score a couple of times on opponents; both times being very late in lopsided games when the opposing coaches, many of whom had become golf buddies, had put their very weakest players in the game in failed attempts to hold down the score. Our one bright spot was a particularly feisty young sprout named Cody, who in spite of the horrible beatings always played like a man possessed. I loved this kid! As fate would have it, Cody was carried from the field early in the fifth game with a broken leg, thus extinguishing our small flame. This sad event led to another "first" in my many football experiences. Following Cody's removal from yet another slaughter, I turned to the bench in search of a replacement.

"Hey Pokey, you wanna get in there and show these chumps what you're made of?"

I shouldn't have been so surprised when Pokey Parmenter, #8 in your programs, responded with,

"Oh God, Coach…please not me!!"

Hell, I didn't blame him a bit!

Chapter 57
Miracles Do Happen

Spring came. It was 1969, and in spite of a couple of scares, Kip courageously carried our third attempt at a family. It was a time when laughter, though frequent was guarded. We held our breath with each small addition to the empty room. We sat quietly as we drove to the weekly visits at St. Francis Hospital for checkups. We thanked God each time the doc would give us the "thumbs up" sign indicating that we were still OK. His sign, accompanied by a big grin always reminded me of Father Bill, and with each passing week, I was assured that he was hovering above us somewhere in that examination room, saying prayers a mile a minute, and possibly wondering what Kip would be preparing for dinner.

During my first year in teaching-coaching purgatory, I had become very interested in the kids I had worked with who very much, like myself as a youth, found education a difficult task at best. I was particularly interested in working with the kids whose home lives I knew to be less than happy. I gravitated to those students, and wanted to help them through their struggles if at all possible. Kip was not surprised when I told her that I wanted to begin graduate school at the nearby University of Tulsa. Of course, she supported me. UT had a renowned graduate school of Clinical Psychology and amazingly enough they accepted my application. How strange that I felt eager to begin graduate studies when I had barely made it through high school. Once again, I knew it was the influence of my wife, and my desire to do something special to show doubters that I was not a loser. Even the 0-10 record at Berryhill had brought me quite a lot of local notoriety, and as a sports writer friend once commented,

"You're the most frequently quoted coach in Tulsa," alluding to various quips I had made like,

"They may be ahead of us 77-0, but we've got a great cafeteria!" and "Do you guys have any idea how sore they're feet are gonna be tomorrow after running for fifteen touchdowns?"

It was sick humor, but beat the hell out of the reality of the miserable beatings we took weekly. In some twisted sort of way, I had begun to like these kids and amazingly enough, not a single player quit the team. They weren't smart enough to.

I was sitting in one of my favorite classes; Introduction to Deviant Behaviors, when the prof's aide stuck her head into the classroom and motioned for me to follow her. My heart sank and I left the class without even taking my book and notes. I remember shaking so badly that I had difficulty walking to the admin office just down the hall in the Psych Building. A sweet lady behind the counter gave me a pleasant smile and pointed into the Dean's office where he sat holding his telephone up for me. Before I could take the first step, the tears just poured. Kip had lost the baby and I wasn't even there to support her. Suddenly, I noticed the big smile on the Dean's face, and holding out the phone to me, he said,

"Better get your butt to St. Francis, Coach! Kip's in labor!"

Dean Jackson knew us both and always joked that he read the Sports Page every Saturday morning in search of a new quote before going on to the "other" funny paper. I was half way out of the parking lot when I realized I had left Dean Jackson holding the telephone which I never took. I knew exactly where I was going. We had been there many times over the last months and I didn't need to chat on the phone. I was out of there.

A hospital guard was yelling at me as I raced into the large hospital. He was yelling something about,

"You can't park on the lawn!" which of course I already knew, but just didn't acknowledge under the circumstances.

Flying out of the third floor elevator, a nurse I recognized at the desk smiled and pointed to a room I knew was the Labor Room. I was trying to be quiet but obviously wasn't doing a good enough job of it as two nurses standing by Kip's bed, immediately made that "S,hhhhh!" thing on their mouths and attempted unsuccessfully to scold me. Kip looked like hell but she was smiling.

"My God, Larry, take a breath!" one of them suggested. All I could do was plead,

"How is she, how is she, how are THEY?"

"THEY are doing fine...just relax!!"

I guess that I was making a scene as the nurses finally forced me out the door and into the waiting room. As they pushed me through the door, I was making this stupid gesture to Kip like I would be waiting right there in the Waiting Room. Where the hell did she think I was going to go???? Kip was doing fine. I was about to have a massive heart attack!

Kip was in labor thirteen hours. With each passing minute, I knew that things were not going well, and each time the nurses or doc would come out to report, they seemed a little more stressed; a little less optimistic. Finally, at four o'clock the next morning, an exhausted Dr. Frederick, whom we had become close friends with over the past months slowly walked into the waiting room and said,

"Well Coach, no Paco.........How about Paquita????"

Again the tears flowed uncontrollably as I fell flat on the

floor of the waiting room. I awoke to the pungent odor of smelling salts, something that I had become accustomed to in my many times of being knocked unconscious on the playing field.

"Are THEY OK, doc?"

"Kip had one hell of a difficult delivery. Paquita was pretty twisted and we're concerned about an arm that lost circulation in the last few hours. She's very small and about the colour of a Notre Dame jersey. All in all though, they're pretty good. You wanna go play golf this afternoon?"

I grabbed Danny Frederick and hugged him so hard he was gasping for air.

"Doc, I owe you!"

"You wanna see 'em?"

"You bet your ass I do!!!"

Neither of us said a word for the longest time. There was not much to say that wasn't wonderfully stated in the tiny bluish bundle tucked under Kip's arm. She was very small with a mop of dark hair that looked more like it belonged on a monkey than a little girl. Unlike the earlier report, she was much more like the colour of a UCLA jersey instead of Notre Dame's royal blue. I had heard people say my whole life that babies were beautiful, but my initial thought as I looked at this miracle nestled beside Kip, that MY baby girl was butt ugly. She was no bigger than a football and her hair was awful. She was however, the most wonderful thing I had ever seen in my life.

"Let's call her Brittany Jane, Jane for your mom, Dorothy Jane."

"I don't care if we call her Bosco! She's our baby girl!"

We christened her Brittany Jane Wood, and after two more weeks in the hospital we brought her home to our beautiful house on Hickory Street in Tulsa, Oklahoma. How strange I thought that she had been born in St. Francis Hospital, named for the same St. Francis where I had attended mission school what seemed like ten lifetimes ago. I decided that maybe there was a God after all, and perhaps he was even a loving God who had blessed us beyond my wildest imagination. Brittany Jane, in her very first breath had erased every heartache and dried every tear I had cried for the past ten years. It just doesn't get any better than this I knew as I gave thanks several times a day for the next many years.

***

Miracle of miracles!!! The following year, my miserable little football team almost won a game. Late in the fourth quarter of the last game, my little hero Cody; healed from the broken leg, miraculously got free and ran for a touchdown, tying us 6-6 with a very poor team from Big Springs. My dwarfs were so excited, they fumbled the extra point attempt and we ended the game with a 6-6 tie. It was like winning the Super Bowl, and the field was covered with exhaltant, and disbelieving fans. The big crowd was filled with sports writers, and right in the middle of the melee were my biggest and best supporters, Kip and Britt! A reporter with a microphone sticking in my face yelled,

"Any plans for next year, Coach?" he asked excitedly.

"Hell yes, man....We're outa here! Me, Kip, Britt: we're outa here!"

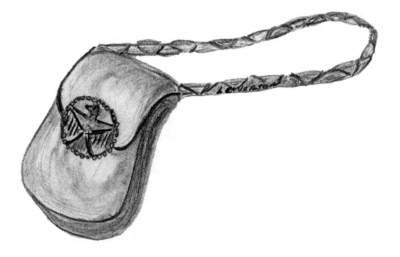

Part XVII
Reflections in the Mill Pond

Chapter 58
Life in the Fast Lane

It's interesting when I look back that I don't remember exactly when or even how the whole financial thing got started. Maybe it was the investment in Saul's Deli back in Indianapolis, or maybe the Hewlett-Packard or Apple stocks. I had made additional investments over the past few years, and each seemed to have the same result; they skyrocketed. Even the pretty home on Hickory Street in Tulsa which we purchased from an old widow our second year there, had doubled in price thanks to the oil and gas boom of the early 1970's. Each year I had rolled my income from the deli into more oil and gas stocks as the price of crude oil was growing rapidly and the supply limited. It was interesting that my second year at Berryhill, the board of directors in their infinite wisdom and generosity had seen fit to raise Kip's and my salaries, to $800.00 a month. The two of us combined were earning less than $20,000.00 a year. While that was not exactly poverty wages in 1970, it was interesting noted, by our tax man, that in the same year we owed federal taxes on roughly $200,000.00 in income. Another interesting thing about our ever growing income was that making money was something that I spent very little time and effort in doing. Living comfortably was nice, and money had its perks for a couple in their early twenties. The acquisition of money was just not the driving factor. Playing golf with a couple of doc buddies our second year in Tulsa, one had asked me,

"Larry, how the hell do you do it?" referring to the fact that everyone seemed to know that Kip and I were making money faster than we could spend it.

"Well, I'm not sure," I answered, and the truth was, I wasn't sure. I told him the story about an old Indian man who once told me that there's one thing in the world that you can trust, and that's the feeling in your stomach. If it "feels" right, I told him, trust it. If it doesn't "feel" right, avoid it. I shared with him my belief that "If you're afraid to lose all of an investment, forget about ever making money." I told him that if you can't laugh at a loss, don't invest in anything, except maybe real estate. I had made investments, that if any one of them had failed, Kip and I would have gone bust. You just can't be afraid. Curious, yes, afraid, no. I had based my strategy mostly on the people I was investing in, as much as the venture. I told him that if you liked the feeling you got from the people you were investing in, and their venture made good common sense; do it. I liked to invest in "working people" as opposed to "scheming people." Someone who knows how to work will capitalize on an opportunity. I told him about a paper boy I had invested in the previous year. The kid was trying to play football for me at Berryhill, but was always exhausted because he was up at 4:00 in the morning to throw a paper route. He rode a rickety old bicycle that barely got him around on the route and after school and practice; he did homework, maintaining almost a B average. His parents were minimally involved. With my help, we upgraded the rickety bike to a Vespa Moped and doubled the size of his route. I was happy, the kid was happy. I had no idea at the time that this kid would graduate from college a few years later with a degree in business. He located me and asked about underwriting the stock in a small oil and gas drilling company he was starting. The boom was really gearing up and this kid knew how to work. The boy went public with his two little drilling rigs and when I finally cashed out years later, the tax alone on the sale of my stock in Mustang Drilling was a staggering amount. This boy couldn't miss. He was a worker and his venture made good sense. In short, the man was as good as the idea.

I also did very well investing in women. In the early seventies when everything was booming, women in business began to realize that they didn't have to be secretaries any longer. Many of them were much smarter than the bosses they worked for, but made a fraction of the income. When given the chance, they went crazy. I never lost a cent investing in a business woman.

Chapter 59
Hopping, Skipping, Jumping

Kip, Britt and I moved back to Oklahoma City the summer following our second year in Tulsa. It had been a fun two years, in spite of the teaching and coaching experience. That had become laughable.

We had decided that we both wanted to continue graduate school; Kip in Special Education and me in Psychology. Of course Kip had excelled as a teacher of special needs kids and would continue to build a reputation as someone who knew what they were doing. On the other hand, I had no clue what I was doing. Kip was going to graduate school, so I would go to graduate school, too.

Working with messed up kids still appealed to me. School didn't, but working with kids did. I liked kids; especially my Britt! The idea of having a Master's Degree did make me feel pretty good, as I still had a need for my family to be proud of me for doing something worthwhile. The plan to go on to a PhD was even more exciting as I would then be addressed as "Dr. Wood." The sound of it was pretty funny as I reminisced over my years of school. From ABC's to PhD, I liked the sound of it. Again it was Kip who made it all possible, even probable.

Upon returning to Oklahoma City, we couldn't find the perfect home. We decided to just build one like we wanted. We moved back into the funny little house by the auction company and bought land in Edmond, Oklahoma, where we would attend school. We had no idea at the time that Edmond was about to have a population explosion. We built a beautiful rambling ranch style on the outskirts of the small town and all the land around it. After all, we had to have room for the dogs and maybe even a horse or two, or ten! Our new home was awesome! Life was good. Britt was the icing on the cake.

In two years we both received Master's Degrees and went to work in our chosen professions: Kip as a key figure in a clinic called the Child Study Center and me as the director of a clinic for troubled kids, which was called The Learning Center. We both made good salaries, but again our salaries paled in comparison to our investment income.

The oil and gas boom was in full blossom when my cousin Mike who was likewise doing very well financially suggested that I join him in the booming oil business. My doctoral pursuit required driving to Oklahoma State University in Stillwater, Oklahoma each day and that kept me away from Kip and Britt too much, so I decided "What the heck," and left my job at The Learning Center to go into engineer training for one of the old Howard Hughes companies, named BJ-Hughes. The company was involved in oil and gas reservoir stimulation and the work fascinated me. I worked hard learning the very technical aspects of the new job, and enjoyed the fact that I was finally making a good salary working at my job, along with the investments.

In the early 70's the oil and gas business was fairly antiquated and had not made a lot of technological advances; especially in the area of reservoir stimulation, and enhanced reservoir recovery techniques. It was very fertile ground for a man with ideas. I was surrounded by ambitious colleagues and everyone was doing very well. My job involved the marketing of our reservoir stimulation services to companies who were drilling oil and gas wells. As the wells were drilled, various companies like Halliburton, Dowell and ourselves would compete for the job of bringing the well to its maximum potential through reservoir stimulation. I loved the work and was very successful in landing a sizable amount of the jobs we competed for. I had become knowledgeable in the field and enjoyed my status as an up and coming player in the rapidly growing business. When I wasn't working on a project, I entertained customers on the golf course, or we took lavish trips together; mostly with our families, to enjoy the monetary benefits of a booming business. It didn't exactly hurt my "competitive edge" that I frequently invested with the same companies I was bidding on for their work. It became a common thing for a company to call and ask if I wanted a "piece" of an oil and gas venture. It went without saying that BJ would automatically do the reservoir stimulation work on the well I was personally investing in. It wasn't exactly "cheating" my competitors; but it did give our company the opportunity to do more work than we could possibly handle. It was good for all of us; especially me.

In the second year of my career with BJ-Hughes, I had become friends with the sales manager of an up and coming new company called The Western Company of North America. It was obvious to everyone in the business that I was getting a disproportionate share of the business available, and The Western Company was eager to employ successful young people to help them expand. I liked The Western Company as they were "pulling out the stops" to gain a market share in a wildly growing business. When offered a job, I simply replied,

"When you guys expand to the Rockies, I'm your boy!"

The call came six months later. I was working on the completion of a deep gas well near Canadian, Texas when my car phone rang.

"You wanna move to Denver?"

I recognized the voice as my friend with The Western Company and asked,

"How much?"

"A shitload!"

"When?"

"Pronto!"

It wasn't my dream of returning to New Mexico, but it was the mountains, and when he told me what the "shitload" amount was, I almost gasped. I told him I needed to visit with Kip, but I knew that Kip was always with me. Hell, I thought, she would have backed me had I told her about my dream of being a guitar player in a Mexican whorehouse. She was just that way.

The new job was not only my first six digit salary; it also meant that after so many years I was finally going home to the mountains and we were going in style.

Kip, as expected was happy for me. Brittany, with her ever present smile didn't have a clue, but seemed to join in our excitement.

A week later, I resigned from BJ-Hughes, and sadly left the many friends I had made working there. I loved those guys and no one resented my good fortune.

We sold the home and property in Edmond and bought a lavish home on Lookout Mountain overlooking Denver. I simultaneously bought property in a new area called Genesee Mountain, which soon exploded with the oil and gas business expanding to the Rocky Mountains.

In management for the first time, I helped procure offices in the penthouse suite of the First of Denver Plaza. My personal office which overlooked the majestic Rockies was roughly the size of our little house next to the auction company, back in Oklahoma City. A professional decorator finished out my office with Persian rugs, English walnut paneling, and a Brazilian Rosewood desk that was big enough to play ping pong on. An attendant parked my expensive company car each morning as I proceeded to the penthouse for my day's work. The Western Company was beyond cool! We had an add that ran frequently on television and suggested,

"If you don't have an oil well, get one! You'll love doing business with Western!"

I loved The Western Company and they certainly did well by Lariano!

Chapter 60
Going Through the Roof

On the home front, Kip was making sure that we enjoyed the fruits of my labours, and kept up the standards of a well-to-do, very young couple. She excelled at that. Britt was beginning pre-school at a cute little place just over the mountain from our home. I agreed that it was pretty much unthinkable that she should begin her education not attired like the little princess she was. Neiman-Marcus was just the ticket for a five year old starting school, and so we coupled a business trip to Dallas with a shopping spree at Neiman's. It awed me to think that the last time I had been in the elegant store; I was in the company of my beloved Old Bea. It was different this time. Not only had we ridden up the elevator, but a store owned limo had picked us up at the Adolphus Hotel, anticipating that Neiman's was about to have a very good day in the kids' department. Christ Almighty, did they ever have a good day! Britt looked like a fashion model as she came and went from the dressing room in beautiful clothes she had picked out. It was one of the best days of my life, watching my little princess strut and spin as she had seen models doing on TV. The salespeople kept turning and making awed faces towards us indicating that they, too, thought she was adorable. She was adorable. We adored her.

Back in Denver we had decided that the lavish home on Lookout Mountain wasn't quite lavish enough so we hired a well known architect to begin drawings on the first of the two homes we would build in Genesee. At work, I accused my superiors of arranging business meetings with families invited just so they could be around Kip! It was probably true even though they never confessed to it. I was a pretty good little businessman, but Kip was outrageously gorgeous and worked a social gathering like a pickpocket at a diamond auction. I didn't mind. I never doubted for a minute that were it not for Kip, God only knows where I would be, quite possibly in that Mexican whorehouse! Kip had all the brains, all the style. I just had the luck to marry her.

In spite of working hard and traveling a lot, we still had time for social events and it seemed the right thing that we should join not one, but two of the nicer country clubs in the Denver area; one in town and one in the mountains just outside of town. Just seemed like the thing to do. Britt had developed a taste for lobster, and insisted that the lobster was always better at "the club" instead of the elegant restaurants we frequented. She also had commented one evening as she was munching her lobster, that the restaurants lacked the "savoir faire" that the clubs offered.

"Where the hell did she learn that?" I gasped. They sure as hell didn't teach me about "savoir faire" at the mission school in Taos!

The first home in Genesee was like something out of a magazine. As a matter of fact, it WAS out of a magazine and appeared in the Denver Post! It was almost as impressive as the SECOND home we built not too long after moving into the first. The first, quite simply had "too many levels" making it hard for the maid to carry in groceries. The second, more of a traditional style was much flatter; and larger. Ay, Chihuahua!!!! Kip had mastered being young and rich! She had absolutely and unequivocally turned it into an art form. I couldn't have cared less. I was the luckiest man in the world.

Tuffy and Troubles had disappeared one day prior to our move to Denver. They had probably run off chasing a rabbit and just never thought about turning around. We were saddened at the loss of the two mongrels and hadn't had a pup since then. When Britt asked for a puppy, of course I agreed. We all liked dogs. Britt chose a small blonde Cocker Spaniel who quickly grew up to be an idiot. House training the moronic dog was impossible, but before trading him in on a Bassett Hound mutt at the dog pound, Honey brought me into a state of "enlightenment." I had followed a curious looking trail of gummed up fur into the den where I found the beast gnawing impatiently at the full length red fox coat Big Kip had bought Britt for her birthday. Over the years and all our good fortune, I had learned to control my temper. Seeing that SOB eating the $3,000.00 fox coat caused a relapse. I had been enlightened. Honey taught me that we had "too damn much money!" The next day, "Honey" was gone, and "Poor Pitiful Pearl," the Bassett hound moved in. Pearl was too lazy to even get up, much less destroy things. We loved Pearl.

Back at work, things were out of control. We were making money faster than we could count it. The only thing keeping us from raking it in faster was the shortage of men and equipment required to perform the large, expensive reservoir stimulation jobs. Our equipment manufacturing facility was located in Ft. Worth, Texas, the home of our company offices. Head of the manufacturing facility was a brilliant young Argentinean engineer named Antonio Arribeau. "Tony" had come from the University of Texas and thought light years ahead of most engineers in the business. I liked him and always enjoyed visiting and learning from him. He and I both knew that our only limitation to further expansion was a shortage of the massive trucks and equipment needed to perform our service. Over lunch one day the idea struck me,

"Hell, Tony, let's build OUR OWN equipment!"

Tony Arribeau paused, and realized I wasn't kidding.

"Lariano," which he always called me, "We're talking several million dollars to even think about it!"

"No problema, my man!" I answered, and asked him how soon he could get me a pro forma approximating the actual cost and rough plan to start our own manufacturing company.

"Well, I've played with some numbers a couple of times, but was just 'playing,'" he told me.

"Game's over!! Get me the numbers!!!"

Two weeks later, Antonio Arribeau met me at the Lakewood Country Club in Denver with a large portfolio containing numbers and plans to begin Condor Engineering. The following afternoon, after having met with a couple of my good friends in the business; older fellows who had made fortunes in oil and gas, I told Tony over the phone,

"You say we'll need about fifteen million, right?"

"Right!"

"I came up with $25 million. When do you want to meet the partners?"

Tony paused for a minute, then answered,

"Tomorrow??"

Tony flew the company jet back to Denver and the next day we met for lunch at the Petroleum Club. He didn't seem too impressed when I introduced him to the three men who joined us dressed in jeans and flannel shirts. I winked at Tony who was looking a little concerned sitting in his Brooks Brothers suit. My friends didn't seem too impressed either with Tony's Brooks Brothers suit, as they had all began as roughnecks in the oil field, and through hard work and common sense amassed an extremely large amount of wealth. I discreetly reminded one of them that I had once seen him write a personal check for $3,000,000.00 as he passed me the bill to sign for the lunch. They were funny guys. They were my kind of guys. Every one had made a large fortune by their own hard work and common sense. I silently laughed to myself when

I looked down next to me and noticed that the gentleman I liked the most, a fellow named David James had put duct tape on an old penny loafer to keep the sole from falling off. We shook hands, called the attorneys for an incorporation conference, and I went home to see Kip and Britt.

Condor Engineering was not a gamble. It was like betting on the opponent in a Berryhill football game. We started it, expanded it, and sold it two years later to a Fortune 500 oil and gas related company for an amount equaling about 8% of their entire stock. We couldn't take cash as none of us could pay the taxes on the income we already had. With the sale of Condor, I had reached another financial milestone. It was almost embarrassing.

We celebrated the sale of Condor with a company meeting in Cabo St. Lucas.

Sitting in the bar of a luxurious hotel, a Mexican kid came up to me and asked if he could shine my shoes. He was surprised that I spoke Spanish and struck up a conversation. I liked this kid immediately. He was a worker and reaching in his pocket, showed me a small roll of $1 dollar bills. He told me he was working to help his mom, who also shined shoes in the fancy hotels in Cabo. They were working to buy a little house for her and her four kids.

"That's her over there," he said, pointing to a lady carrying shoe shine accoutre mon in a box with a shoulder strap. The lady smiled and nodded graciously.

"You got a minute, kid," I asked.

His mom watched curiously and the boy ad I walked to the desk of the hotel. I asked for the manager, and he joined me at the front desk.

"What's your mom's name, hito?"

"Rosaria, Rosaria de la Cruz."

"You and your mom be here at this desk tomorrow at noon and ask for this gentleman. He will have an envelope for you.

He didn't even inquire about the envelope, only said,

"Gracias, Señor"

As he turned to walk away, I asked him,
"Hito, cómo te llamas? What's your name?
"Paco, Señor."

The boy had no idea what was going on, but I checked the desk the next day and the manager assured me that he had given Paco's Mom the envelope. I thanked him and hoped they would find a nice place to live for $100,000.00.

Chapter 61
Enough's Enough

"What do we do now, Kip?"

We were exhausted after the trip to Cabo, and I took a few more days off work to sit around the deck of our beautiful mountain home enjoying my lovely wife and daughter. I had spent too little time doing that. Taking this break from work and relaxing, it was hard to imagine how far we had come, and how fast we got there. I was not yet 35 years old. Kip was 30. Britt was a rambunctious 7. We weren't sure about Pearl.

"What do you want to do, Kip?"

"Wow, I'm really not sure. Maybe you should retire?"

The thought of "retiring" had never crossed my mind. Old people retire I thought to myself.

Kip had started taking post grad classes at the University of Colorado in Boulder. She had always been a brilliant student. I encouraged her as she had done so much to make me successful and my life wonderful. I felt ashamed that so much of what we had done, and what we had achieved was focused around me. I had spent far too little time being a good husband to her and helping her reach personal goals of her own. I had really never even inquired about her desires and the more I thought about it, the worse I felt. I made a vow that the rest of our lives I would do for her what she had done for me. There was no way to measure the love I had for my wife and daughter. We were waste deep in the pot of gold Old Bea had predicted and now it was Kip's turn to shine.

The day I returned to work, I made an appointment with my accountant to see more or less where we stood financially. I confided in the man who had done our books and handled my investments for the past few years that money had never been my goal. He knew a little about my background from days we had golfed together. I had shared with him that I had always felt that I was never quite good enough in the eyes of my family, and that I had used the dollar sign as a measuring stick to prove my worthiness. He just laughed. It still wasn't funny to me, and in spite of my successes, I still harboured old feelings of being a loser. When he asked me,

"How much do you think is enough?"

I told him that I really didn't know as every time I hit a new milestone financially, I still felt like I was still a loser in the eyes of some of the people in my family.

"I wouldn't exactly call you a loser, man!"

"I thought when I made a million dollars that might do it. Now, I'm thinking more along the lines of 8 digit money."

"How did someone as stupid as you ever get so rich?" he laughed. "You had 8 digit money before you ever sold Condor!!"

"No shit??"

"No shit," he responded.

Part XVIII
Reflections in the Mill Pond

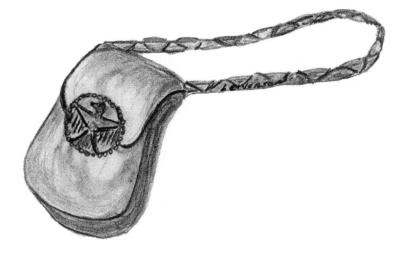

Chapter 62
Harvest Time

"Hey Kip, I quit my job! Did you hear me, Kip? I quit my damn job!"

Our home on top of Genesee Mountain was so huge that it was hard for the three of us to find each other, much less Pearl even though she made a habit of lying in the middle of the kitchen floor just waiting to be made fatter and more immobile. The intercom didn't really help much as a typical intercom conversation would go something like,

"Hey Britt! Can you hear me?"

"Yes, Daddy!"

"Where are you, Baby?"

"I'm on the deck, Daddy!"

"Which deck, Sugar?"

"The one by the bedroom with the picture of Grandma."

"Britt, there's seven bedrooms and Grandma's picture is all over the place. Where ARE you?"

"I'm by the den with the big fireplace."

"You're doing good, Sweetie! The upstairs den or the downstairs den?

"The one with the fireplace!"

"Sweetheart, they both have fireplaces!"

"Where's Mommy?"

"She's on the phone."

"Sugar, which phone?"

"The one in the bedroom, Daddy!"

"Britt, there's a phone in ALL the bedrooms!"

"Daddy, hit the All Call!"

"What the hell is that, Sweetie?"

"That's naughty, Daddy!"

"Britt!!! Do you know EXACTLY where Mommy is?"

"Yes, Daddy!"

"Then where the hell is she??"

"You shouldn't say that word, Daddy."

"I'm sorry Sweetheart, Daddy just got a little frustrated."

"What's FRUSTRATED, Daddy?"

"Britt, Honey, SweetPea....would you ask Mommy to meet me in the kitchen?"

"Sure, Daddy!"

"Daddy, are you still there?"

"Yes, Sugar...Daddy's still here!"

"Hey Daddy!"

"Yes, Britt!"

"Which kitchen?"

"Hey Britt...tell Mommy to meet me in the goddamn bar!"

"Hey Daddy."

"Yes, Britt!"

"You shouldn't talk like that."

"The Goddamned bar, Britt, and I mean RIGHT NOW!!!

In a twisted sort of way, I had almost come to resent the life we were living. I loved Kip and Britt more than I had ever loved anything in life, but having SO MUCH didn't simplify our lives. On the contrary, it complicated them. I just wanted to stop everything we were doing and move to a simple log cabin, somewhere deep into the mountains where we could all just spend time together enjoying the peace and quiet we so richly earned. Each in our own way we had both worked our butts off, and I had no intention of spending the rest of my life running around chasing my tail. I needed to ride a good horse, sit by the fire, and catch a Brook Trout on a tiny Caddis fly. I needed to find the peace and contentment that I had only known as a young boy, playing along the sand streets of Taos, New Mexico. I wanted to walk the paths, smell the piñon and most of all I wanted to take Kip and Britt to the little adobe home they had never seen, and let their beautiful faces be added to all those other beloved reflections in the mill pond.

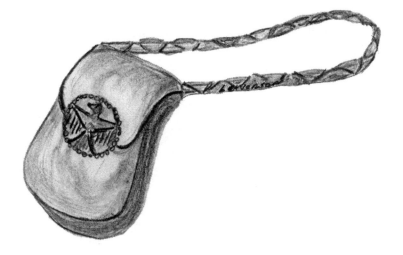

Chapter 63
Cabin in the Woods

Our next door neighbor, if you could call it that in Genesee, was a guy named Pete. He was my age and had made his fortune the old fashioned way. He received it as a gift from a grandmother, upon graduation from an Ivy League college. I loved Pete. He taught me the difference between Ripple and Chateau LeTour. One of my favorite remembrances of him is hearing him say in total sincerity,

"You don't really have to spend much to get a good French wine. Forty or fifty bucks will buy you some really decent stuff!"

Pete was of course referring to a "bottle," not a case! His lovely wife, Bonnie was a striking blond, and ran in the same circles as Kip. They made one hell of a pair darting around Denver in their 450 SEL's. Pete had bought two amazing properties that were nestled alongside the 15th green on the Eagle Vail Golf Club. We played tennis daily, and spent many winter days skiing in Vail. When Kip met me at the door one day after playing tennis with Pete, she excitedly said,

"Larry, I've got an idea for the CABIN!"

Kip had spent the day with Bonnie, and the two of them

had dreamed up an amazing plan. The plan was to build "Retirement Homes," sitting side by side on the golf course in Vail! It wasn't exactly what I had in mind for a cabin, but her excitement made me laugh, and all I could respond with was,

"Sure, Darling, whatever you guys want to do!"

I had doodled out a couple of sketches of the cabin I had dreamed about, but there were some remarkable differences between my doodles, and the sketches that she and Bonnie had hurriedly come up with.

The next morning, the four of us sat in the offices of an expensive architect in Denver turning the sketches into architectural drawings. Looking curiously over at Pete, who sat beside me, I whispered,

"Holy shit, Pete! Are we as rich as they think we are?"

"We damn well better be!" he whispered in a muffled Boston accent.

My two bedroom rustic cabin, with no damn intercom turned out to be a seven bedroom, six bathroom, sprawling Spanish Colonial showplace on the 15th green in Vail. It was lovely, I do admit, but it was a little more than I had hoped for in retirement, and still not a log in sight. Between Kip, Bonnie, and the architect, they had thought of every detail except for the occasional errant golf ball that too frequently would bounce off the back deck and on more than one occasions cause me to spill a Gin & Tonic. I put up a glass "deflection" wall, and not unlike the Queen of England, enjoyed my afternoon gin. We both preferred Bombay Sapphire.

Part XIX
Reflections in the Mill Pond

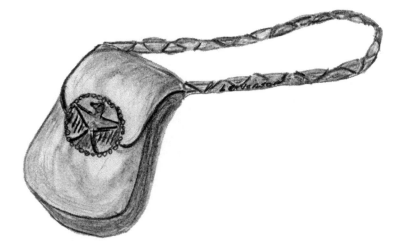

Chapter 64
All Good Things....

We lived the summer and fall of 1979 in the fairytale retirement home in Vail. The days were getting shorter and the afternoon breeze drove us from the golf course with the first hints of winter. An occasional light snow fell, bringing the deer and elk onto the 15th green for their last taste of summer. It was delightful. Our phone rang off the wall from friends, old and new, who essentially invited themselves to visit us when ski season began. We always welcomed visitors, whether we had actually invited them or not. We had been blessed, and were not selfish in sharing our blessings.

Britt was a great little skier, and of course Kip had become so skilled that she had worked a little as a ski instructor in a special program for handicapped skiers back in Winter Park. Like many young, well-to-do families...we skied a lot.

"Larry, do you know how Britt got that bruise on her hand?" I heard as I walked in one afternoon from the firewood stack beside the house.

"Probably fell off her bike!" I yelled back.

"Don't think so, Dear, she says she doesn't remember falling."

"I'm sure it's nothing, Sweetheart!"

"Would you look at it, Sweetie," she implored me.

"Sure, Sweetheart! Come here, Pumpkin, let Daddy have a look."

It was sort of a nasty looking bruise, and in examining the dark spot on the back of her right hand, I noticed that she had a similar one on the left.

"Come here for a minute, Kip. This is really strange."

"What do you think, Kip?"

"I don't know what to think. It's pretty unusual."

"What do you want to do?"

"I want to go ride my bike," Brittany interrupted.

"Kip, what do you want to do?"

Britt had experienced all the normal childhood maladies; the colds, the flu, occasional crash while skiing or playing. She was a tough little nut, and we had always suspected she had gotten that from me. I was as tough as they come....... .physically. When I was sitting at the kitchen table looking at something I didn't understand, that involved the health of my baby, I was a total and complete pantywaist. The spots just looked like bruises. I had seen thousands of bruises. A bruise is a bruise. For some reason though, Kip and I knew these were no ordinary bruises!

An hour later, we were packed and driving over Vail Pass headed for Denver Children's Hospital. Britt sat in the back seat of the big Mercedes touring car. She was playing with a sack full of Muppet toys she had brought along. Kip sat staring straight out the window of the car. I sat staring straight out the window of the car. We didn't speak all the way to Denver.

While we assured ourselves, it was a long drive for nothing, we chose the Emergency Room entrance in an obvious, non-verbal statement of our anxiety. We were told there, of course, that we only needed to make an appointment to see a pediatrician as bruises were certainly no emergency.

At the front desk of Children's Hospital, I made a call to Dr. Frank Austin, who had seen Britt before when we lived in

Denver. His nurse told us to come on over as they always had time to see Britt. It was what we wanted to hear, and we drove the short distance to his office. Dr. Austin examined Britt's hands with curiosity, then after what seemed like an eternity, he looked up to us and said,

"I really don't think it's anything to be concerned about. Lots of kids get what's called "Osteomyelitis." It's a mild bone infection that they usually just grow out of."

"It is interesting," he added, "that she has it exactly alike on both hands. Really interesting!"

"Just tell us, doc, that it's nothing to worry about and we'll gladly go home."

"It's nothing to worry about, guys. Be careful driving home over the pass."

I took a normal breath for the first time in several hours. Kip looked like a hot air balloon with all the air let out. She hugged Dr. Austin, and we drove home feeling very much like we used to feel after a Berryhill football game. We were emotionally wiped out.

That evening back home in Vail, I sat for a long time on the deck that overlooked the frosted green. The late October evenings were cool now and I had wrapped myself up in a large down comforter from one of the guest bedrooms. Kip had read the story about the Velveteen Rabbit to Britt, and the two of them lay snuggled up and sound asleep on Britt's big canopy bed. As I looked in on them before coming onto the deck, it occurred to me that everything I loved in the world was laying there on that canopy bed. It had been a very frightening day and it had exhausted us all. More so, it had made me aware of the frailty of our happiness. We had literally everything monetary wealth afforded you. We had it all, and we had it on a very large scale. Still, the fear that Kip and I felt as we drove our princess to the hospital in Denver, paralyzed us both. We could lock the front door to the million dollar home, and drive to Denver in a $60,000.00 car, but we were helpless, God Forbid, that some disaster happen to any one of us.

Chapter 65
The Boys

There was something about that day we drove Britt to the hospital in Denver that stayed with us. Even a passing thought of losing this child who had been the answer to our prayers had more or less brought a quiet to our home. It was like we were walking on pins and needles, almost afraid to breathe when Kip suggested Thanksgiving morning,

"Let's adopt some kids!"

We had known since shortly after Britt was born that she would be our only biological child. We had Britt, so we accepted that and gave thanks every day for the blessing. Now we were wading in a sea of wealth, and yet Britt had no one to play with. It was the logical thing to do. Again, the next morning, we're back in the Mercedes headed for Denver. This time we drove to the Social Service Office in Golden, Colorado. We still had residency in Jefferson County and friends who had adopted a lovely little girl there a couple of years before. Noticing the big Mercedes, and glancing at the bottom line of a financial summary I filled out for them, a nice lady quickly responded,

"I think we can help you!"

"Do you folks like boys?"

"Sure, we do! We love boys!"

Britt shot me a look that was supposed to be a frown."

"How many would you like?"

"Well, that depends. How many you got?"

"Uhhhhhh.......what about 3?"

"Holy shit!"

In our 13 years together, I had never heard Kip use that expression! As for me...often. As for Britt...a couple of times followed by a serious chastising.

"Are you serious?" Kip asked nervously.

"As a heart attack!" the Social Worker answered.

"It's a very unusual case of abandonment we've been working on for a couple of years now. Three baby brothers were essentially left to die, and it's taken months to track down the parents for relinquishment of parental rights. These poor little guys have been stuck in foster care for a long time. I have a feeling we could put something together pretty fast."

"What's fast?" Britt asked.

"You want to see them?" she asked.

"You bet!" we all three answered simultaneously.

The Social Worker went on to say that we would have to undergo quite a lot of paperwork, and go to court, do a home visit, etc., etc., but if we wanted to act now, she thought things could be expedited a lot. She also said that until certain paper work was underway, we couldn't "meet" the boys, only "observe" them in a neutral meeting place.

"When?" Britt asked.

"Let me make a call," the Social Worker answered.

An hour later we sat with the Social Worker in a booth at a nearby McDonalds. After about fifteen minutes of eating our fingernails, a blue Chevy pulled up and parked. We could see one little guy sitting in a car seat next to the driver. He was clapping his hands and looking excited about coming to McDonalds. The back door opened slowly and a little larger child tumbled from the back seat onto the pavement. We knew them to be around 2 and 3 years of age. There was no third. Kip's instinct and a beautiful heart compelled her to rush out the door and help the little guy who had fallen face down in the hard parking lot. She couldn't. The Social Worker held up her hand in a "Stop" motion, and we just sat there watching these two little guys, now both walking, make their way into the McDonalds. The larger of the two, who had fallen on his face, had pulled himself up laughing. In a heartbeat, I knew that tough little rascal was mine. The smaller guy was so cute, Kip had to turn her head away as the tears flowed. Britt just sat there with her mouth wide open. She flashed me a quick grin but immediately turned back to these little guys who needed a family.

"We're taking them home today," Britt matter-of-factly informed the lady sitting at the table with us.

"Sorry, Sugar, your parents have to do a lot of paperwork first."

"Well, can we just BUY them?" Britt insisted. "Daddy will pay you a lot! He's got a shitload of money!"

"BRITTANY JANE!" Kip and I both blurted simultaneously.

It was embarrassing as heck for her to say that in front of this lady we were doing our best to impress as decent people. At least, our darling daughter had shocked us so much, Kip had immediately stopped crying to look sternly at our sweet child, and make a VERY mean face. Britt just didn't get it. I guess she thought that we had bought everything else, so we might as well make a run at the Social Worker with some kind of offer.

After a week of paper work and a million or so calls coming into the Social Service office assuring Jefferson County that these boys had just hit a home run, we set up a home visit for the boys to come spend three days with us in Vail. It was a trial outing. We had learned after seeing these guys the first day that the third brother, who was almost 5, had been so traumatized by the abandonment, that sadly, he would not be eligible for adoption. It broke our hearts, but we accepted the bad news.

Several days later, we set up the home visit, picked the boys up at the foster home and headed for Vail. It was one of the happiest occasions of my life. We vacillated between loud raucous laughter and muffled tears. It was going to be very difficult to return these two little monkeys after the three day visit. We could have cared less about the three day trial and already knew beyond a shadow of a doubt that these guys were staying. That fact almost came to an abrupt halt when not thirty minutes into the visit, Kip screamed at me yelling,

"Larry, Larry, come quick. Joey's drowning in the commode!"

It scared the hell out of me, but Kip had already pulled the little guy out by his feet and was giving him mouth to mouth. Joey was laughing by this time, and I knew he would survive, if Kip didn't kill him trying to save him! Joey, age 2, had watched his big brother going to the potty in the bathroom that adjoined their room. Evidently he figured that now he had his own room and own bed like a big boy, he should go to the potty like a big boy. Regardless, he had climbed up and fallen in head first with only his little tennis shoes sticking out. Thank God, Britt had heard the commotion and screamed for help.

For a long time after the commode drowning incident, I imagined what I might have said in the phone call to Social Services. I imagined that it might have been something like,

"Hello, Jefferson County Social Services. May I help you?"

"Well, yeah, maybe. This is..uh..Larry Wood..over here in Eagle County.....and, uh...you know we just got a couple of..... uh..little guys..uh..from you folks."

"Oh, of course, Mr. Wood. How are things going?? I bet you're having a lot of fun with Jeff and Joey!"

"Well..actually, uh...we ran into a little problem with Joey...uh..just now, uh....and thought that maybe...uh...we would call."

"Of course, Mr. Wood! What can we do to assist you?"

"Well...you remember, Joey...uh...he's the..uh..little one?"

"Of course I remember Joey, Mr. Wood, he is soooo cute!"

"Yeah, uh...he's pretty cute."

"How is little Joey doing, Mr. Wood?"

"Well, uh.....he..uh...he   just   drowned   in   the commode!!!!!!!"

Part XX
Reflections in the Mill Pond

Chapter 66
Learning New Words

"Learning new words, we'd never heard;
listening to facts that sound so absurd,
so dazzled by fear, our vision is blurred,
in hearing those words we'd never heard.
Having to hear what no parent should hear;
about our dear one whom we hold so dear,
the pain, the torment, the anguish, the fear,
of having to hear what no parent should hear.
Trying to cope as we harbour the pain;
we can't run away, it's all so insane.
Yesterday's sunshine has turned into rain,
praying for daylight to come once again.

Things certainly livened up around the Wood house with the addition of the boys! After the initial scare of losing Joey in the commode, we learned to watch them pretty cautiously and no conversation lasted very long without the constant inquiry,

"Where are the boys?"

These little guys had turned out to be even better than our wildest hopes. They were cute, funny, loving and definitely added entertainment. They adored their big sister, Brittany! Britt immediately loved them too and only once did she inquire,

"Is it too late to take them back?"

It was some silly incident that had caused her to question our sanity in taking kids two at a time. The boys promised to quit playing dress up with Britt's clothes, and for that matter to stay completely out of her room and possessions. We made a big deal of placing a Keep Out! sign above her door, but of course our little monkeys couldn't read it. After days of sitting at her door looking imploringly at their big sister, she took the sign down. It didn't work too well anyway.

"Larry, look at this," Kip was pointing to Britt's hands.

"Oh brother," I responded, seeing the bruises had returned.

In a short while, we were driving back to Denver, unsatisfied that the bruises that had left for a while had now returned. Dr. Austin this time had referred us to a bone specialist for a second opinion and we stayed in town until we could see him.

The specialist had concurred with Dr. Austin's diagnosis of Osteomyelitis, but added Asymmetric Osteomyelitis which still failed to comfort us with his suggestion that she would probably grow out of it. To appease our anxiety, he prescribed a strong antibiotic in hopes of solving the problem. The antibiotics didn't help at all, and we saw another specialist. The third doctor, while fascinated by this condition, again assured us that it was nothing to be overly concerned with. The fourth and fifth doctors concurred.

"Now what, Kip?"

In spite of the numerous reassurances, we were not satisfied. In less than a week we were on a jet headed for St. Jude's in Memphis, Tennessee to see if the best names in pediatric medicine could make us feel any better.

"This is a very rare occurrence," we were told upon examination at St. Jude's."

"We are familiar with Osteomyelitis, but have to admit that seeing it duplicated exactly on both hands is somewhat of a mystery."

"What now, docs?"

"We think it's a waste of time and money, but just to make us all feel better, we might do a bone marrow aspiration?"

"What the hell is a bone marrow aspiration?" I inquired.

"We take a sample of bone marrow from your daughter's spine to see if it might tell us what's going on here. It's done with an aspiration syringe and is not a pleasant thing to undergo."

Kip was as white as a sheet, and I was having trouble breathing as we assessed the horrified looks on each other's faces.

"Doc, you can cut my heart out with a rusty scalpel, but please don't hurt my baby!"

"Mr. and Mrs. Wood, we think it's the thing to do."

The painful procedure was performed in less than an hour. Britt took the horrendous aspiration like the brave little girl she was. Kip and I sat in the next room; holding on to each other like a hurricane was passing. Two hours later, one of the physicians walked into the waiting room and motioned to Kip and I to follow him into a consultation room.

"Mr. and Mrs. Wood, there is no doubting that Brittany has a bone infection in her hands. She definitely should grow out of that. What we found in the biopsy is more disturbing.

"Oh Dear God," we gasped simultaneously.

Two physicians and a friendly nurse took turns pointing to dots on a chart; the results of the bone marrow aspiration, and though we understood little of the explanation, we heard words we recognized as a condemned person might recognize the "whir" of an ax falling upon his neck.

"Acute Lymphoblastic Leukemia of the T Cell, the most difficult type of cancer to treat."

***

We spent the next few days consulting with the best physicians in the country both at St. Jude's and on the phone to them wherever they were located. Everyone concurred. In the evenings, we drove around Memphis, seeing the sights and eating lobster, Britt's favorite, in all the best restaurants. As soon as Kip and the boys retired, I went straight to the chapel at St. Jude's and prayed long into the night to St. Jude, the Patron Saint of Desperate Causes.

Having made the decision that Britt would begin treatment immediately in Oklahoma City at Children's Hospital, we flew back home. At "Children's" she would receive the same treatment offered at St. Jude's, and would be close to family and old friends. The terrible phone calls were made to loved ones, along with the promise that very soon, for the third time, we would be moving back to Oklahoma City.

A favorite cousin, a physician who also practiced in Denver came to our rescue and quickly bought the Vail house. In perfect silence and immeasurable fear, we packed and moved.

Chapter 67
The Clegern Mansion

In the earlier part of the 20th Century, the governor of Oklahoma had built an estate in Edmond, the town where Kip and I had attended college. It was also the town where Kip, Britt, and I had lived prior to the move to Denver. The lovely old English Tudor estate was on the market and I wrote a check for it. Clegern Manor was old, stately, covered with large trees, ponds, fountains, and had a wishing well tucked secretly amongst a grove of magnificent Magnolia and Pine trees. Small cobblestone streams connected the fountains and ran through the property much like trout streams did in the faraway mountains of New Mexico. I entertained the notion of having trout flown in from the Rockies, but soon realized they would not survive in the warmer waters of Oklahoma. I settled for a 30 hour one stop trip to Santa Fe and back accompanied by my brother-in-law, Chad whom I dearly loved and admired. Chad had known tragedy in his own family, and the bond we shared was unbreakable. He would have made the trip daily to help assuage our desperation. In Santa Fe, we bought a load of piñon wood which we loaded in his truck before making the drive home to Oklahoma.

Somewhere in my now frazzled memory, I had remembered the words from my mother's funeral that said,

"I shall look onto the hills, from whence commeth my strength," and I was pulling out the stops to get any kind of strength I could muster. Maybe the smell of piñon smoke would take me back to a time of peace and security I had known in my youth, and the long drive would be well worth it if it could give me any kind of comfort. The endless prayers didn't seem to be helping much.

Kip, as I had always suspected was much stronger and braver than I was and her positive insistence that we would "beat this thing," only served to emphasize my cowardice. As Britt began the long and painful treatments to cure her of Leukemia, I began drinking and taking ever increasing doses of Valium in order to keep up a positive front. Neither was helping much, and shortly into the treatment, I sadly accepted that I was, in fact, the loser that my dad had helped my family perhaps to think I was.

Being around a loving family was helping a little and my cousin, Mike Holbrook and I formed a little oil company we named "Brookwood," in hopes that working might impede my freefall. In short time, I proved myself worthless. In spite of Kip's love and the support of family and friends, my desperation had rendered me totally and completely useless. I had decided beyond question, that if anyone was going to leave this life, I wanted it to be me.

In spite of all the successes I had known and the personal challenges I had overcome in my life, when it came to the possibility of losing what I loved most in the world; my family, I was defenseless. I had heard so many times over my lifetime that hardship builds character, and that character is what sustains us through trials and tribulation. This was not so in my case. The losses I had encountered had not made me stronger. They were open wounds which had never healed and left me very weak and vulnerable to another tragedy. A doctor friend had once commented that I had expended so much strength at the loss of my mother; likening that loss to escaping a shark attack, that I might find myself vulnerable to the "minnows." It wasn't "minnows" I was faced with. It was another shark, and even the possibility that I might lose Britt was unacceptable. While I loved Kip and the boys with all my heart and soul, Brittany WAS my heart and soul.

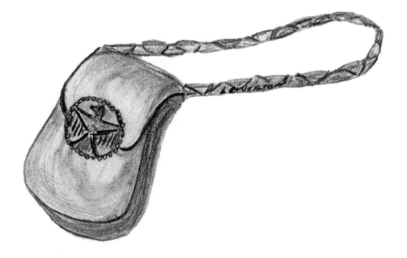

Chapter 68
A Ray of Hope

A few months into treatment, we were told about a lady doctor in Bombay, India who was doing experimental bone marrow transplants using sheep's blood to separate good cells from diseased cells. It had never been attempted in the US, and the costs, even if Dr. Mina Kapoor would come would be many, many millions of dollars. Experimental Medicine, of course I soon learned was not covered by the expensive family insurance that I had carried on all of us through Blue Cross and Blue Shield. That didn't even faze me as I begged the doctors who had now become personal friends to make the call to Bombay. We had become close to all the medical community who was taking Britt's sickness on a more personal level. Children's Hospital, a public institution served a mostly indigent population, and the newly gained awareness that a family that belonged to the same country clubs, and lived the same lavish lifestyles as them could fall victim to such a tragedy stuck them that they too, could be vulnerable. We all suffered together and held our breath with each day's treatment.

Mina Kapoor did come to Children's Hospital. It required

the hospital's addition of an Isolation Treatment Facility and other highly experimental paraphernalia which I simply wrote a check for and donated to the hospital. It also required that Britt obtain "remission" and stay in remission until a suitable bone marrow donor could be found. While the Isolation Facility was in construction, Kip and I did bone marrow aspirations in hopes that one of us might match. Mine failed. Kip's passed. Again, she had proven herself the better of us. In my miserable, drug and alcohol induced state, I began to resent her and all the courage, strength, and beauty that had caused me to love her so desperately. Away from the hospital, I spared no opportunity to search for shortcomings I hoped I could find in her to make her like the miserable person I had become. In my rage, and all too often, drug induced state, I attacked the love of my life. Kip, putting all of her strength into saving the life of our Britt was defenseless against my emotional brutality. The week prior to the first bone marrow transplant, I packed my clothes and left my family behind to fend for themselves in the Clegern Mansion. I went on Auto Pilot and left the controls to Jack Daniels.

The first transplant went well. Britt was "living" in a tent in the Isolation Facility. To visit her required going through a surgical scrub and adorning cap, gown, and gloves just to get inside the tent. Everything was sterile and I hoped that the surgical mask covering my face during daily visits would disguise the smell of alcohol on my breath. I never missed a visit but I didn't slow down my abuse either. Kip and I were like passing ships in the hospital. I had hurt her beyond description. What I had done to her, the boys and Britt had no explanation, understanding, nor forgiveness. The daily copies of "On Death and Dying" which anonymously showed up at the door of my apartment along with multiple copies of "Why Bad Things Happen to Good People," had little impact on my behaviour. In my mind there was no right or wrong. There was only the minute in which I was living, and the hope that the next drink would be readily available.

To add to my despicable demonstration of unworthiness, I had met what turned out to be an incredibly loving young woman, who in total naivety and sympathy for my miserable state, threw away her own personal dignity and became my constant companion. Angels come in all forms and I still don't understand why she interrupted her life to attempt to save mine, but I do believe that she was "sent" for whatever reason to sustain me.

"Mr. Wood, can we chat for a minute?" Mina Kapoor had called me into a conference room.

We were alone there and I noticed Valentine Cards that kids had made were hanging from the walls of the little room. It was the day before Valentine's, 1983.

"Britt's transplant has failed."

Dr. Kapoor suggested that we attempt remission again and attempt a second transplant. I just nodded my head affirmatively and left the hospital.

The next morning, I arose pretty early. I spread every picture I had of Kip and the kids very neatly on a coffee table. I overdosed on Valium, drank a bottle of gin, and hung myself from the upstairs balcony. It required very little thought, very little effort, and very little resignation. In the past months I had done very little right. That included failing to lock the door to my apartment and when an Avon lady heard the thrashing of a dying man suspended from a rope, she opened the door and called for help. I had failed again.

Several hours later, I awoke to familiar faces. I was in the emergency room of University Hospital right next door to Children's. The dour faces around me I recognized as the docs and nurses from the Oncology Clinic across the street where Britt lay dying. I woke up in hell, but at least I was surrounded by caring friends. I had no recollection of the Valium I had taken along with the liter of gin. I was later told that the numerous lethal doses I had ingested had "clumped" instead of dissolving and were simply pumped out of my stomach. The neck wound would heal. Regrettably I had not hung long enough to die.

Britt attained remission for the second time. While she waited for the second transplant, also donated by Kip, I sat secured to a chair in the Psychiatric Ward of University Hospital. Britt had been mercifully told that I had become ill, and each day when the psych attendants rolled me up to the window where I could see her, she waved cheerfully and blew me kisses. Every night, strapped to my bed, I said prayers that my daughter would miraculously be healed, or that I would not see the light of another day. Neither prayer was answered.

The second transplant failed after only a few days, and I knew something was happening when the nurses came in on the morning of the 21st with the wheel chair.

"Now what?"

"Mr. Wood, let's go see Brittany," a nurse suggested.

"What's going on?" I begged.

"Please, Mr. Wood."

We rolled out of University Hospital and into Children's as the nurses tried to make small talk. I had de-toxed to the point of awareness when things were out of the ordinary. Going up the elevator and onto the floor with the Isolation Unit, I gasped at the sight of practically everyone we knew standing in the waiting room. All the family was there and incredibly enough, they treated me with the respect and kindness I had always known from them. As the nurses unfastened the straps holding me to the wheelchair, I took what I prayed would be my last breath. Instead, they helped me walk inside to the Isolation Room where I saw Kip and the doctors standing beside my Britt. Waving me in, I noticed none were wearing masks or gowns. A nervous smile on Kip's face for a brief moment gave me hope that my prayers for her recovery had somehow been miraculously answered. As I approached her bed, I realized this was not the case. The doctors and nurses whom we had grown to know so well over the past 18 months were avoiding eye contact with me. Frantically, I prayed that it was just to demonstrate their disgust for what I had become.

It wasn't that either. It was then I noticed that every one of the medical persons at her bedside had tears streaming down their cheeks. As I watched them slowly and lovingly remove the many tubes attached to my Britt, and take the oxygen from her face, I knew it would soon be over. The final injection that was placed in her tiny pale arm can only be known by parents who have suffered this same immeasurable tragedy. Our child was dying before our very eyes, and all the holding, pleading, praying, and begging we did could not hold her back. All I could say, as I struggled to stay on my feet and continue breathing was,

"Fly away little bird, fly away to Heaven."

Britt flew away at 11:00AM, May 21st, 1983. She became an angel at age 12.

Chapter 69
Scattered Pieces

We were allowed to say our goodbyes after all the people had left the small plastic tent where our most cherished possession had spent the last three months of her life. I held Kip in my arms and wanted to tell her I loved her and beg for forgiveness for my weakness. The words didn't come and we walked away knowing that Britt's passing was but one of the fatalities of our tragedy. Any hope that we would ever find happiness again, either together or apart was dead. Kip could never in a million years forgive me for what I had done. I could never forgive myself.

The boys couldn't really grasp what had happened on that tragic day. In the waiting room, we both held them and told them we loved them, but our assurances fell on innocent, non-understanding ears. I refused to ride back to the clinic in the wheel chair. I insisted that I would walk. I did. Some miraculous energy had overtaken me and having just witnessed the passing of the bravest person I had ever known, I told myself that I could at least walk like a man even if I couldn't act like one. I owed my daughter at least that much.

Returning to the clinic, I walked into my room and

gathered the few clothes I had there. Having done so, I walked to the desk and informed the staff that I was leaving.

"Please, Mr. Wood, please stay a while longer. We can't release you today."

I responded with,

"It's perfectly OK. Don't worry that I'll try again to kill myself. I'm already dead."

I left the hospital AMA...Against Medical Advice.

One of the doctors from the hospital drove me back to my apartment. Everything had been neatly cleaned and the photographs I cherished put away.

"Are you going to make it?" he asked, as he gave me a big hug and patted my back.

"I'm going to make it," I responded. "I died and went to hell the day I moved out on Kip. Whatever life brings me now will be relatively easy. I don't want to die again anytime soon. I want to live for a very long time remembering every day just how much I hurt the people who loved me."

The doctor patted me on the back and left the apartment. I lay on the couch for a long time until there was a knock at the door. Opening it, I was surprised to see my friends from a little company I had started to handle my financial affairs. I had called it Timberline, the name of a little pub in Bergen Park, Colorado where Kip and I used to dance; Timberline Energy

"Larry, we've got bad news," they said apologetically.

"So what's new?" I responded, almost laughing.

"Penn Square Bank was just closed by the FDIC. We're in big financial trouble!"

Penn Square Bank was the first of the big oil and gas banks to fail following the recent collapse of the oil business. To people in the business it was like the stock market collapse of the late 20's.

"How much did we loose, guys?"

"Everything!"

"It'll be OK," I lied.

I told my employees to salvage anything they could and keep it for themselves. I had no interest in having anything that might remind me of earlier days. My good friends left with tears in their eyes. They were good people. I had always managed to surround myself with very good people.

We buried Britt a few days later and I found myself in the embarrassing position of having no money for a funeral. Once again, my brother-in-law Chad, in spite of what I had done to his sister, picked up the large expense. I don't remember the funeral except that one of the many poems I had written during the past months appeared on the back of the handout at the service. It was titled "Dove With A Broken Wing." It pretty much summed up my state of mind. I didn't cry at Britt's gravesite. I just didn't have any more tears.

Just as I didn't remember the funeral, I hardly remember the next few months. Friends had given me an office to come to each day and I did. I spent some time in another friend's home at Sea Ranch north of San Francisco as it was the consensus that I would eventually get healthy and we would all make money again in the now, non-existent oil exploration business. They even paid me a modest salary in hopes that I would regain an interest. It didn't work. Finally one day a few months after Britt's death, I was visited by God who graciously blessed me with a rather severe heart attack. I remember the jubilation I felt as I lost consciousness and fell to the floor in a little house I was renting. Unfortunately, a tennis friend was there and called an ambulance.

I woke up a while later and recognized that I was in the ER of Baptist Hospital not far from my house. I also recognized an ER doc as being one of my former tennis and golf buddies.

"Dan," I asked, "Am I finally going to die?"

"Well, you little bastard, looks like you might get 'er done this time."

Sighing a big sign of relief, I told him,

"Dan, there's one thing I want and I'm very serious about it."

"No, I'm not bringing you a gin & tonic into the ER!"

"That's not it, Dan!"

"So what?"

"I want to go home, Dan. I want to go home."

"What the hell are you talking about?"

"I want to go home. I want to go home to New Mexico."

"Larry, listen carefully. You'll never make it to the parking lot!"

"I can make it, Dan. I've got to make it!"

An hour later two daughters of good friends walked into the ER. I had known and loved these girls as much as I had loved their parents. I had helped one of the girls through a serious drug problem, and they both adored and supported me. They were willing, though not eager to take me home. As they rolled me out of the hospital I flipped the high sign to my doctor friend, indicating that I could in fact make it to the parking lot.

At my request, the girls drove by my little house where they were able to locate $38.00 and a box of Snicker Bars. With me slipping in and out of consciousness in the back seat of the Audi, we hit the four lane headed west.

It wasn't exactly the homecoming I had planned with Old Bea some 24 years earlier, but no mistake about it; I was going home. There was no forgiving the terrible things I had done in the past two years. Even if I had been forgiven by the ones I hurt the most, I could never forgive myself. The God that I had forsaken in my anger hopefully would allow me one last look at the Sangre de Cristo Mountains and that thought sustained me.

Part XXI
Reflections in the Mill Pond

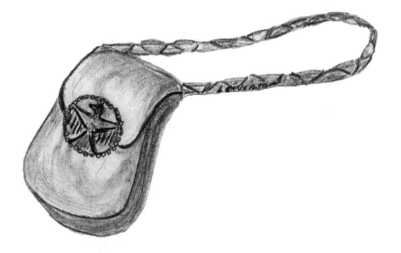

Chapter 70
The Best of Plans.....

As the sun peaked in the rear window of the speeding car, I thought I could see the faint image of mountains rising in the west. I had rested a little during the night and awoke only once to notice an exit sign to Shamrock, Texas. The multiple memories of Shamrock, Texas actually gave me a sense of peace as I thought of how not once, but twice, the little town had figured greatly in my life. We passed the exit sign and I thanked God I would never see the name again.

"Would you kids like me to drive for a while?"

Kathy Marple, age 20, turned and looked at me like she had seen a ghost.

"My God, Larry, we thought you were dead!!!"

"Not yet, kids! I've got to make it to Terrero!"

"What in hell is Terrero?" asked Jenny Compton, who was driving at the time.

"That's where you guys let me off. It's the jumping off place to the Pecos Wilderness area and that's as far as you guys are going."

I was sitting up in the seat of the car now, and even though I felt like I had been kicked in the chest, I knew for sure that I was going to make it home.

"Oh crap, and then what??"

"It's beautiful up there this time of year and that's where I'm going to make peace with God."

"Larry, don't make us do this!"

"Girls, it's a done deal. I'm very, very tired, and if you like me at all, you'll do just as I ask."

The girls were quiet for the last 60 miles of the trip except for an occasional sniffle. I couldn't believe how good I felt as we entered the Sangre de Cristos from the east. The morning sun was dancing on the aspen trees that sported their fall colours of brilliant yellows, reds, and golds. The huge pines swayed gently to an occasional morning breeze and their big branches seemed to reach out to me; pulling me further and further into the Sangres. There was no doubting that the exhilarating pleasure of my homecoming would be short lived. I had accepted that, and even welcomed the idea that I would not have to worry about the rigors of everyday life. Mercifully, I was being spared that. We crossed the Pecos River and entered the little community of Pecos, New Mexico, the gateway to the Pecos Wilderness Area. Terrero was just a short distance up the road.

"Please don't do this!!"

The girls were getting uncomfortable with the reality that I had not only made it to New Mexico, but now had every intention of making a one way trip into the Pecos Wilderness. I thanked them with all my heart, and asked them to be as happy as I was about coming home and escaping the horror of spending my last days in an Oklahoma hospital. With a big hug for each, and a peck on their tear covered cheeks, I put my Snicker Bars into a small backpack and crossed a cattle guard leading into the forest. I didn't turn around to wave. I took a deep breath as I heard the sound of the Audi turning around to leave, and I prayed that my strength would hold out until I got to where I was going.

It had been many years since I had seen this little road, and I had no recollection of the small adobe building that sat alongside. A blue Buick with Massachusetts plates sat out front. The modest sign hanging from the front porch read Pecos Lounge. How curious, I thought that this small cantina would be sitting here at the entrance of the wilderness. Terrero had nothing but a gas station so I surmised this was a hikers last shot at a drink before hitting the back country. As I walked past the place it dawned on me that I still had the $38.00 in my billfold. I carried very little else except for a picture of the four people I had loved more than anything else in the world. The boys wore coonskin caps with long tails. I had found the hats in a shop in Cheyenne, Wyoming. Britt wore a baggy knit beret that covered what was left of her beautiful hair after extensive radiation. Always beautiful, Kip smiled for the picture even though I knew her heart was breaking.

It suddenly struck me that while the bears might enjoy my earthly remains, and certainly would find pleasure in an entire box of Snicker Bars, they had no use whatsoever for $38.00. The money was in my pocket and a small flashing sign in the window said...Cold Beer!

A friendly looking Hispanic lady behind the bar greeted me with,

"Bienvenido! ¿Cómo está?"

"Bíen bastante, well enough," I answered thinking that was a pretty absurd response when you're dying. The cantina was completely empty except for an attractive young lady I guessed of Aztec decent who sat in a corner booth crying. It was a curious scene, but thinking if she rejected the offer to buy her a drink, I wouldn't have too long to suffer the humiliation.

"May I buy you a drink?" I offered quietly.

She looked surprised and even a little embarrassed, but after an uncomfortable pause answered,

"OK."

Her name was Theresita Medina, but said I could call her "Laurie." As we sipped the first margaritas, she told me that she was a "missing person," who had run away from Tufts Medical School in Boston. She went on to tell me that her father was a surgeon in Cuenca, Ecuador, and he had insisted on her coming to the states to get an education. After graduating from Duke, she had gone on to Boston to become a doctor like her father. It was not her choice but had done so at his insistence.

"I'm sick of doing what he wants me to do. I just ran away. How about you?"

"I came here to die."

My response sounded so ridiculous that she laughed. Then we both laughed. We laughed out loud and the more we thought about the absurdity of our situation, the louder we laughed.

"You're not really going to die are you?"

"Well, I'm supposed to according to a doctor friend."

We laughed again. Every time we laughed, I felt a little stronger. A few hours before, I lay in an ER in Oklahoma City being told I would never make it to the parking lot. Now I was sitting in a bar near Terrero, New Mexico laughing out loud with an Ecuadorian runaway. The more we shared our pathetic stories, the more we laughed. The more I laughed, the stronger I felt. Laurie Medina, myself, and the misery of our mutual circumstances had become laughable.

Somewhere between the fifth and sixth margaritas, Laurie gave me a serious look and said,

"I don't think you should die. I think we should go to Santa Fe and find a place to stay."

By this time, the margaritas and my physical condition had rendered me pretty much immobile. I lacked the strength for further conversation, and simply responded,

"OK!"

In five minutes we were in her blue Buick headed for Santa Fe. My $38.00 was gone, but Laurie still had one of her dad's credit cards. We rented a cutely furnished apartment with a view of the Sangres and moved in with only the clothes on our backs. Laurie more or less carried me into the little apartment and I only woke once in the next two days as Laurie rolled me over to put newly bought Wal-Mart sheets on the bed where I slept.

On the third day in the apartment, I awoke to a gentle nudge. It was Laurie Medina.

"Hey," she whispered, "If you really want to see your home again, you need to get well."

I could barely see her face. My eyes were swollen, and my head was pretty fuzzy from the prolonged sleep. I struggled to focus on the pretty face above me whom I had shared my story and my plan with.

"Do you really want to see your home, again," she asked.

"Yes, I want to go home."

"I will help you go home, but first you have to do something for me."

"What could I possibly do for you Laurie?"

"You have to live."

I drifted off to sleep again, and didn't wake until around 4:00PM. I could smell something coming from the kitchen, and recognized it to be green chile stew. A crackling sound I had not heard in a long time, I knew was sopapillas frying in hot oil.

"Can we get you up to eat a little?"

"Absolutely!"

With Laurie's help, I walked into the kitchen and sat down to one of my favorite meals. I couldn't remember when I had last dined on green chile and sopapilla, and as I began to savor those old familiar flavours, a little voice in my head kept whispering,

"You're going home, you're going home."

"Thank you, Laurie."

"De nada, Lariano!"

Chapter 71
Rehab

It began with very short walks around the small apartment. We were on the ground floor, so within a week, with her help, I was walking outside into the fresh autumn air. By early October, Laurie would drive us into town where we walked around the Plaza, occasionally stopping to sit on a bench and watch the very last of the tourists who had come to see the changing of the Aspen leaves. In the evenings we would sit by the little kiva fireplace in our apartment, enjoying the aroma of burning piñon and sharing our stories.

With Laurie writing, we began to document the events that would record the roller coaster history of my life. With each recollection of Tony Two Hats, my grandfather, Father Bill, Bernie and eventually the account of those I had loved the most, I knew it was almost time to make that final journey to the place where it had all begun.

"What about today?" Laurie asked as I wakened to the smell of coffee and bacon frying in the kitchen.

"What about today?"

"Do you want to go home today?" she asked softly.

The thought of making that final leg of the journey was

almost frightening, but with her support, I knew I could do it. I also knew that Laurie, who was much younger than I, needed badly to return to school and become the healer that she was born to be. She had brought me back to life and needed to share her gift with others.

I had previously called a friend back in Oklahoma and told him that I was still alive and needed money. A few thousand dollars arrived by wire within the hour. With that I would begin a new life.

The thought of saying goodbye to the angel who had given me life again was sad, but necessary. Before leaving though, she would help me make the final leg of my journey, and today we would make the drive through the Rio Grande Canyon to Taos and home.

Chapter 72
Reflections in the Mill Pond

We left Santa Fe early in the afternoon and were soon in the canyon that would lead us to Taos. It was about 2:00PM when we drove past the St. Francis Church where the long abandoned mission school had been. I smiled and pointed to the church. Laurie smiled back and nodded affirmatively. In a few more minutes, we made the turn off the pavement and drove onto the little dirt road that now had a sign indicating, Hatchery Lane. A lot had changed, but as we made the final turn into what had once been the trout hatchery, I saw the adobe house that had been my home. It was now a well kept apartment, and behind it, suspended from the huge willow tree, I saw the old rope swing hanging gracefully next to the pond. Everything was still there. It was much smaller than I had remembered, but it was still there. I was home.

"Do you want me to go with you" Laurie asked softly.

"No thanks, I need to do this myself."

Laurie parked and watched me walk the short distance. Arriving at the edge, I lowered myself into the swing and took a long, relaxed breath.

"I'm home, Grandfather. It's me...I've come home. It's me Tony, I've come home."

Though no one was there, I knew they could hear me and in my mind I could see each and every one of their reflections in the still water. Everyone was there and the smiles on their faces assured me that they knew I had finally come home. From my pocket I drew out the picture I carried with me and showed them the smiling faces of the wife and children I had loved so much. Now all my loved ones were there together on the surface of the water, reflecting back at me with all the love they had filled my life with.

The serenity of the moment was broken by the sound of young voices behind me. Turning, I saw the curious faces of three young children, two little dark faced boys, and a cherubic faced young girl I guessed to be about four.

"What are you doing here, Señor?"

"I've come home to visit my loved ones," I responded.

"Where are they?" the little girl asked as she looked around curiously.

"They're right here. They're right here with me," I said pointing to my heart.

"I can't see anyone," she insisted.

"Come look into the pond and maybe you'll see them better," I suggested.

At the edge of the pond, the children looked into the water and saw their reflections.

"Are WE you're loved ones?" she asked with a puzzled look.

"Yes, sweetheart, we're ALL someone's loved one and you must never forget that."

"I won't Señor, I won't ever forget that," she said as the children turned to walk away. To my surprise, this little angel walked up to me and gave me a hug.

"I won't ever forget that," she repeated as she turned to leave. "And I won't ever forget our Reflections in the Mill Pond."

THE END

***

EPILOGUE

Many years have passed since I made that first return voyage to visit the Mill Pond. In the almost three decades which had passed since I had been there with family, friends, and loved ones, the pond had become much smaller I thought. It had not. I had simply grown much bigger. The world I was living in had grown much bigger, and the simple childhood notions that life didn't exist beyond the canyon leading to Santa Fe, or beyond the crest of Wheeler Peak, which stands sentinel above the little town of Taos, proved to be very incorrect.

The world outside Taos, New Mexico is a very large and sometimes perplexing place. It can be just as exciting, and even mysterious as learning in the spring of each year, when the ice is gone from the mountain streams, that the Brook Trout are still there!

And so life has gone on for the many people whose lives intersected with mine. While the great majority of my immediate family is gone, many of the friends and loved ones remain; making their own journey, and even perhaps documenting it as I have done.

Brittany's mother, the love of my life, returned to school

and received her doctorate. She excels in her field, and works at a very prestigious university. The "boys," twice abandoned, are making their own journeys in an ever challenging world. Judith Lorain Wood, my beloved sister, lost a long and brave struggle fighting the cancer that devastated our family, but left four wonderful children who miss her as much as I do. The few remaining nieces, nephews, and cousins make summer pilgrimages to the mountains where we hike the trails, fish the streams, and marvel at the beauty of God's creation.

After coming home, I spent the following years before retiring working with children in their quest for security and happiness. It was quite simply what I was meant to do.

This book is dedicated to the bravest person I have ever known:

BRITTANY JANE WOOD: July 15, 1970-May 21, 1983

About the Author

Born in Duncan, Oklahoma in the mid 1940's, the author considers "home" to be the ancestral home of his grandparents, Taos, New Mexico.

While he has lived in a variety of places including Texas, Oklahoma, Colorado and New Mexico, he resides at the foot of the Sangre de Cristo Mountains close to the Colorado, New Mexico border where he has lived for many years.

The author attended schools in Texas, Oklahoma, and Colorado receiving undergraduate and graduate degrees in Foreign Languages and Psychology. After a number of years in the booming oil and gas industry of the 1970's the author returned to his long time dream of working with young children and painting the unique scenes of the American Southwest in oils and watercolors. While achieving some success in both areas, he began to document events of his life in story form.

During the flamboyant days of the oil and gas boom of the 70's, the author published technical articles dealing with enhanced oil production through reservoir stimulation. In the 1980's, the author penned a series of poems of which several were published by organizations including Hospice. The author submits periodic articles to a variety of local publications.

"Reflections in the Mill Pond" is the author's first venture into a full length novel. He is currently writing a second.